The Diffusion of E-commerce in Developing Economies

To the future: my daughters Rana, Reem and Ruba
and to
my past, present, and future: my husband Victor.
To them, I dedicate this book.

Zeinab

To the two most important people in my life who truly believed in women participating in their society: my late father Sheikh Khalid and my mother 'Um Sultan'.

Lubna

The Diffusion of E-commerce in Developing Economies

A Resource-based Approach

Zeinab Karake Shalhoub

American University of Sharjah, United Arab Emirates

Sheikha Lubna Al Qasimi

Minister of Economy, United Arab Emirates

Edward Elgar

Cheltenham, UK • Northampton, MA, USA

Published by
Edward Elgar Publishing Limited
Glensanda House
Montpellier Parade
Cheltenham
Glos GL50 1UA
UK

Edward Elgar Publishing, Inc.
William Pratt House
9 Dewey Court
Northampton
Massachusetts 01060
USA

A catalogue record for this book
is available from the British Library

Library of Congress Cataloguing in Publication Data
The diffusion of e-commerce in developing economies : a resource-based
approach / edited by Zeinab Karake Shalhoub and Sheikha Lubna Al Qasimi.
    p. cm.
    Includes bibliographical references and index.
    1. Electronic commerce—Developing countries. 2. Developing countries—
Economic conditions. I. Karake Shalhoub, Zeinab. II. Al Qasimi, Lubna
    HF5548.325.D44D54 2006
    381'.172091724—dc22

2006011743

ISBN-13:   978 1 84376 514 1
ISBN-10:   1 84376 514 4

Printed and bound in Great Britain by MPG Books Ltd, Bodmin, Cornwall

Contents

Foreword

Something special was celebrated in 2005. August 2005 was celebrated worldwide as the 10th anniversary of the Internet. While the technological core of the Internet dates back to the early 1960s, it was in 1995 that many of the everyday names of today's Internet economy were formed or formally listed – Yahoo!, Amazon and eBay to name a few.

Think back to how life was just a mere 10 years ago. Think about a time when one could not access email on the road, when one could not get information in real time, when one could not download music, when no chat-rooms or blogs existed and when online commerce was a dream. Today all of these examples seem to be 'normal' aspects of our everyday lives. However, none of them would have existed without the innovations unleashed by the Internet. Indeed, the last decade has seen some of the most innovative years in human history.

Many of these innovations have been triggered by the ability of the Internet to provide global connectivity and real-time interactivity. The world is more connected than before and these interconnections are spurring innovative business models – such as the rise of off-shoring. Real-time interactivity is enabling global e-commerce to blossom and allowing like-minded citizens to come together to drive change, in both business and politics.

For example, the Internet is changing the fundamental nature of innovation. Innovation is increasingly open, global and community based. Innovation is less and less proprietary and the privileged domain of firms and their professional staff. The community-based model of innovation relies upon the open, collaborative and often voluntary efforts of multiple individuals. Open source software development is a frequently quoted example of successful community-based innovation. Such trends are also prevalent in other domains such as the design of sports equipment where sports enthusiasts are collaborating to allow rapid development, simultaneous experimentation and diffusion of winning ideas.

The Internet is a global phenomenon. The total number of Internet users worldwide already exceeds 1 billion and the centre of gravity is moving east. For example, India and China together contain a

500 million plus strong middle class that is technology savvy and hungry for new Internet products and services. If you want to look at the leading edge in broadband and mobile Internet services, don't head to Silicon Valley. Go instead to Asia. Korea already boasts of the most sophisticated broadband society in the world. The number of Internet users in 2005 exceeded the number of personal computers on a global level, as compared to 1999 when the situation was the reverse. Whereas the global number of personal computers grew in the years 1999–2005 by more than 50 percent, the number of persons accessing the Internet grew about four times during the same period. In comparison, the number of telephone mainlines grew only about 25 percent.

The Internet has also impacted on the productivity and development of nations. Countries such as India have transformed their economies, in large measure owing to the benefits of the Internet and technology revolution. Others, such as Ireland and Israel, have experienced similar benefits and emerged as centres of technology. Some countries, such as Singapore, the United Arab Emirates and Hong Kong, have incorporated the key ingredients of the Internet revolution in order to provide an optimal environment for the functioning of critical stakeholders, especially businesses. Many countries in Africa and other emerging regions are leapfrogging with new technology and are providing new opportunities for all. Ethiopia, despite being one of Africa's poorest countries, is spending about one tenth of its Gross Domestic Product (GDP) on Information Technology (IT) every year. The government of Rwanda has identified Information Communication Technology (ICT) as being a key enabler of its goal to transform itself into the Dubai of East Africa, providing a knowledge-intensive, technology enabled and service-orientated business environment.

All of the above factors increase the importance of this book. In *The Diffusion of E-commerce in Developing Economies*, Professor Zeinab Karake Shalhoub and UAE Minister of Economy Lubna Al Qasimi, provide a timely and valuable perspective on how technology and the Internet revolution are changing business and spurring development across the world, especially in emerging economies. This book utilizes a framework grounded in rigorous theory to provide a fine-grained understanding of electronic commerce adoption processes by public and private sector entities in developing countries. In doing so, the authors consider how each exchange encounter is shaped by, and in turn shapes, relational characteristics which form the bases for growth and development.

The challenge for corporations is to change their business models and to leverage the power of technology to create new value for their customers across the globe. This book will provide both managers and academics with useful inspiration for such change.

Soumitra Dutta
Dean of Executive Education
Roland Berger Professor of Business and Technology
INSEAD
Fontainebleau, France

1. Establishing the context

INTRODUCTION

The end of World War II marked the launch of a post-industrial society most commonly designated as the Information Age. The main drivers of this period are two explicit forms of technology, namely Communication Technology (CT) and Information Technology (IT). More broadly, CT consists of the hardware equipment, organizational structures and social values by which individuals collect, process, and exchange information with other individuals. In contrast, IT largely denotes computer and electronics-based technology, generally encompassing the development, installation, and implementation of computer systems and applications (Webster's, 2003). These two forms of technology came together within the Information Age, creating a new type of technology known as Information Communication Technology (ICT), which facilitates the exchange of information on a many-to-many basis specifically through computer and electronics-based communication systems.

Rapid cycles of technological innovation, particularly with the advent of electronic commerce (e-commerce), have seen ICT become recognized by business owner/managers as a vital element of business (Johnson et al, 1999). Perhaps most significantly, the Internet is praised as a unique and powerful form of ICT which, despite the collapse of the 'dot-coms', is continuing to advance at an ever-increasing pace and is making electronic commerce attractive to even the smallest of businesses, which stand to gain tremendous business advantages from implementing Internet technology. Similarly, despite the slow growth of mobile commerce, the importance of cellular phones as a form of business ICT is becoming more pronounced. While the emergence of the Internet, cellular phones and other forms of ICT have significantly altered the way in which both small and larger businesses operate, divergent views exist as to whether the impact of such technological developments is indeed favorable or not.

ICT may be considered 'a tool to enhance life' given its desirable direct impacts. In particular, it is claimed that ICT improves productivity, enables business to be conducted outside of an office, and creates new industries. The correlation between ICT and business growth is noted for a number of developing countries; however, the direction of this effect is unclear. A growing literature examines the link between growth and the convergence of communication and computer technology, particularly within the United States.

The 1980s and 1990s are seen as a period of advanced development. This period witnessed major processes of transition from industry-based to knowledge-based economies. There are a number of indicators, both quantitative and qualitative, that point to these transition processes – such as the increasing number of knowledge workers, the shifting of importance between human capital and fixed assets, the investment in information technology, the creation of new knowledge-based businesses, the creation of new professions, and the introduction of institutional changes at the macro level. These changes are described as two interwoven society-wide development processes: (1) transformation of knowledge for economic and social development, and (2) the emergence of the Internet as the core of a world-wide digital information infrastructure.

The concept of the division of knowledge is a determinant in analyzing and describing the dynamics of societal processes of interaction by which knowledge is effectively generated and used. In the new millennium, the information and the speed with which corporate executives receive it will be extremely important to charting the course of any company. John Donovan, professor at the Massachusetts Institute of Technology and chair of the Cambridge Technology Group, maintains that information executives were the only people who could improve the competitive position of US corporations during the 1990s and beyond (Donovan, 1989). The Internet has opened up avenues for commerce that were unimaginable just a few years ago. In essence, the Internet has created opportunities for seamless business collaboration between buyers and sellers as well as the collection of service companies that have constituted traditional supply chains. New business models inspired by the new technology break down traditional boundaries between business partners, in essence making all participants in a business transaction part of an expansive extranet. In theory, these business partners will be able to easily and securely communicate and complete end-to-end transactions from within their respective companies – streamlining communications, increasing the precision of forecasts, and driving cost out of day-to-day operations.

The changes brought about by the Internet have even broader implications. With the advent of Internet technology, every company becomes a global company, with the means and opportunity to buy and sell from, or strike an alliance with, any company, anywhere, anytime. This golden opportunity brings with it a level of complexity that surpasses anything that all but the most far-flung global enterprises have experienced to date.

The recent explosion of information and IT has induced corporate management to utilize its ingenuity in creating the best available means to manage the flow of information, control flow channels, and integrate the different assets (both hardware and software) of IT utilized by the different departments and divisions of the corporation. As companies invest heavily in information-based systems, they are vesting more control in technology strategies and new business models, especially those related to electronic commerce, or e-commerce.

E-commerce is considered the star of the IT revolution and the Internet. The most established components of e-commerce–electronic data interchange and electronic corporate payments have been growing for over a decade at rates of around 20 percent a year and are rapidly reaching critical mass. As that happens e-commerce becomes a competitive necessity not an option. In the 1990s, those proven and steady applications of e-commerce were accelerated and extended by the combination of low-cost, high performance telecommunications and personal computers plus the astonishing emergence of the Internet as both a marketing channel, a telecommunications infrastructure that opens up e-commerce to small firms, and a vehicle for companies to rapidly develop internal and external information and communication systems. The recent growth in use of the World Wide Web (the Web) signals that the Internet is a massive mass market for just about every type of business

E-commerce is the most effective way to do business in an era where telecommunications allows more and more options for customer contact, elimination of documents and all the overhead and administration costs associated with them, and computer-to-computer processing of transactions between customers and suppliers and, though to a far lesser extent as yet, between companies and customers. If it's the best way to do business, then it's obviously something that every manager needs to make part of his or her thinking. That is what this book is about: providing business managers with a non-hype, non-technical, reliable, and interesting guide to this new business territory.

The adoption of the Internet and e-commerce is widespread around the world. Most countries, especially the developing nations, are making substantial investments in modernizing and boosting IT infrastructure, building a strong telecommunications infrastructure, promoting Internet and e-commerce adoption in businesses, government, and various communities. This wide use of ICT has accelerated the growth of e-commerce in many parts of the world, transforming businesses, increasing economic prosperity, and facilitating communication within a country, and among countries. The world is rapidly moving toward Internet-based economic structures and knowledge societies, which comprise networks of individuals, firms, and countries linked electronically in interdependent and interactive relationships (UNCTAD, 2003). In addition, electronic commerce promises to be the drive behind a new surge of economic growth and development.

To examine the impacts of adopting new information technologies including e-commerce, two independent schools of thought have developed over the last decade. Proponents of the first school have emphasized models of diffusion of technology integrating theories from change management, innovation, and technology diffusion literature (Larsen, 1998). The second school of thought identifies the impact of innovation or new technologies where innovations are the means of changing an organization, either as a response to change in the external environment or as a pre-emptive action to influence the environment (Rogers, 1995).

The spatial implications of the communication revolution are profound but still uncertain for the developing world. Lower transaction and communication costs, combined with goods production that is increasingly based on flexible specialization, tend to favor the dispersion of economic activities. Yet, real-time information about consumers, easier outsourcing and the proliferation of producer-support services tend to favor locating production near to large markets and urban centers. Concerning services, the ICT revolution is likely to promote the dispersal of services that can be delivered remotely and effectively, even while inducing further concentration of others, such as activities that are driven by innovation, tacit knowledge, and face-to-face interactions. Location-independent work or telecommuting is growing in industrial countries. One estimate suggests that about 5 percent of all service-sector jobs in industrial countries will be contestable by developing countries (ILO, 2001).

Beyond enabling global trade in services, advanced information infrastructures are increasingly important in attracting foreign direct investment, facilitating technology diffusion, and developing innovation clusters. Geographic regions are, more than ever before, emerging as gateways to services, learning, and innovation. Regions are also differentiating and competing on a global scale, giving rise to global urban networks. For example, Singapore envisions its future role as an intelligent island and a regional hub for information-intensive services. The 'walled' cities of China are opening up to all kinds of information flows; for example, Shanghai has a 'smart' growth strategy that will attract knowledge-based and information services industries, enhance access to information infrastructure, and enrich learning opportunities.

PARADIGMS OF E-COMMERCE

Despite controversies surrounding e-commerce and the burst of the 'dot. com' bubble, many countries continue to deploy e-commerce extensively in their economic activities and develop Internet-enabled initiatives to manage the various aspects of economic activities, to strengthen online integration, and to design and customize products and services in an effort to serve citizens more effectively. While sizeable investments in e-commerce are being made, researchers and practitioners are struggling to determine whether and how these expenditures improve the performance of an economy both at the micro and macro levels. There has been much guesswork, but little empirical data to determine the magnitude and distinctiveness of e-commerce initiatives and their impact on economic performance, especially of developing countries. Due to the complexity of determining what data to assemble, and of essentially collecting them, most of the existing literature regarding what determines the success of e-commerce initiatives tends to be fragmented and qualitative in nature. Case studies on countries such as Costa Rica, Bolivia, Egypt, Nepal and Uganda have provided insights into the benefits of e-commerce, but the findings of these case studies are specific to just a few firms in the particular economy. In this book, a series of hypotheses will be formulated and tested in an effort to determine the success factors of e-commerce in developing economies.

The rise of e-commerce, the development of the Web, and the software to support initiatives is so startling in its economic implications that it may reasonably be considered a breakpoint in the way that we do business. This breakpoint is an abrupt and defining moment that obliterates standards and accepted commercial practices and replaces them with the essential business paradigm for the new era. The immediacy and growth of the Web have profound implications for businesses of all sorts. If you are a business strategist in the e-commerce age, you are confronting the fact that, almost overnight, your potential customer base has exploded in size, the choices available to those customers have multiplied many times, and hundreds of new competitors are suddenly clamoring for their attention. To thrive in this world, you must be online, and your online presence must be a powerful one. Way back in those pre-Web years of 1993 and 1994 the big question was 'why do we need an electronic presence?' Now, it's a question of 'what can we do to leverage our Internet presence and online customer relationships (and how much will it cost us to do it)?'

The adoption of e-commerce is occurring at a frenetic pace in companies of all sizes, and countries with varied degrees of development. Success in an environment that changes so fast requires individuals who are generalists but who can penetrate deep down into the technological foundation when needed. The strategic challenge is to understand a broad range of technologies, judge them quickly – especially emerging ones – make decisions about them, champion a direction, and provide leadership, all without losing track of the core business objectives, and the fundamental growth perspectives.

Many essays concerning the implications of IT in general and e-commerce in particular, assert that these implications take a particular form and that the broad outlines of the future with e-commerce can be discerned fairly rapidly. The review of the literature on this issue uncovers an array of different conclusions. According to the various authors, the implications could either be centralizing or decentralizing, either deskilling or upgrading, either enhancing or threatening democracy, and so on, through a list of oppositions. The literature reveals three distinct perspectives on the implications of IT, in general. These perspectives can be applied to the implications of adopting e-commerce and electronic government at the macro (country) level. The three such viewpoints are labeled the *Continuity, Transformation,* and *Structural* schools.

For Continuists, IT exemplifies an incremental step on a long course of technological development. The important determinant for IT innovation here is how technological changes can meet: (1) users' needs, (2) the structure of factor costs, and (3) the availability of managerial, technical, and work force skills (Miles, 1989, p. 224). Countries that do not jump on the wagon of IT innovativeness will risk the problem of losing their competitive edge and jeopardize their potentials for economic growth. This is the main reason that developed countries spend respectable percentages of their budgets on technological research and development (R&D).

Transformationists tend to put less importance on structures and strategies than on their underlying values and perspectives (Miles, 1989). Consequently, there has been ample research into perceptions of the 'impact' of IT on the workplace. Following the 1982 Versailles Summit, a major program of research into the acceptance of new technologies was launched. The latter was particularly inspired by concerns that public resistance to change was the root of slow innovation (Miles, 1989, p. 225).

A major assumption of the Structuralists is that many of our current uncertainties relate to being at the point of transition between structural doctrines; the stagnation and limits of old structures could be clearly seen, but the viabilities of new models are hard to assess. New technologies imply learning processes and organizational changes to capitalize on their potential; new areas of demand are needed to establish new patterns of growth. Structuralist analysis typically attempts to identify key features of an emerging paradigm and to outline the enabling constraining factors around appropriate changes.

These three schools of thought differ in assessing the implications of IT in general and e-commerce in particular on formal work in an economy (including different economic sectors), the social structure of a country, international interdependence among nations, and globalization. It would be inappropriate to draw many conclusions from existing research, however. What is apparent is that there has been uneven development of research and that this adds to the intrinsic difficulties associated with assessing the implications of e-commerce and a knowledge society.

Most practitioners and theorists are in agreement that the majority of developing countries in the new millennium will continue moving from the industrial society to the information/knowledge era, or the third wave. Many advocate the use of IT and e-commerce as an effective way of coping with the changing environment, locally, regionally, and globally. These authors go one step further by stating that the adoption of electronic commerce at the national level plays a critical role for countries to survive in a hostile, complex, and turbulent global environment.

E-COMMERCE: BENEFITS VERSUS ECONOMIC VALUE

E-commerce technologies have received much attention from both academia and practice in the last few years. Of significant importance to our understanding of e-commerce technologies is the analysis of the benefits that they confer upon adopting economies. As a by-product of technology, information is an over-riding consideration for national leaders and managers.

Through the years, national leaders and managers have generally been preoccupied with specific types of information rather than focusing more broadly on information itself. An unfortunate consequence of this tendency has been the haphazard, 'bits-and-pieces' management of information at the macro and micro levels. Costly inefficiencies resulting from the collection of irrelevant or redundant information have too often been the result. Information management specialists have responded to this state of affairs by recommending that information be viewed as a resource. Prior research values IT on the design of firm business processes and the value of decision support systems provides a useful starting point in conceptualizing how much value from an investment can be realized by the firm (Davamanirajan et al, 1999; Davern and Kauffman, 2000). In addition, our understanding of theory that conditions expectations of value in a competitive marketplace is important – especially the role of technological standards. Related research on IT value emphasizes the extent to which customer and firm adoption of an IT innovation in the marketplace is a major determinant of its success for the firm (Dos Santos and Peffers, 1995). Other related research (Lucas, 1999) highlights the importance of organizational factors and the capabilities of management.

In the e-commerce context, the issues become even more interesting because they span multiple levels of analysis, all of which must be understood in order to make sense of value accrual and investment performance. These include the level of the individual user and the experience that one has with the qualities of the human-computer interface of an e-commerce-related technological innovation. The analysis must also consider the level of impact of the innovation in the marketplace, where it may alter the fundamental ways in which firms and individuals interact. At this level, the issues of interest are business process designs, technological standards, firm-to-firm competition, and alternative organizational strategies. Understanding them, along with the extent to which the marketplace is prepared to adopt (sometimes dramatically) new innovations, and whether the users of a new technology are prepared to buy in, is important.

A variety of benefits are provided by e-commerce: better profits, improved communications, an evolving understanding of information requirements, a test bed for system evolution, and cost reductions. The information provided by new advanced technology has characteristics that are important to national leaders and managers. It supports decision making by identifying areas that require attention, providing answers to questions, and giving knowledge about related areas. It provides relevant, timely information. In addition, IT has improved communications in several ways. It is used to facilitate the sharing of information with customers and suppliers, at the micro level, and among firms and various governmental entities, at the macro level.

Before we move further, it is important to differentiate between the benefits of information and e-commerce technologies and the value of these assets. Benefits of information and e-commerce technologies are evaluated by using a number of economic analysis techniques, such as return on investment, net present value, and the payback period. These techniques are based on assessing monetary costs and benefits of the various investments in technologies and conducting a structured benefit/cost analysis. Value of investment in technologies, on the other hand, goes beyond measurable benefits to include a number of intangible factors and impacts. One important factor is the strategic match of a specific investment whereby the degree that a proposed investment responds to established national strategies and goals is assessed. Competitive advantage is another intangible factor that is hard to quantify. Evaluating the competitive advantage of an investment calls for an assessment of the degree to which the proposed investment provides an advantage in the global marketplace. The management of information is another intangible factor. This is an assessment of an investment contribution to management's need for information on essential activities. Finally, competitive response is an important intangible element. This evaluates the degree of economic, social, and political risk associated with not undertaking the investment.

In general, to evaluate a technology investment, it is necessary to consider both tangible and intangible factors. The emphasis should be on the value of this technology investment, not solely on its benefits. When governments start assessing the value potential of an e-commerce proposal, they have to consider the impacts of inner and outer characteristics – that is, the inner characteristics of the economy and the outer characteristics of the e-commerce value flow. We identify two classes of limits to value for the e-commerce technologies valuation process: national and global barriers. The value potential of a specific IT investment is often limited by scarcity, cost, and path-dependency of co-specialized assets that are necessary to obtain the benefits of the technology (Clemons, 1991). Other barriers are generated by the industrial structure of the economy that may favor technologies that 'plug in' to the existing systems to the detriment of other, non-standard but innovative technologies (Brynjolfsson and Kemerer, 1996). Similarly, the adoption of new technology depends on the standardization of technologies that are complementary to them (Katz and Shapiro, 1986). In addition, industrial structure of the economy might also generate negative externalities limiting the potential value of the technology (Bakos and Brynjolfsson, 1993; Riggins et al, 1994).

On the other end of the spectrum, unique characteristics of firms as economic players, such as organizational routines and norms, market and product expertise, customer and supplier relationships, and human capital, can lead to different potential value estimates for the same investment in technologies (Brynjolfsson and Hitt, 1995, 1998; Clemons, 1991). Effective implementation of e-commerce projects may require extensive redesign of current business processes around technologies' new capabilities (Barua et al, 1996; Brynjolfsson and Hitt, 1995, 1998; Clemons, 1991). These changes can create inefficiencies and trade-offs that end up embedded in organizational routines (Leonard-Barton, 1992; Porter, 1996) and reduce the benefits of current as well as future technology investments.

When economies implement systems, they aim to convert the potential value of the technologies in which they have invested into realized value (Davern and Kauffman, 2000). However, this process is fraught with conversion contingencies, which influence the amount of potential value that can be successfully transformed into realized value by the economy undertaking the implementation. With these perspectives in mind, we next identify three limits to value in the conversion process: resource, knowledge, and usage barriers. E-commerce projects require additional investments in specialized resources, such as new processes and human capital (Barua et al, 1996; Brynjolfsson and Hitt, 1995, 1998). These resources are probably the single most important limit to value of new technologies, but they do not ensure that the economy will realize potential value. This viewpoint is underscored in the 'productivity paradox' work of Brynjolfsson and Hitt (1998) and other authors, who remind us that success with IT implementation and realization of value requires far more than just sophisticated leadership visions about how technology can be leveraged for strategic and operational advantage. Training and other efforts to increase 'awareness' of how to obtain value from these investments are often hamstrung by insufficient resources.

Secondly, the redesign of processes requires employees to learn new skills and the economy to develop new routines – and thus creates knowledge barriers (Attewell, 1992). New technologies require complex understanding and mental representations (Weick, 1999) that may be hard to manipulate due to limited information-processing capabilities of human employees (Simon, 1997). Knowledge barriers also stem from a lack of absorptive capacity, which is developed over time by acquiring related knowledge and expertise in diverse areas (Cohen and Levinthal, 1990). Building and retaining human capital through training and human resources policies help economies eliminate such barriers. However, these activities require significant investments, which in turn will create a resource barrier for the implementation of e-commerce at the national level.

Thirdly, it is only through a high level of technology usage that value is realized. Usage barriers are often related to user perceptions regarding the technology and the responsibilities that must be shouldered when it is used. Unfavorable perceptions will result in users not adopting the technology solution (Chircu et al, 2000; Davis, 1989; Moore, 1998; Rogers, 1983), even if they are capable of acquiring the requisite knowledge for using it. Ackoff (1967) states that poorly designed technologies can increase information overload, thus making them unattractive, even though they may be easy to use. Moreover, because users have different levels of tolerance for innovation and organizational change (Rogers, 1995), their personal characteristics may predispose them to be reluctant adopters. Each of these usage barriers prevents the potential value of an e-commerce investment from being realized at the national level.

Notwithstanding the arguments made above, the value of e-commerce can be difficult to measure and even more challenging to explain. Some of the reasons for the mystery about e-commerce result from the fact that:

1. E-commerce is not just a single technology or tool; as a matter of fact, it is a combination of technologies, applications, processes, and business strategies. Managers who are fully knowledgeable about business processes and strategy may not know much about and even be intimidated and put off by the jargon of e-commerce technology.
2. E-commerce cannot be accomplished by any single enterprise working alone, regardless of the quality of its technologies or its business strategies. It is fundamentally about business relationships. Managing the relationship is the starting point for managing e-commerce. Then, managing processes and technology becomes the priority.
3. E-commerce systems and procedures must be consistent with the practices, relationships and, in many instances, power and influence structures of industries. E-commerce is about the relationships between enterprises. As a result, its progress depends heavily on industry associations and working groups to define the standards – formats and procedures – for electronic relationships. Progress in using electronic data interchange (EDI) in health care, for instance, was for long blocked by the fragmentation of the industry: hospitals, insurers, governmental agencies, and others. By contrast, much of the impetus in EDI came from power players in an industry encouraging and even forcing their suppliers to move. When General Electric or Ford invests in e-commerce, the action inevitably changes its suppliers' role in the supply chain and their necessary e-commerce investments.

E-commerce is a means to a business end. Improving costs, relationships, channels, processes, and economic growth is the objective. Technology is the enabler.

E-COMMERCE AND GLOBALIZATION

E-commerce has become a driving force for the globalization of the world economy, and countries that do not engage in e-commerce may put the competitiveness of their economies at risk. As a result, many firms and organizations in developing countries have become integral parts of global networks of production supply chains that increasingly use e-commerce mechanisms. Through these networks, entities in more developed countries induce developing-country enterprises to adopt new information technologies, organizational changes, and business practices. Recent forecasts estimate that e-commerce would represent about 18 percent of worldwide Business-to-Business (B2B) and retail transactions in 2006 (UNCTAD, 2003). The Internet is the prime source for conducting e-commerce. According to

UNCTAD (2003), some 150 million additional people began using the Internet between 2001 and 2002, of which developing countries accounted for almost one third, bringing the number of Internet users worldwide to 655 million by the end of 2002. This means that around 10 percent of the world was online in 2002, and that the growth of new users continues at a rapid pace. In developing countries, however, Internet penetration rates remain far below the penetration rate of 50 percent (and above) seen in more developed economies.

Today's technological advances are faster (Moore's law) and more fundamental (breakthroughs in genetics). They are driving down costs (computing and communications) at an unprecedented pace. Leading these transformations are the accelerated developments in ICT, biotechnology and just-emerging nanotechnology.

Information and communications technology involves innovations in microelectronics, computing (hardware and software), telecommunications and optoelectronics – microprocessors, semiconductors and fiber optics. These innovations enable the processing and storage of enormous amounts of information, along with rapid distribution of information through communication networks. Moore's law predicts the doubling of computing power every 18–24 months, due to the rapid evolution of microprocessor technology. Gilder's law predicts the doubling of communications power every six months – a bandwidth explosion – due to advances in fiber optic network technologies.

Individuals, households and institutions are linked in processing and executing a huge number of instructions in imperceptible time spans. This radically alters access to information and the structure of communication, thus extending the networked reach to all corners of the world. Today's technological transformations are intertwined with another major historic shift – economic globalization – that is rapidly unifying world markets. The two processes are mutually reinforcing. The late twentieth century integration of world markets was driven by trade liberalization and other dramatic policy changes around the world, such as privatization and the fall of communism in the former Soviet Union. The new tools of information and communications technology reinforced and accelerated the process.

Globalization propels technological progress with the competition and incentives of the global marketplace and the world's financial and scientific resources. The global marketplace is technology based, with technology a major factor in market competition. Developing countries that can develop the requisite infrastructure can participate in new global business models of intermediation, business process outsourcing and value chain integration. In developing countries, as the user base expands, costs fall and technologies are adapted to local needs, the potential of ICT will be limited only by human imagination and political will.

The organization of work must be revamped if national economies are to perform more effectively in a global market. Practitioners, theorists, and futurists alike concur that the challenge for countries that want to maximize their global presence involves structuring relationships and the flow of information so that the right parties can obtain it at the right time. Information technology and e-commerce initiatives play critical roles in the strategy of global competition. Countries reap the biggest benefits not by superimposing computers on top of old work processes but by restructuring those processes and the national culture. This strategy, over time, develops entirely new economic and business capacities.

In a 'plug-and-play' economy, sourcing major business processes (design, finance, manufacturing, scheduling, logistics, insurance, sales, marketing), will be as easy as opening the *Yellow Pages*. This specification, automation, and outsourcing of processes with global economies of scale will bring big growth in the number of strategies for assembling businesses. The number of potential businesses and marketplaces will grow exponentially. Another crucial step is to establish standard specifications for business processes, that is the ways in which messages are generated and acted upon once they are received. For example, there will emerge specifications for how purchase orders (POs) or invoices are dealt with. The processes will be described so explicitly that machines can interpret and act upon them. That's not to say that businesses will do everything in precisely the same ways. Rather, they'll use a modular architecture to build competitive strategic business processes from a standard set of explicitly defined process elements. For example, the systems that run electronic auctions can use the same components as those that run purchase orders – acknowledgment processes – only they will do it simultaneously with several companies. Businesses will take elemental pieces and rearrange them to create new competitive processes.

The ultimate goal is to have virtual companies and governmental agencies that assemble, with efficiency and effectiveness, the right sets of business processes at the right times from large numbers of market participants. This vision assumes fundamental changes in the way that business people behave. It requires sophisticated, non-technological abilities to conceptualize new businesses. It requires more people to become risk takers and a greater willingness to engage frequently in all sorts of new business relationships. It requires that people trust the marketplace to deliver goods or services that they need while also protecting their proprietary interests.

Technology is not the limiting factor here. The extent to which processes become automated depends almost entirely on the willingness of people to be open and explicit about their intentions. A buyer's ability to find the right supplier depends fundamentally on his or her willingness to send out a request for quote that explains, in detail, the competitive advantage that he or she is trying to exploit. It depends, as well, on how explicitly a supplier is willing (and able) to describe itself to the market at large. If the buyer is doing everything possible to make objective, knowledge-based purchasing decisions, then the rules governing those decisions can be made explicit, and the process can be automated. If that happens, then, over time, machines will be able to learn as they go, recognizing patterns in human decision-making and writing their own precise and effective business rules (neural networking).

Through the standardization of messages and business processes, today's market makers will create interoperability among markets. They will serve also as guarantors of predictable, trustworthy behaviors among trading partners, giving entrepreneurs the confidence that they need to take their great ideas into the market and build virtual businesses. Another crucial step is to establish standard specifications for business processes – the ways in which messages are generated and acted upon once they are received.

Technology to support this vast interconnected global commerce network is maturing rapidly due, in large part, to the great progress being made in establishing standard specifications for building commerce messages such as requests for quotes, purchase orders, contracts, invoices and so forth. Soon there will be libraries from which businesses can build and dispatch electronic messages that any other businesses in the world can accept and act upon with ease.

Economic globalization has affected information management in unexpected ways. The rapid growth of global corporations in both number and degree of influence has been accompanied by an unprecedented flow of information across international borders. The American Express Company, for instance, authorizes more than 1 million credit card transactions daily from around the world. This sort of globalization of information has raised questions about privacy protection and national sovereignty. Some nations, such as Brazil, have responded with regulations that threaten to interfere with the timely and efficient flow of information from one branch of a multinational corporation to another. Other countries are even considering taxes and tariffs on corporate data flowing across their borders.

The economic impact of the e-commerce revolution is beginning to surface significantly on the global front. As a result, many developing countries have developed or are in the process of developing national IT policies. These policies are being developed based on two different understandings of the role of IT in general. The first considers IT policy as an integral component of a microeconomic 'industry' policy, and the second looks at IT from a broader social view. Fundamentally, all observers agree that the introduction of IT policies on the global front will inevitably facilitate the utilization of IT more efficiently and productively.

One of the global consequences of IT, however, is the international concern about the risks and dangers that developed as well as developing economies may face in the wide application of IT. One such risk may be dehumanization (Ogura, 1989). Regardless of what has been stated, the international repercussions of corporate information and IT promise to remain an uncertain and sensitive issue for the foreseeable future.

ECONOMIC DEVELOPMENT AND GROWTH

Many studies suggest that the key determinants of economic development are the accumulation of physical and human capital and technological improvements. Traditional neoclassical growth theory emphasizes physical capital accumulation whereas endogenous growth theory presumes that investment in human capital and technological progress are the main sources of economic growth. More recently, and as an extension to neoclassical models, Mankiw et al (1992) have shown that physical and human capital are important determinants of growth. Nevertheless, it still remains an open question whether these factors are the real sources of economic development.

There is reason to believe that if physical or human capital enrichment or technological improvements are taking place, the real growth factors must already have been unbound. Accordingly, physical and human capital and technology should be seen as proximate causes of growth. The still open questions are:

- What speeds up capital accumulation?
- What conditions are necessary for technological improvements?
- What are the ultimate causes of economic growth?

The changing value proposition in the knowledge economy is triggering a revolution in the way businesses and governments carry out their jobs. The Internet has always had its own complicated ethics, and those ethics were set aside by old-style management. This is radically shifting. They are, in part, becoming the rules of the game. For example, not only does B2B supply-chain management provide huge efficiencies and significant bottom line enhancement, but its deep integration allows partners to see into and through other organizations. As a consequence, decision makers are often privy to their competitors' internal strengths and weaknesses, trade secrets, unique know-how, market positioning, key personnel, and other valuable economic assets.

In summation, perhaps the most profound ethical changes in the New Economy are going on internally, inside the organization and at the firm level. In the New Economy, where knowledge, not equipment, drives profits, employees can no longer be considered 'outsiders'. They are the source of competitive advantage. The traditional command-and-control model of management is rapidly being replaced by decentralized teams of individuals motivated by their ownership in the corporation.

Value in the New Economy is being fundamentally redefined. As a result, transparency is becoming one of the keys to success in the twenty-first century. In e-business circles, transparency is no longer a rhetorical word. It is the rule of the game.

It is unarguably recognized that the IT revolution will have significant long-run effects on the economy and that the principal effects are more likely to be 'microeconomic' than 'macroeconomic'. As a result, the New Economy will require changes in the way the government provides property rights, institutional frameworks, and 'rules of the game' that underpin the market economy. Two main reasons underlie these changes; first is the pace of technological progress in the IT sector, which is very rapid and will continue to be very rapid for the foreseeable future. For example, at the end of the 1950s, there were 2,000 computers processing 10,000 instructions per second. Today, 300 million computers are processing several hundred million instructions per second. In addition, instructions per second rose from 20 million to 90 quadrillion – a 4 billion fold increase in 40 years. This translates into an annual growth rate of 56 percent per year. As the IT sector of the economy becomes a larger share of the total economy, the overall rate of productivity growth will increase toward the rate of productivity growth in the IT sector. Secondly, the computers, switches, cables, and programs that are the products of today's leading sectors are general-purpose technologies. As a result, advances in high-technology affect all aspects of the economy, thereby leading to larger overall effects. These microeconomic effects will have long-lasting and far-reaching impacts on the economy. As a result, the role of the government in developed and developing economy alike needs to be re-examined. Since the creation of knowledge is cumulative, the importance of intellectual property rights becomes more critical in the New Economy. Three issues are interrelated: property rights over ideas, incentives to fund research and development, and the exchange of information among researchers.

The New Economy is 'Schumpeterian' rather than 'Smithian'. In a Schumpeterian economy, the production of goods exhibits increasing returns to scale. Under these conditions, the competitive equilibrium is not the likely outcome – setting price equal to marginal cost does not allow the firm to recover the large fixed costs. However, government regulation or government subsidies to cover fixed costs destroy the entrepreneurial spirit and replace it with 'group-think and red-tape defects of administrative bureaucracy'. In addition, when innovation becomes the principal source of wealth, temporary monopoly power and profits may be essential to stimulate innovation. In a recent Brookings study on the economic impact of the Internet, a group of scholars estimated that the increased use of the Internet could add 0.25 to 0.5 percent to productivity growth over the next 5 years. Most of the impacts come from reducing the cost of data-intensive transactions (ordering, invoicing, accounting, and recruiting), from improved management of supply chains, from increased competition, and from increased efficiency of the wholesale and retail trade. In addition, many of the benefits of IT may result in improved standards of living, even though measured gross domestic product (GDP) is unaffected. Examples include reduced error rates in medical care delivery; a reduction in accidents, crime, and fraud prevention; and additional conveniences for consumers in the use of time and space.

The emergence of the information economy has been a key feature of faster productivity growth for many economies, developed and developing. Information technology has affected productivity in two ways. First, the IT sector itself has contributed directly to stronger productivity. Computers and other IT hardware have become better and cheaper, leading to increases in investment, employment, and output of the IT sector. Secondly, advances in technology have also increased productivity in the more traditional sectors of the economy: financial services, business services, and the retail and distribution industries. In the US, economic policy has contributed to a revival in productivity growth. Policies to maintain domestic competition and increase international competition have been stressed. Funds have been provided to support basic research and education. Also, and most importantly, the mix of monetary and fiscal policy has lowered interest rates and encouraged investment. The information economy can improve the effectiveness of monetary policy by allowing the private sector to better anticipate future central bank actions. Central banks typically operate by affecting overnight interest rates. By affecting current overnight rates and, most important, by affecting market expectations of future rates, monetary policy can affect financial market prices such as long-term interest rates, exchange rates, and equity prices. These prices will have the greatest effect on economic activity.

To summarize, the recent advances in IT will lead to continued strong productivity growth, and, therefore, overall economic growth. In addition, the gain in productivity will come from reducing the number of non-production workers per unit of output.

ECONOMIC DEVELOPMENT AND THE DIGITAL DIVIDE

All estimates relating to the growth of e-commerce have a central theme: exceptional growth over a very short period of time. Existing indications, though, show a widening gap between developing and developed economies in terms of competitiveness in this area. The absence of significant and far-reaching soft infrastructure in the developing economies could lead to the loss of existing industry and failure to attract new industries. This would mean a reduction in employment and tax revenue, with obvious negative consequences for overall economic performance in these countries.

In order to create the right environment to assist and to promote the widespread use of ICTs, a number of areas need to be addressed: the provision of adequate telecommunications infrastructure; procedures to promote the development of e-commerce and business prospects; the placement of appropriate enabling measures to smooth the progress and development of, use of, and access to applications using ICTs; adoption of legislative arrangements to support those enabling measures; development of electronic delivery methods for public services; and a variety of support activities. The authors believe that addressing these key areas will provide the necessary environment within which large elements of commerce and public service delivery will be developed in the future.

Many of the developments related to the information/knowledge society, such as Internet growth and the emergence of e-commerce, have arisen only over the last 5 or 6 years. The nature of these developments and the speed with which they occur impose new demands on the ability of governmental entities to keep abreast of them and to seek to influence and respond to them. The quick rate of development and the unquestionable necessity to act in response to the changes mean that additional resources are essential in key areas if we are to deal adequately with the range of issues identified and help accomplish the objective of any country being a key player in the information/knowledge society.

It is generally accepted that critical developments in the area of ICT and, in particular, those concerning e-government will take place over the next few years. This puts the burden on the shoulders of governments and requires them to commit resources immediately if they are to be adequately positioned to influence and respond to these developments and to make sure that their economic performance is not negatively affected through a failure to keep abreast of them. Those countries that ignore current developments in the marketplace will find themselves playing catch up with those who have taken the earliest lead. Even if such a catch-up were possible, the resources required at a later stage to take corrective action may well be considerably greater than those needed now to take anticipatory measures.

The uneven diffusion of information and communications technology – the digital divide – has caught the attention of academics, practitioners and politicians alike. Bridging this divide is now a global objective. However, the uneven diffusion of technology is nothing new. There have long been huge differences among countries. As a result, the world's 200 or so countries face the challenges of human development in the network age starting from very different points. In addition to the differences across countries, there are considerable disparities within countries.

When talking about the digital divide, a distinction has to be drawn between two different dimensions. The first is the international divide. The issues here are quite similar to those addressed in the classic discussion about the 'relatively slow and irregular' spread of technical progress from the originating countries to the rest of the world, about catching up and about the importance of not falling too far behind. The whole of Africa, for instance, has less international bandwidth than São Paulo, Brazil. Latin America's bandwidth, in turn, is roughly equal to that of Seoul, Republic of Korea, which is the worldwide leader in broadband Internet access (UNDP, 2001). The second (but surely no less important) dimension is the domestic divide. The discussion in this connection is about universal inclusion, about growing with equality and about averting the emergence of yet another form of exclusion. This second focus is of major importance in regions with such harsh social and economic inequalities. The digital divide can be assessed from many different standpoints. Income and Internet use are positively correlated, with countries that have lower income levels tending to have lower Internet penetration rates as well. Countries in Eastern Europe, for instance, do not have much higher per capita incomes, but their connectivity rates are relatively higher than those in Latin America.

The above discussion indicates that access to ICT infrastructure is not exclusively determined by income. Other resources seem to account for the fact that some countries make fuller use of its economic potential than others. Alongside this international dimension of the digital divide, a similar situation is found between different groups of citizens within a given society. The Latin American and Caribbean region has the most unequal income distribution in the world (ECLAC, 2002). This inequality is reflected, and often replicated, in its inhabitants' access to the 'heart of the information society'. The available figures and estimates regarding the domestic divide give grounds for serious concern about the creation of another form of exclusion. According to various estimates, almost 30 percent of the richest 15 percent of the Latin American population already had Internet connections, compared to an overall connectivity rate of around 6 percent for the aggregate. Extrapolating these numbers into the future, this discrepancy can be expected to increase significantly. For example, the top income group in Brazil is expected to reach a connectivity rate of 82 percent by 2005, in comparison to an estimated overall connectivity rate of just 12 percent. In addition to income, the digital divide is reflected in many other socio-economic, demographic and geographic characteristics. One of the most evident correlations is between ICT use and educational level. While it is true that, especially in Latin America and the Caribbean, there is also a very high positive correlation between income and education, the educational level has an independent effect on ICT use. Even within the same income group, ICT use is significantly higher among more highly educated people.

In this context, it is also noteworthy that illiteracy can be a major contributing factor to the digital divide. It is often overlooked in current discussions on the subject that illiteracy is one of the fundamental barriers to participation in the information society. Illiteracy rates in Latin America and the Caribbean vary widely (from as low as 2 percent to as much as 50 percent or more of the total national population). Especially among minority and marginalized groups (such as indigenous women), illiteracy rates are very high. It should also be pointed out, however, that ICTs offer a way of tackling long-standing problems such as illiteracy and, in fact, ICT-based literacy methods and projects are already being implemented in Latin America. Advancements in text-to-voice and voice-to-text software may eventually provide a useful tool for mitigating this long-standing form of social and economic exclusion.

The global reach of e-commerce is also double-edged in its impact on consumers. While e-commerce can bring far flung and highly competitive suppliers to the buyer's doorstep, this may be at the cost of uncertain recourse in the event of a dispute. Tracking down a delinquent trading partner and pursuing litigation in a different state or a foreign country may be prohibitively costly, particularly if the value of the transaction is relatively low. Digital River – a US-based online wholesaler selling software and music worldwide – has resorted to using software that tracks the national origin of prospective customers, in order to evaluate the potential for fraud. Chief Information Officer Randy Womack reported that the system thwarted more than US$13 million in attempted fraud in 1999, by identifying and giving extra scrutiny to potential buyers from countries that are responsible for a high proportion of online scams (Dalton, 1999).

The above discussion illustrates how the characteristics of the Internet can exacerbate the hazards facing those who transact through e-commerce, but there is a general consensus in the developed countries that government intervention in e-commerce should only be undertaken as a 'last resort', and that e-commerce companies and other intermediaries can be effective in mitigating the hazards raised by online markets. However, we should not discount the role of public institutions in supporting the development of e-commerce. Researchers in the New Institutional Economics (NIE) emphasize the critical role governments play in creating environments that foster private investment (North, 1990).

Indeed, there is little doubt that consumers' confidence in the integrity of e-commerce transactions would be greatly diminished were it not for a generally supportive national legal environment. It is precisely because consumers (and producers) believe that the courts can handle serious cases of fraud that new intermediaries are effective in creating confidence in e-commerce.

To narrow the digital divide, the 1969 United Nations Commission on International Development remains valid today – namely, a major effort is needed to revitalize education and increase the capacity to absorb, adapt and develop scientific and technical knowledge in developing countries. Information and communication technology is an important tool in helping to achieve this objective. Access is a key challenge. More than 95 percent of Internet hosts and secure servers used for electronic commerce reside in Organisation for Economic Co-operation and Development (OECD) countries.

While the public sector will play a role, it is believed that the private sector will play a key role. Getting private sector involvement will depend on good governance. Applications of the rule of law, market liberalization, fair competition laws, an appropriate regulatory framework, a well functioning financial sector, and so on, are all part of that good governance infrastructure. As developing countries start educating people, building good clean governance, applying the rule of law, liberalizing telecommunications markets, creating an environment for private investment, the digital divide will start to close.

E-COMMERCE DIFFUSION AND IMPEDIMENTS

The term diffusion is generally defined as 'the process by which an innovation is communicated through certain channels over time among the members of a social system' (Rogers, 1995, p. 5). The traditional economic analysis of diffusion focuses on unfolding and forecasting the adoption of products in markets. In particular, the question which factors affect the speed and specific course of diffusion processes is of central concern. Traditional diffusion models are based on similar assumptions. Generally, the number of new adopters in a certain period of time is modeled as the proportion of the group of market participants that have not yet adopted the innovation. Based on this fundamental structure, three different types of diffusion models are most common (Lilien and Kotler 1983; Mahajan et al, 1990). The exponential diffusion model (also external influence model or pure innovative model) assumes that the number of new adopters is determined by influences from outside the system, eg, mass communication. The logistic diffusion model (also internal influence model or pure imitative model) assumes that the decision to become a new adopter is determined solely by the positive influence of existing adopters (eg, word of mouth). The semi-logistic diffusion model (also mixed influence model) considers both internal and external influences. In general, network diffusion models can be divided into relational models and structural models. Relational models analyze how direct contacts between participants in networks influence the decision to adopt or not to adopt an innovation. In contrast, structural models focus on the pattern of all relationships and show how the structural characteristics of a social system determine the diffusion process (Valente, 1995).

Besides the analytical economic research approaches described above, a set of empirical studies of diffusion processes can be found in various research areas (for an early overview of existing empirical studies refer to Rogers and Shoemaker, 1971). Most of the studies are based on the critical mass approaches which analyze the diffusion rate of innovations, collective behavior, and public opinion (Marwell et al, 1988). A long research tradition exists in the area of network models of diffusion of innovations. Subsequently, network analysis in this context is an instrument for analyzing the pattern of interpersonal communication in a social network (for concepts of sociological network analysis).

There are a number of obstacles to the diffusion of e-commerce and e-governments in developing economies. Thus governments have an important role in speeding Internet diffusion and setting appropriate policies and complementary services, particularly affecting the telecommunications sector, other infrastructure, human capital, and the investment environment severely constrain Internet access in developing countries.

The major impediment to the growth and success of e-commerce in developing economies is poor telecommunications infrastructure. Required telecommunications services include transmission facilities connecting a country's domestic network to the greater Internet, the domestic Internet backbone, and connections from homes and businesses to the backbone network. The defects of domestic telecommunications services may be less important for the larger firms in developing countries; these firms may find it profitable to invest in telecommunications facilities (such as wireless) that bypass the local network. A growing number of African Internet sites are hosted on servers in Europe or the US because of poor infrastructure. Hence, even traffic that originates and terminates domestically can cost the same as international transmission. The high cost of Internet access, the lack of local loop infrastructure necessary for basic dial-up modem access, and the poor quality of the local loop infrastructure that does exist all impede connections to the domestic backbone. Country comparisons show a strong relationship between usage price and Internet penetration. For many developing countries, the most important issue is the lack of telephone service to homes and businesses. Despite increases in rates of telephone line penetration during the 1990s, more than one-third of the 130 developing countries (excluding small islands) with data for 1998 had fewer than 5 telephone lines per 100 inhabitants.

The most popular alternatives by which developing countries can overcome inadequate local loop infrastructure have been either shared facilities or wireless local loop. Shared facilities, which involve local entrepreneurs selling the use of a computer with Internet access, are a fast and relatively cheap way of increasing Internet use. Wireless and satellite technologies also provide an alternative to the high costs and inefficiencies of many domestic telecommunications systems. Although currently used primarily for voice, mobile phones are increasingly acting as better devices for many of the usual Internet applications. Cellular phones in some developing countries have experienced strong growth rates and relatively high penetration, similar to those in industrial countries. In the United Arab Emirates (UAE), for instance, mobile phone penetration rate is 65 percent (Karake Shalhoub and Qasimi, 2003). On average, however, for developing countries as a group, mobile phone penetration remains well below industrial country levels. Sub-Saharan Africa averages 5 cellular phones per 1,000 people, compared with 265 cellular phones for every 1,000 people in high-income countries (World Bank, 2000).

Poor infrastructure services (other than telecommunications) are an important constraint on e-commerce in developing economies. Frequent and long power interruptions can seriously interfere with data transmission and systems performance; many Bangalore software firms, as an example, have their own generators (Panagariya, 2000). Mail service can be unreliable, expensive, and time consuming in many developing countries. For example, the unreliability of postal services in Latin America has meant that more expensive courier services must be used to deliver goods ordered over the Internet, and in response, international courier services are setting up special distribution systems in Miami (Lapper, 2000). The lack of safeguards against fraud can severely restrict credit card purchases, the most common means of conducting transactions over the Internet. For example, many consumers in the Gulf countries of Saudi Arabia, UAE, and Kuwait are unwilling to purchase goods over the Internet because credit card companies will not compensate holders for fraudulent use of cards (in many industrial countries, cardholders have only a limited exposure to loss).

A critical mass of highly skilled labor is needed in developing countries to supply the necessary applications, provide support, and disseminate relevant technical knowledge for e-commerce. The workforce in many developing countries lacks a sufficient supply of these skills, and the demand for this specialized labor from industrial countries has further strained the supply of this labor in developing countries. In the mid-1990s North America and Europe had unfilled demand for professionals trained in IT. In addition, the Internet also facilitates the mobility of skilled labor services. Workers can choose to remain in their own country while exporting labor services to higher-paying industrial countries.

Several regulatory impediments to the widespread adoption of e-commerce exist in many developing countries. Duties and taxes on computer hardware and software and communication equipment increase the expense of connecting to the Internet. For example, a computer imported into some African countries may be taxed at rates exceeding 50 percent (UNCTAD, 2003). The overall environment for private sector activities is a significant determinant of Internet service diffusion. An open foreign direct investment regime helps promote technology diffusion, which is important to the growth of e-commerce.

Foreign direct investment is also one channel that could facilitate certification of domestic firms for access to online auctions. Governments also can play an important role in supporting the certification of firms by providing information on certification procedures, promoting access by domestic firms to international organizations and firms that provide certification, and perhaps subsidizing the costs of certification to demonstrate the kinds of resources available in the domestic market. This role will be particularly important (at least in a transitional sense) as the intermediaries that formerly helped connect developing country firms to international markets are replaced by web-based intermediaries that may have less information on developing countries. Governments must provide a supportive legal framework for electronic transactions, including recognition of digital signatures, legal admissibility of electronic contracts, and the establishment of data storage requirements in paper form, intellectual property rights for digital content, liability of Internet service providers, privacy of personal data, and mechanisms for resolving disputes.

That most Internet business is conducted in English is currently an important constraint on using the Internet. Estimates of the share of English used on the Internet range from 70–80 percent, but only 57 percent of Internet users have English as their first language (ITU, 2000). Per capita Internet use averages about 30 percent in those industrial countries where English is common, compared with about 5 percent in other industrial countries. Conversely, Internet content is limited in the local language of most developing countries. From a commercial aspect, Schmitt (2000) found that just 37 percent of Fortune 100 websites support a language other than English. The amount of non-English material on the Web is growing, however. Spanish websites in particular are increasing, in part to serve the large Spanish-speaking community in the US (Vogel and Druckerman, 2000). Improvements in translation services (by people and machines), as well as web browsers that recognize characters of different languages should ease language constraints. There is growing recognition that English-only content is insufficient for a global economy.

WHY ADOPT E-COMMERCE?

There are three different perspectives with which developing countries have viewed ICTs and e-commerce. The dominant perspective has been one of promoting the growth of ICTs as one of the key sectors of a country's economy. According to this perspective, the ICT sector presents a great opportunity for a country to enhance its economic growth and employment as has been shown by India and Egypt (to a lesser extent). The ICT sector can also become a major source of earning foreign exchange and offer products and service that can be deployed by other sectors of the economy.

A second perspective that has emerged in the last 5 years is the deployment of ICT for delivering government services. Improvements in the delivery of government services are an important issue for many developing countries as the largest cost of inefficiency is borne by the poor. Electronic delivery can improve efficiency, cut delays for citizens, lessen corruption, and increase transparency. Applications that focus on the online delivery of services to citizens, to businesses, and to different arms of government are covered within the broad definition of electronic government. E-government is about a process of reform in the way governments work, share information and deliver services to external and internal clients. Specifically, e-government harnesses information technologies (such as Wide Area Networks, the Internet, and mobile computing) to transform relations with citizens, businesses, and other arms of government. The resulting benefits can be less corruption, increased transparency, greater convenience, revenue growth, and cost reduction.

The third perspective defines the role of electronic media and communication within a society. Within the ambit of this view, governments have to deal with issues such as convergence of different technologies, private control over media, and censorship. This book is concerned with the second viewpoint and focuses on the role of governments as enablers, regulators, and providers of ICT-based services.

Investment in ICTs and the *productivity paradox* has been a well discussed topic; for example, see Brynjolfsson (2003) who looked at the ongoing debate over whether IT contributes to productivity growth. His ongoing research, based on data from more than 1,167 large US companies, finds a statistically significant correlation between the intensity of IT used in a company (IT capital per worker) and that company's overall productivity. There is an emerging consensus among economists that IT has been the biggest single factor driving the productivity resurgence, although debate continues about the exact magnitude of its contribution. Brynjolfsson and Hitt (1998) argue that the focus should be on how to make ICT more effective rather than more productive (in terms of efficiency). They hypothesize that computerization does not automatically increase productivity, but it is an essential component of organizational changes that do lead to productivity increase. Hence, business and organizational processes must be re-engineered in co-ordination with IT investments in order to increase the probability of improved performance. Hitt and Brynjolfsson (1996) separate the value dimensions of investment in IT into three: (1) the effect of IT on productivity; (2) the effect of IT on profitability; and, (3) the effect of IT on consumer surplus. The authors believe that this multidimensional approach is more realistic because, depending on one's point of view, one, two, or three dimensions may be realized or one dimension may be more important than the other. Although this school of research is becoming more prominent, the relationship between investment in information communication technologies and performance is still vague and requires more research.

RESOURCE-BASED VIEW

The resource-based view argues that the performance of a firm is a function of the resources and skills that are in place, and, of those firm-specific characteristics which are rare and difficult to imitate or substitute (Barney, 1991). This concept is basically based on Coase's theory of the firm, which maintains that the firm is a combination of alliances that have linked themselves in such a way as to reduce the cost of producing goods and services for delivery to the market-place (Coase, 1937). An enhancement of this resource-based view is that a firm or an economy can create a competitive advantage by building resources that work together to generate organizational capabilities (Bharadwaj, 2000). These capabilities permit firms and economies to adopt and adapt processes that enable them to realize a greater level of output from a given input or, maintain their level of output from a lower quantity of input.

Capabilities afforded by ICT are one major component of organizational and economies' capabilities; and recent studies have identified a number of specific ICT capabilities that provide competitive advantage. Bharadwaj (2000) classifies an entity's key ICT capability as comprising: (1) a physical IT infrastructure, (2) human IT resources (including technical IT skills, and managerial IT skills), and (3) intangible IT-enabled resources (such as customer orientation, knowledge assets, and synergy).

Viewed from a growth perspective, resource-based theory is concerned with the origin, evolution, and sustainability of firms (Conner and Prahalad, 1996; Peteraf, 1993). Firms experiencing the highest growth have added new competencies sequentially, often over extended periods of time. Resource-based sequencing is important for achieving sustainable growth. In a changing environment, firms must continuously invent and upgrade their resources and capabilities if they are to maintain competitive advantage and growth (Agryris, 1996; Robins and Wiersema, 1995; Wernerfelt and Montgomery, 1988). This sequential development of resources and capabilities can make a firm's advantage inimitable (Barney, 1991). Competitors cannot simply buy these resources and capabilities without acquiring the entire firm. This is because the resources and capabilities are built over time in a path-dependent process that makes them inextricably interwoven into a firm. This facet of resources and capabilities development makes it theoretically impossible for competitors to imitate completely (Dierickx and Cool, 1989).

Until recently, little research using a resource-based-view framework has examined strategy differences in the social context of developing economies. As with most resources that create competitive advantage, resources for competitive advantage in developing economies are, on the whole, intangible. However, they are not necessarily market or product specific, as might be expected. Although some qualifications are standard regardless of the level of development (for instance, first mover advantages), others are particularly important in developing economies. Global and multinational firms that are able to manage some of the imperfect conditions in developing economies benefit from being first movers; some the benefits include economic advantages of sales volume and domination of distribution and communication channels.

In developing economies, however, such advantages are difficult to establish without good relationships with home governments. Early relationships give tangible benefits, such as access to licenses, whose number is often limited by a government. In addition, local competitors may have developed capabilities for relationship-based management in their environment that substitute for the lack of institutional infrastructure. Developing distribution mechanisms may protect a domestic firm in a developing economy against entry by foreign firms. Furthermore, focusing on a market that has not yet reached the globalization stage might allow a domestic firm in an emerging economy to dodge the onslaught of multinational rivals. Additionally, competing in a global market may be possible in a commodity area where natural resources or labor give a low-cost advantage (Aulakh et al, 2000). In essence, a firm must understand that relationship between its company assets and the changing nature of the institutional infrastructure as well as the characteristics of its industry. In so doing, the emerging economy firm may be able to become an aggressive contender domestically or globally by using its resources as sources of competitive advantage.

The resource-based view of the firm sees a firm as a bundle of resources and capabilities. Resources are firm specific assets and competencies controlled and used by firms to develop and implement their strategies. They can be either tangible (eg financial assets, technology) or intangible (eg managerial skills, reputation) (Barney, 1997). Resources are heterogeneous across firms, and some resources are valuable yet rare, difficult to imitate, or non-substitutable, giving the firms that have them distinctive core capabilities. Resources that provide sustainable advantage tend to be: (1) causally ambiguous (eg transformational leadership), (2) socially complex (eg culture), (3) rare, or (4) imperfectly imitable (Barney, 1997). Capabilities are a firm's abilities to integrate, build, and reconfigure internal and external assets and competencies so that they enable it to perform distinctive activities (Teece et al, 1997). The resource-based approach focuses on the characteristics of resources and the strategic factor markets from which they are obtained.

Past research using the resource-based view associates rent potential, (ie greater than normal returns) with two possible paths. The first involves external factors, including buyer and supplier power, intensity of competition, and industry and product market structure, that influence what resources the firm selects, as well as how they are selected and deployed. The second path to the capture of rents involves creating idiosyncratically productive combinations of resources.

Firms cannot expect to garner rents by merely owning and controlling resources. They should be able to acquire, develop, and deploy these resources in a manner that provides distinctive sources of advantage in the marketplace. The traditional conceptualization of the resource-based view has not looked beyond the properties of resources and resource markets to explain enduring firm heterogeneity. In particular, past research has not addressed or examined the process of resource development (Oliver, 1997). Firms' decisions about selecting, accumulating, and deploying resources are characterized as economically rational within the constraints of limited information, cognitive biases, and causal ambiguity (Peteraf, 1993). Additionally, the traditional resource-based view is limited to relatively stable environments. Barney (1997, p. 171) warns, 'if a firm's threats and opportunities change in a rapid and unpredictable manner, the firm will often be unable to maintain a sustained competitive advantage'.

Only recently have researchers begun to focus on the specifics of how some organizations first develop firm specific capabilities and then how they renew competencies to respond to shifts in the business environment. The dynamic capabilities approach (Teece et al, 1997) is an extension of the resource-based view of the firm that was introduced to explain how firms can develop their capability to adapt and even capitalize on rapidly changing technological environments. Dynamic capabilities emphasize the key role of strategic management in appropriately adapting, integrating, and reconfiguring internal and external organizational skills, resources, and functional competencies within a changing environment. The development of such capabilities is limited by the firm's existing base of capabilities, and is shaped by its current market position and past history of developing capabilities (Grant, 1991; Teece et al, 1997). The difference between the traditional conceptualization of the resource-based view of the firm (Barney, 1997; Grant, 1991; Wernerfelt, 1984) and the dynamic capabilities view (Teece et al, 1997) is that under the traditional view, current firm resources and capabilities are exploited to the opportunities in the marketplace, whereas under the dynamic capabilities view, the firm needs to develop new capabilities to identify opportunities and respond quickly to them.

Although Teece et al (1997) outlined the dynamic capabilities approach, they did not provide empirical evidence to help understand how these capabilities are developed. Following this approach, a handful of models have been proposed to explain how resources and capabilities are built up over time (see, for example, Oliver, 1997). All these models are empirically grounded; however, they have all followed a factor-oriented, or variance theory, approach. Process theories are less common in the resource-based view of the firm literature, and have yet to be developed for explaining the resource and capability development process. Process theories focus on sequences of activities to explain how and why particular outcomes evolve over time.

The literature review undertaken did not identify a single process model of capability development. The prevailing wisdom seems to be that capability development is a lengthy, complex process influenced by multiple organizational dimensions.

BOOK SUMMARY

This book aims to take a step toward an empirical/theoretical framework for understanding the impact of IT in general and e-commerce in particular on the growth and development of emerging economies. Basically, a framework that is grounded in strong theory is developed. The framework uses core constructs that appear central to resource-based and technology diffusion literature and provides a fine-grained understanding of e-commerce adoption processes by public and private sector entities in developing countries. In so doing, this book considers how each exchange encounter is shaped by, and in turn shapes, relational characteristics, which form the bases for growth and development.

This book is aimed at the 'low-to-middle'-level rigor. It is not designed to compete with extremely sophisticated modeling or quantitatively oriented books. Actually, this book does not know of any competitor. This level of rigor makes the book attractive to any student, professional, practitioner, or policymaker interested in finding answers to questions such as:

(1) Why are some developing countries successful at e-commerce while others toil?
(2) What are public and private sector entities doing differently in adopting and adapting to e-commerce?
(3) How are successful countries moving from traditional applications to the new breed of integrated e-commerce architectures?

The major thrust of the book, which evaluates the experience of e-commerce in developing economies from a resource-based theory perspective, is unique and innovative in nature. The features of uniqueness and innovativeness, coupled with the radical changes in the use of governmental resources to improve the effectiveness and efficiency of an economy, and the effects of these changes on the economic structure of a country make this book useful to many disciplines.

The book is inspired by a number of factors:

1. The importance of the subject at hand.

2. The lack of empirical research on the subject. Most of the work done is descriptive in nature. The book brings economic concepts into the picture of adopting an e-commerce model, by using resource-based theory as a vehicle of analysis.
3. While most writers have focused on the nature of business models such as e-business and e-commerce in developed, advanced economies, this will be the first published book on analyzing the impact of e-commerce on growth and development of emerging economies.

As e-commerce matures and its tools and applications improve, greater attention is given to its use to improve the business of public institutions and governments. The main goal is to provide citizens and organizations with more convenient access to government information and services, and to provide delivery of public services to citizens, business partners and suppliers, and those working in the public sector. E-government applications extend over a wide spectrum: (1) government-to-citizens (G2C), (2) government-to-business and business-to-government (G2B and B2G), (3) government-to-government (G2G), and (4) government-to-employees (G2E).

As in the industrial age, in many instances it will be up to governments to lead the transformation to the new information/knowledge age. Public sector organizations will have to adjust their relationships with citizens, businesses, employees and other public agencies – indeed, the US government is in a unique position to be a catalyst for change. To this end, the information/knowledge society has prompted many countries to adopt e-government initiatives.

The value of the book is twofold. First, it will cover the experiences of a number of developing countries (DCs) and newly industrialized countries (NICs), or emerging economies that adopted e-commerce and e-government initiatives early on, such as Singapore, Malaysia, Taiwan, Hong Kong, and the UAE. Some fragmented literature exists on the subject, but there is no unique book evaluating it from a comparative analysis, resource-based perspective. The book will add value to existing literature by accomplishing this goal. In addition, the book will cover the different approaches governments in the various countries have taken based on their own social, cultural and economic contexts. Some countries have adopted a gradual approach to e-government starting with the *Publish phase*, moving on to the *Interact phase*, and ending with the *Transact phase*, whereas others have taken a *basket* approach by going through the three stages simultaneously. The book will cover the experiences of those countries from the inception of the idea, to the setting of vision, to the formulation of strategy, through implementation, and ending with assessment of the costs and benefits of the initiative from a resource-based theory perspective.

Secondly, the book aims to take a step toward an integrative theoretical framework for understanding the impact of e-commerce on economic development from a resource-based perspective. A large stream of research in organization theory, information systems, organizational sociology, economics, and technology management has contributed substantially to our understanding of organizational adoption of innovations. A close examination of the research would suggest three broad themes: (1) a number of organizational and environmental factors influence organizational adoption of innovations; (2) institutional pressures from the environment do influence technology adoption; and (3) firms and governments often fail to respond effectively to environmental changes, including new technology.

In this book, the authors extend theoretical developments in the resource-based view to investigate why some countries respond better to new technologies, in general, and e-commerce, in particular. Technological opportunism, a sense and respond capability of decision makers with respect to new technologies, is an important determinant of e-commerce/ e-government adoption. To assess the incremental contribution of technological opportunism in explaining e-commerce adoption, variables such as the perceived usefulness of e-commerce as a technology and complementary assets that help generate value from e-commerce are integrated in the model.

Electronic marketplaces, e-commerce and e-governments are (and will be) playing a significant role in determining the success (or failure) of corporations, governmental agencies and, even, nations. Management and government officials need to learn that the real challenge surrounding electronic marketplaces, in particular, and e-commerce, in general, is the task of making it happen. The book targets professionals, academicians and researchers. It can be used as a recommended reading in Electronic Commerce classes, Information Economy classes, Management of Change classes, Economic Development classes, Macro economic classes, as well as Marketing classes. The book is a great reading for small and medium size businesses that are considering moving into e-commerce and are looking for a real case study. In addition, the greatest benefit could be gained by governmental officials of developing and NICs contemplating e-government initiatives. The book's timeliness and insights into the changes in organizational and governmental practices make it appealing to a broad management and to geographic markets: (1) senior and mid-level managers and strategic planners who are charged with developing business strategies; (2) corporate executives who must drive their firm's competitive future; (3) government officials, especially in developing economies; and (4) IT managers, both in the public and the private sectors, who need to lead their teams with strategic decisions.

The book is geared toward professionals in the private and public sectors, researchers, and academicians. It refrains from technical complexity and this makes it readable and understandable. With respect to competition, we do not know of any book analyzing the empirical impact of e-governments and electronic marketplaces on the economic, cultural and social texture of an economic entity from a strong economic theory such as resource-based approach. The book is unique and we believe it will open the door to other researchers to explore research and study experiences of other economic entities.

A major competitive advantage of this book is the fact that it is the collective product of an academician/consultant who is knowledgeable of the latest development in e-commerce theory and application, and a practitioner/leader who is applying bleeding edge e-government technology and leading the implementation of one country's e-government initiative. The two authors form the perfect team.

CHAPTER OVERVIEW

E-commerce and economic development uses a theory-based, empirical investigation to describe the linkage between the adoption of e-commerce and economic growth and development and a number of country specific characteristics (resources). The book's six chapters are organized as follows:

Chapter 1
This chapter provides an overview of the entire book and establishes the context for the whole book. Importance of the research at hand is emphasized along with the theories used, the geographic area of implementation, the methods used and the methodology applied.

Chapter 2
This chapter provides an overview of the move to the *digital economy* and the move from the marketplace to the marketspace. Coverage of the changes that e-commerce has introduced into economic systems will be emphasized in this chapter, starting with the economic roles of markets, extending into changes of the processes used in supply change and the various components of digital ecosystems, to factors of competition on marketspaces and critical success factors in the digital economy. This chapter will highlight the experience of developing countries from the practical side.

Chapter 3

This chapter reviews the literature on resource-based theory and diffusion of radical technologies in developing economies.

Chapter 4

This chapter is devoted to the development of hypotheses, discussion of methodology, identification of variables, and data collection. In addition, reliable measures of this construct are identified.

Chapter 5

This chapter is devoted to model testing, data analysis and presentation of the results; the analysis should reveal why some countries are more technologically opportunistic than others and what countries can do to become more technologically opportunistic.

Chapter 6

This chapter consists of a summary, concluding remarks, practical implications of findings, and recommendations for future research.

CONCLUSION

The e-business revolution is not only changing the technology of the workplace, but fundamentally redefining the way that countries design their growth and development strategies. Electronic governments, the B2B world with its e-markets, customer focus, and deeply integrated corporate and economic relationships are driving growth and development of economies at e-speed and creating value in different ways. The key to survival in the new e-business environment depends upon governmental leaders' ability to adapt to a new, more collaborative, corporate-type, and transparent competition model. This new reality presents major challenges to traditional ways of governing and leading economic growth and development.

Economic development is the process of creating wealth by mobilizing human, financial, physical, natural, and capital resources to produce (generate) marketable goods and services. The government's role is to influence the process for the benefit of the various stakeholders in the country. Economic development, then, is fundamentally about enhancing the factors of productive capacity – land, labor, capital, and technology – of a national, state or local economy.

Early economic development theory was but merely an extension of conventional economic theory which equated 'development' with growth and industrialization. As a result, Latin American, Asian and African countries were seen mostly as 'underdeveloped' countries, ie 'primitive' versions of European nations that could, with time, 'develop' the institutions and standards of living of Europe and North America.

Economic growth is caused by improvements in the quantity and quality of the factors of production that a country has available, ie land, labor, capital and enterprise. Conversely, economic decline may occur if the quantity and quality of any of the factors of production falls. Increases in the supply of labor can increase economic growth. Increases in the population can increase the number of young people entering the labor force. Increases in the population can also lead to an increase in market demand thus stimulating production. However, if the population grows at a faster rate than the level of GDP the GDP per capita will fall. It is not simply the amount of labor and skills that will lead to economic growth. It is often the quality of that labor. This will depend on the educational provision in countries. Improving the skills of the workforce is seen as being an important key to economic growth. Many developing countries have made enormous efforts to provide universal primary education. As more and more capital is used, labor has to be better trained in the skills to use them. It should always be remembered that education spending involves an opportunity cost in terms of current consumption and thus it is often referred to as investment spending on human capital.

REFERENCES

Ackoff, R.L. (1967), 'Management misinformation systems', *Management Science*, **14**(4), 18–21.

Agryris, N., (1996), 'Evidence on the role of firm capabilities in vertical integration decisions', *Strategic Management Journal*, **17**, 129–50.

Attewell, P. (1992). 'Technology diffusion and organizational learning: the case of business computing', *Organization Science*, **3**(1), 1–19.

Aulakh, Preet S., Masaaki Kotabe, and Hildy Teegen (2000), 'Export strategies and performance of firms from emerging economies: evidence from Brazil, Chile and Mexico', *Academy of Management Journal*, **43**(3), 342–61.

Bakos, J.Y. and E. Brynjolfsson (1993), 'From vendors to partners: information technology and incomplete contracts in buyer-supplier relationships', *Journal of Organizational Computing*, **3**(3), 301–8.

Barney, J. (1991), 'Firm resources and sustained competitive advantage', *Journal of Management* (March), 99–120.

Barney, J. (1997), *Gaining and Sustaining Competitive Advantage*, Reading, MA: Addison-Wesley.

Barney, J.B. (1991), 'Integrating organizational behavior and strategy formulation research: a resource based analysis', *Advances in Strategic Management*, **8**, 39–61.

Barua, A., B. Lee and A.B. Whinston (1996). 'The calculus of reengineering', *Information Systems Research*, **7**(4), 409–28.

Bharadwaj, A. (2000), 'A resource-based perspective on information technology capability and firm performance: an empirical investigation', *MIS Quarterly*, **24**(1), 169–96.

Brynjolfsson, E. (2003), 'The IT productivity gap', *Optimize*, July (21), 793–808.

Brynjolfsson, E. and L.M. Hitt (1995), 'Information technology as a factor of production: the role of differences among firms', *Economics of Innovation and New Technology*, **3**(4), 183–200.

Brynjolfsson, E. and L. Hitt (1998). 'Beyond the productivity paradox', *Communications of the ACM*, **41**(8), 49–55.

Brynjolfsson, E. and C.F. Kemerer (1996), 'Network externalities in microcomputer software: An econometric analysis of the spreadsheet market', *Management Science*, **42**(12), 1627–47.

Chircu, A.M., G.B. Davis and R.I. Kauffman (2000), 'Trust, expertise and e-commerce intermediary adoption', *Proceedings of the 2000 Americas Conference on Information Systems*, Long Beach, CA: Association of Information Systems, pp. 10–13.

Clemons, E.K. (1991), 'Evaluation of strategic investments in information technology', *Communications of the ACM*, **34**(1), 22–36.

Coase, R.H. (1937), 'The nature of the firm', *Economica*, new series, **4**(16), 386–405.

Cohen, W.M. and D.A. Levinthal (1990), 'Absorptive capacity: a new perspective on learning and innovation', *Administrative Science Quarterly*, **35**(1), 128–52.

Conner, K. and C. Prahalad (1996), 'A resource-based theory of the firm: knowledge versus opportunism', *Organization Science*, **7**(5), 477–501.

Dalton, G. (1999), 'Overseas fraud finders', *Information Week*, September 27, 382–3.

Davamanirajan, P., T. Mukhopadhyay, C. Kriebel and R.J. Kauffman (1999), 'Systems design, process performance and economic outcome', Carnegie-Mellon University, Graduate School of Industrial Administration, working paper, Pittsburgh, PA.

Davern, M.J. and R.J. Kauffman (2000), 'Discovering potential and realizing value from information technology investments', *Journal of Management Information Systems*, **16**(4), 121–43.

Davis, F.D. (1989), 'Perceived usefulness, perceived ease of use, and user acceptance of information technology', *MIS Quarterly*, **13**(3), 319–41.

Dierickx P.J. and K. Cool (1989), 'Asset stock accumulation and the sustainability of competitive advantage', *Management Science*, **35**, 1504–11.

Donovan, J. (1989). 'From the back room to the boardroom', *Computerworld*, **17** (April), 83–4.

Dos Santos, B. and K. Peffers (1995). 'Rewards to investors in innovative information technology applications: first movers and early followers in ATMs', *Organization Science*, **6**(3), 241–59.

Economic Commission for Latin America and the Caribbean (ECLAC) (2002), *Statistical Yearbook of Latin America and the Caribbean*, New York: United Nations.

Grant, Robert M. (1991), 'The resource-based theory of competitive advantage: Implications for strategy formulation', *California Management Review*, **33** (Spring), 114–35.

Hitt, Lorin M. and Erik Brynjolfsson (1996), 'Productivity, business profitability, and consumer surplus: three different measures of information technology value', *MIS Quarterly*, **20**(2), 121–42.

International Labor Organization (ILO) (2001), *World Employment Report – Life at Work in the Information Economy*, Geneva: ILO.

International Telecommunications Union (ITU) (2000), *Telecommunication Indicators Database*, Geneva: United Nations.

Johnson, M.J., R.L. Schwab and L. Foa (1999), 'Technology as a change agent for the teaching process', accessed March 2002 at www.apple.eom/education/LTReview/fall99/tech/11index.html.

Karake Shalhoub, Z. and Al Qasimi, L. (2003), *The UAE and Information Society*, ESCWA Report, Beirut, Lebanon: United Nations.

Katz, M.L. and C. Shapiro (1986), 'Technology Adoption in the Presence of Network Externalities', *Journal of Political Economy*, August (98), 822–41.

Larson, M. (1998), 'Search for the secure transactions: Barriers to e-commerce falling', *Quality*, **37**(8), 61–3.

Leonard-Barton, D. (1992), 'Core capabilities and core rigidities: a paradox in managing new product development', *Strategic Management Journal*, **13** (Summer), 111–25.

Lilien, G.L. and P. Kotler (1983), *Marketing Decision Making. A Model Building Approach*, New York: Harper & Row.

Lucas, H.C., Jnr (1999), *Information Technology and the Productivity Paradox: assessing the Value of Investing in IT*, New York: Oxford University Press.

Mahajan, V., E. Muller and F.M. Bass (1990), 'New product diffusion models in marketing: a review and directions for research', *Journal of Marketing*, **54**, 1–26.

Mankiw, N.G., D. Romer and D.N. Weil, (1992), 'A contribution to the empirics of economic growth', in *Quarterly Journal of Economics*, **107**(2), 407–37.

Marwell, G., P. Oliver and R. Prahl (1988), 'Social networks and collective action: a theory of the critical mass', *American Journal of Sociology*, **94**, 503–4.

Miles, I. (1989), 'Social implications of information technology', in M. Jussawalla, T. Okuma, and T. Araki (eds), *Information Technology and Global Interdependence*, Westport, CT: Greenwood Press, pp. 222–35.

Moore, K.R. (1998), 'Trust and relationship commitment in logistics alliances: a buyer perspective', *International Journal of Purchasing and Materials Management*, **34**(1), 24–37.

North, Douglass C. (1990), *Institutions, Institutional Change, and Economic Performance*, New York: Cambridge University Press.

Ogura, K. (1989), Information technologies and international relations', in M. Jussawalla, T. Okuma and T. Araki (eds), *Information Technology and Global Interdependence*. Westport, CT: Greenwood Press, pp. ix–xiii.

Oliver, Christine (1997), 'Sustainable competitive advantage: combining institutional and resource-based views', *Strategic Management Journal*, **18** (October), 697–713.

Panagariya, A. (2000), 'E-commerce, WTO and developing countries', *The World Economy*, pp. 959–78.

Peteraf, Margaret A. (1993), 'The cornerstones of competitive advantage: a resource-based view', *Strategic Management Journal*, **14** (March), 179–91.

Porter, M.E. (1996), 'What is strategy?', *Harvard Business Review*, **74**(6): 61–78.

Riggins, F.J., C.H. Kriekel and T. Mukhopadhyay (1994), 'The growth of inter organizational systems in the presence of network externalities', *Management Science*, **40**(8), 984–98.

Robins J.A. and M.F. Wiersema (1995), 'A resource-based approach to the multi-business firm: empirical analysis of portfolio interrelationships and corporate financial performance', *Strategic Management Journal*, **16**, 277–99.

Rogers, E.M. (1995), *Diffusion of Innovations*, (4th edn), New York: Free Press.

Rogers, E.M. and F.F. Shoemaker (1971), *Communication of Innovations*, (2nd edn) New York: Collier-Macmillan.

Schmitt, E. (2000), 'The multilingual site blueprint', *The Forrester Report* June, accessed at www.forrester.com.

Simon, H. (1997), *Administrative Behavior: A Study of Decision Making Processes in Administrative Organizations*, 4th edn New York: Free Press.

Teece, D.J., G. Pisano and A. Shuen (1997) 'Dynamic capabilities and strategic management', *Strategic Management Journal*, **18** 7, 509–33.

United Nations Conference on Trade and Development (UNCTAD) (2003), *E-commerce and Development Report*, New York: United Nations.

United Nations Development Programme (UNDP) (2001), *Electronic Commerce and Development*, New York: United Nations.

Valente, T.W. (1995), *Network Models of the Diffusion of Innovations*, Cresskill, NJ:.

Vogel, Thomas T. and Pamela Druckerman (2000), 'Latin Internet graze sets off alarm bells', *Wall Street Journal*, February 16, p. 7.

Webster's New Millenium Dictionary of English (2003), preview edn (v0.9.6), Los Angeles: Lexico Publishing Group LLC.

Weick, K. (1999), 'Technology as equivoque: sense making in new technologies', in P.S. Goodman, L.S. Sproull (eds), *Technology and Organizations*, San Francisco: Jossey-Bass.

Wernerfelt B. and Montgomery C.A. (1988), 'Tobin's q and the importance of focus in firm performance', *American Economic Review*, **78**, 246–50.

Wernerfelt, Birger (1984), 'A resource-based view of the firm', *Strategic Management Journal*, **5** (April–June), 171–80.

World Bank (2000), *Entering the 21st Century: World Development Report 1999/2000*, Washington, DC: World Bank.

2. E-commerce and e-government: a review

INTRODUCTION

The best-selling authors in business topics agree that the structure of the workplace must be revamped if corporations are to perform more effectively in a global cyber-based market. Peter Drucker writes of the 'networked organization', Michael Hammer and James Champy write of 're-engineering the corporation,' Peter Senge talks of the 'learning organization', and Don Tapscott talks of the 'internetworked business'. Other thinkers, drawing upon complexity theory, contend that companies must emulate biological systems such as neural networks and eliminate rigid hierarchy. Leading corporate strategists promulgate the view that individual workers must be empowered and that the patterns of communications within a worldwide organization must resemble *knowledge ecology* more than a flowchart.

Practitioners, theorists, and futurists alike concur that the challenge for businesses that want to maximize their global presence involves structuring relationships in such a way as to ensure that the right information is delivered to the right people at the right time. In all these views, information technology (IT) and electronic commerce (e-commerce) initiatives play critical roles in the strategy of global competition. If there is a common denominator to the global view of IT initiatives and e-commerce, it is that companies reap the biggest benefits not by superimposing computers on top of old work processes but by restructuring those processes and the corporate culture. This strategy, over time, develops entirely new business capacities.

New strategic courses of action were stimulated by a number of world events during the past two decades. Following the breakup of the Soviet Union in the latter half of the 1980s, the nations of Eastern Europe began implementing means of free market economic policies; mainland China adopted an open door policy and assumed market mechanisms; and even the well-to-do nations of Western Europe steadily minimized the role of government and encouraged the privatization of public entities. With these developments, economic liberalization has rapidly become a worldwide trend. Within a free economic environment, free international trade has become a goal that nations around the world are striving to achieve. In the European Union (EU), passage of the Maastricht Agreement in 1991 accelerated economic integration, and the nations of Eastern Europe are gradually being incorporated into the EU. In the western hemisphere, the United States, Mexico, and Canada signed the North American Free Trade Agreement (NAFTA) in 1994, and the five South American nations of Argentina, Brazil, Paraguay, Uruguay and Chile formed the Mercosur trade bloc in 1995. In Asia, the Bandung declaration passed at the 1994 Asia-Pacific Economic Cooperation (APEC) conference announced that developed and developing nations would complete deregulation of trade and investment in 2010 and 2020, respectively.

The Association of Southeast Asian Nations (ASEAN) regional grouping also hopes to achieve complete regional deregulation of trade during the early part of the twenty-first century. At a global level, following the passage of the General Agreement on Tariffs and Trade (GATT), the World Trade Organization (WTO) was established in 1995. In a free and open global economic environment, industries in all nations will face even stiffer competition. In order to increase competitiveness, individual nations will be compelled to further deregulate and globalize the flow of money, manpower, resources, and information. In light of this trend of increasing liberalization and competition, one of the greatest challenges of the twenty-first century will be to enhance national competitiveness through ensuring economic development and the use of IT (UNCTAD, 2003).

We are at the early stages of a knowledge revolution that will have more invigorating implications than any other single industrial development in the history of the world. New configurations and business models are evolving, but, unlike in previous times, these developments are taking place expeditiously. In order to harvest the benefits of these changing events, new and flexible decision-making processes are needed. The rate of change is such that rapid response is needed, both from public and private sectors, to ensure that citizens and businesses can avail themselves of the benefits of the information/knowledge society, thus contributing to the ongoing improvement of societies and economies.

In the new information/knowledge age, the countries that are first to adapt and change are the countries that will reap the rewards. Governments around the world have windows of opportunity to bring about the changes needed to position a country as a leader in this information/knowledge age. Failure to take action could mean that much of the strong economic performance of recent years could be lost, particularly as global companies would be likely to move their operations to other countries. Failure to act would also mean missing out on the opportunities to improve the social inclusion process through the use of information and communication technologies (ICTs).

The Internet is considered the backbone of globalization, and e-commerce is chosen as the perfect tool.

Several terms describe business that takes place on the Internet: e-commerce, the information economy, the online economy, and Internet commerce. Literal interpretations of these terms denote particular domains of activity, and little rigor is applied to their application. The term e-commerce should be understood to include the conduct of business with the assistance of telecommunications and IT; it is not limited to business conducted on the Internet.

RULES FOR THE ELECTRONIC ECONOMY

With the emergence of the electronic economy (e-economy) and new ways of competing, the market is rewarding those organizations that are effectively incorporating new business models. Five rules for the electronic economy are presented that every electronics and high-tech organization should evaluate in creating new business models: (1) vertical disintegration, (2) return on intangible assets, (3) increasing returns to scale, (4) nearly perfect information, and (5) time to market (Lorack, 2000).

Vertical Disintegration

Vertical disintegration is emerging in support of new business models necessitated by e-commerce. Rather than owning the entire value chain, companies are recognizing the value in building a network of best-of breed partners that specialize and excel in links of the value chain. These business partners then can be easily plugged in as needed. Not only is this approach cheaper, easier, and more efficient, but it also allows the organization to create value based upon its core competencies. The key to the new business environment is disintegration. After World War II, economists promoted the theory of vertical integration in which manufacturers would take on all the stages of production, from processing the raw material to distributing the finished item. This approach was popular with corporations for 40 years. However, the current direction has turned, especially for the IT industry. Now the emphasis is on continuous technological enhancement to make products that appeal to better-educated consumers who have an awakened sense of product quality. This change, coupled with the fast pace of current markets, has meant that companies using a vertically integrated business model are having difficulties meeting the needs of consumers. Why? Because vertically integrated companies tend to have gigantic structures, slow speeds, and rising costs – all of which reduce competitiveness. The opposite of vertical integration is disintegration, and this trend has had a strong impact on many companies, particularly in the IT industry.

The infrastructure of the early IT industry was created by a few companies that were built on vertical integration strategies. Then personal computer (PC) companies gradually began to replace proprietary computing environments with open systems. In other words, instead of using their own custom-built materials, the manufacturers started to assemble computers from standardized components made by other firms. This changed the industry's entire infrastructure. If the IT business had remained vertically integrated, the users, publishers, distribution channel members, and academic institutions that are now the computer industry's guiding force would not have been able to influence the industry in such a vital way.

In a PC's value chain – from component, to finished product assembly, to distribution – design and manufacturing used to add a lot of value. However, in today's value chain, these stages turn out to provide the least value. Now the most value-added comes in the creation of component parts – the software, microprocessors, memory chips, storage devices, displays, motherboards, and so forth. Companies are able to successfully compete and provide added value to PC products on the component side of the business, except for the microprocessors and software, which are controlled by US companies.

On the other end of the value chain, no country, so far, has made any inroads against US domination. As the industry settles into the twenty-first century, how enterprises use their manufacturing capabilities to create value through global marketing efforts is an issue worthy of important consideration.

In the grand disintegration mode, the market is full of opportunities, in different segments, large and small. No single giant company can be involved in all segments of the business, and that has given many companies room to develop and even become world leaders in certain areas. In the computer industry, if we had not gone from vertical integration to the disintegration mode, leading companies would never have had the chance to stand up and compete.

Return on Tangible Assets

Tangible assets such as property, plant, and equipment may no longer determine a company's value. The e-economy rewards companies that create value based on intangibles, such as intellectual property, brand equity, knowledge capital, and customer experience. These assets can be easily and cheaply leveraged across a global customer base. In this information/knowledge age, money is made from ideas and the way that we apply them.

This is quite different from the industrial age, when profit went to the owner of capital and land, and labor efficiency was more important than the creation of new goods and services. In the information age it is essential to identify and protect intellectual property to ensure ongoing profits for the company. Many large, international and global companies have most of their assets tied up in patents and copyrights. These companies realize that the intellectual capacity of a company is now more valuable than its buildings, machinery, and fixed assets, as it gives them the ability to control the actions of their competitors.

Virtual assets, such as intellectual property, information, and customer relationships, can drive increasing returns to scale in the e-economy. With virtual assets, production costs are minimal, after initial investments in development. Since the Internet enables information assets – such as research and investment and information services – to be reproduced at practically no cost, firms can theoretically grow without limit, and incremental unit costs can approach zero.

Economies are increasingly based on knowledge. Finding better ways of doing things has always been the main source of long-term growth. What is new is that a growing chunk of production in the modern economy is in the form of intangibles, based on the exploitation of ideas rather than material things: the so-called weightless economy. In 1900, only one-third of American workers were employed in the service sector; now more than three-quarters are. More and more goods also have an increasing amount of knowledge embedded in them, in the form of design or customer service. Economists have a problem with knowledge because it seems to defy the basic economic law of scarcity. If a physical object is sold, the seller ceases to own it, but when an idea is sold, the seller still possesses it and can sell it over and over again. However much knowledge is used, it does not get used up. Yet the market system as described by Adam Smith 200 years ago was based on the notion of scarcity, including a cost structure in which it is more expensive to produce two of anything than one.

Increasing Returns to Scale

Traditional economic theory assumes that most industries run into 'diminishing returns' at some point because unit costs start to rise, so no one firm can corner the market, but an increasing number of information products (anything that can be transformed into a string of zeros and ones), such as software, books, movies, financial services, and websites, have increasing returns. Information is expensive to produce but cheap to reproduce. High fixed costs and negligible variable costs give these industries vast potential economies of scale. A new software program might cost millions of dollars to develop, but each extra copy costs next to nothing to make, especially if it is distributed over the Internet. There is nothing new about increasing returns. The value of many information goods, such as fax machines or software packages, increases as more people use them.

Nearly Perfect Information

The Internet empowers customers with greater knowledge and expanded choices, limiting much of the power that companies traditionally had in the selling process. At the same time, however, the Internet gives companies a tremendous new advantage by enabling them to get closer to their customers. Well-designed websites provide detailed account and service information to customers, while at the same time capturing information on customer interests. This information is then used to enable one-to-one marketing approaches with the goal of building customer loyalty and extending revenue per customer. This explosive growth of the Internet promises a new age of perfectly competitive markets. With perfect information about prices and products at their fingertips, consumers can quickly and easily find the best deals. Price dispersion is often as wide on the Internet as it is in the shopping mall – or even wider. Moreover, the retailers with the keenest prices rarely have the biggest sales. Such price dispersion is usually a sign of market inefficiency. In an ideal competitive market, where products are identical, where customers are perfectly informed, and where there is free market entry, a large number of buyers and sellers, and no search costs, all sales are made by the retailer with the lowest price. Consequently, all prices will be driven down to marginal cost. Search costs on the Internet might be expected to be lower and online consumers to be more easily informed about prices. So price dispersion online ought to be narrower than in conventional markets, but it does not seem to be.

A paper by Michael Smith and Erik Brynjolfsson of the Massachusetts Institute of Technology's Sloan School of Management and Joseph Bailey of the University of Maryland looks at the main research on this topic (Smith et al., 2000). The study found that price dispersion for books, compact discs (CDs), and software is no smaller online than it is in conventional markets. Another finds that prices for identical books and CDs at different online retailers differ by as much as 50 percent on average, by 337 percent for books and 25 percent for CDs. Clemons et al. (1998) of the University of Pennsylvania's Wharton School, found that prices for airline tickets from online travel agents differ by an average of 28 percent.

There are many possible reasons for this price dispersion. One could be that the studies are not comparing like with like. Not so. Even after controlling for differing arrival and departure times or connections, the study of online travel agents finds that prices for airline tickets vary by an average of 18 percent. The study of books and CDs deliberately focuses on identical products. Indeed, it finds that retailers that charge more offer service terms that are no better than cheaper ones.

Convenience could also explain the price spreading. Some websites offer better search tools, product reviews, and samples, such as book chapters or audio clips. However, in a frictionless market, consumers could use these services to choose what they want to buy and then buy from the cheapest site. So such services would explain price dispersion only if there were significant search or switching costs online. Time to market was listed as another rule for the e-economy. New communications technologies have made channel and alliance development easier, faster, and more effective. As a result, the barriers to entry have been lowered. We have an ample list of companies that will help any merchant market a product over the Internet by advertising the site, handling order fulfillment, and delivering the goods worldwide. All the merchant needs to do is create the catalog pages, and the service provider will offer instant global reach and immediate time to market.

Time to Market

Doing things faster and more affordably may seem to be good, but it also may mean nothing more than the production of things that nobody really wants at high speed. Factors other than speed seem to have major impact on successful uses of e-commerce sites; convenience and the effective use of human capital seem to be the lead candidates.

The effective use of human capital demands an extended enterprize view of the world in which each project is a series of concentric circles. Information flows out from the center, and waves carry more detailed information back. Transparency lets everyone view all of the relevant information, and the flat structure helps keep outside distractions to a minimum. At its core this is a democratic system, messy but effective.

E-commerce companies can make these new rules work for them by reinventing themselves and work at adding value by new means. Only those able to frequently adjust their customer value proposition will be able to preserve their market share and maintain their success in the cyber-based economy.

To summarize, the metamorphosis to e-business is at the heart of the Internet economy. Every organization can be a player in this economy, depending on the extent to which it digitizes its business operations and takes advantage of the essential elements of an online world: information, knowledge, relationships, and increased velocity of operations throughout the value chain. Unfortunately, there is a widespread erroneous belief of the failure of a number of highly publicized 'dot.coms' as the demise of the Internet economy. Dot.coms, defined as electronic retailers and/or electronic intermediaries who earn at least 95 percent of their revenues over the Internet, account for a small percentage of the total revenues generated by the Internet economy. Thus, there is substantial potential to expand the Internet economy as more and more traditional businesses adopt e-business practices. Ultimately, when every business becomes an e-business enterprize, there will be no distinction between the Internet and traditional economies.

E-GOVERNMENT: PRACTICE AND FRAMEWORK

Information technology (IT) has become one of the core elements of managerial reform, and e-government may figure prominently in future governance. Information technology has opened up many possibilities for improving internal managerial efficiency and the quality of public service delivery to citizens. It has contributed to dramatic changes in politics (Nye, 1999; Norris, 1999), government institutions (Fountain, 2001), performance management (Brown, 1999), red tape reduction (Moon and Bretschneider, 2002), and re-engineering (Anderson, 1999) during the last decade. The Clinton administration attempted to advance e-government, through which government overcomes the barriers of time and distance in providing public services (Gore, 1993). Recently, some studies have found widespread diffusion of various IT innovations (mainframe and PC computers, geographical systems, networks, web pages, etc) in the public sector (Weare et al., 1999; Musso et al., 2000; Landsbergen and Wolken, 2001; Layne and Lee, 2001; Nunn, 2001; Peled, 2001).

On June 24, 2000, President Clinton delivered his first web-cast address to the public and announced a series of new e-government initiatives. One highlight of these new initiatives was to establish an integrated online service system that put all online resources offered by the federal government on a single website, www.firstgov.gov. The initiative also attempted to build one-stop access to roughly US$500 billion in grants: (US$300 billion) and procurement opportunities (US$200 billion) (White House Press Office, 2000). Following the federal initiative, many local governments also adopted IT for local governance. For instance, they have created or improved their websites and provide Web-based services to promote better internal procedural management and external service provision.

Despite this continuing move toward e-government, the development, implementation, and effectiveness of e-government at the local level are not well understood.

E-government is one of most interesting concepts introduced in the field of public administration in the late 1990s, though it has not been clearly defined and understood among scholars and practitioners of public administration. Like many managerial concepts and practices in public administration (total quality management, strategic management, participative management, etc.), the idea of e-government followed private-sector adoption of so-called e-business and e-commerce. The *Global Survey of E-government*, a recent joint research initiative for global e-government by the United Nations and the American Society for Public Administration, provides a broad definition of e-government:

> Broadly defined, e-government includes the use of all information and communication technologies, from fax machines to wireless palm pilots, to facilitate the daily administration of government. However, like e-commerce, the popular interpretation of e-government is one that defines it exclusively as an Internet driven activity ... to which it may be added that improves citizen access to government information, services and expertise to ensure citizen participation in, and satisfaction with the government process ... it is a permanent commitment by government to improving the relationship between the private citizen and the public sector through enhanced, cost-effective and efficient delivery of services, information and knowledge. It is the practical realization of the best that government has to offer. (UN and ASPA, 2001, p. 1)

Similarly, e-government is narrowly defined as the production and delivery of government services through IT applications. However, it can be defined more broadly as any way IT is used to simplify and improve transactions between governments and other actors, such as constituents, businesses, and other governmental agencies (Sprecher, 2000). In her book, Jane Fountain (2001) suggests the concept of the 'virtual state', that is, a governmental entity organized with virtual agencies, cross-agency and public-private networks whose structure and capacity depend on the Internet and the Web.

Largely speaking, e-government includes four major internal and external aspects: (1) the establishment of a secure government intranet and central database for more efficient and cooperative interaction among governmental agencies; (2) a Web-based service delivery; (3) the application of e-commerce for more efficient government transaction activities, such as procurement and contract; and (4) digital democracy for more transparent accountability of government (*The Economist*, 2000). Various technologies have been applied to support these unique characteristics of e-government, including electronic data interchange, interactive voice response, voice mail, email, Web service delivery, virtual reality, and public key infrastructure.

The functionality and utility of Web technologies in managing the public sector can be divided into two categories: internal and external. Internally, the Web and other technologies hold promise potential as effective and efficient managerial tools that collect, store, organize, and manage an enormous volume of data and information. By using the function of upload and download, the most up-to-date information and data can be displayed on the Internet on a real-time basis. Government also can transfer funds electronically to other governmental agencies or provide information to public employees through an intranet or Internet system. Government also can do many mundane and routine tasks more easily and quickly, such as responding to employees' requests for benefits statements.

Externally, Web technologies also facilitate government's linkages with citizens, other governmental agencies, and businesses. Government websites can serve as both a communication and a public relations tool for the general public. Information and data can easily be shared with and transferred to external stakeholders (businesses, non-profit organizations, interest groups, or the public). In addition, some Web technologies (such as interactive bulletin boards) enable the government to promote public participation in policy-making processes by posting public notices and exchanging messages and ideas with the public.

There are various stages of e-government, which reflect the degree of technical sophistication and interaction with users: (1) simple information dissemination (one-way communication); (2) two-way communication (request and response); (3) service and financial transactions; (4) integration (horizontal and vertical integration); and (5) political participation (Hiller and Belanger, 2001).

Stage 1 is the most basic form of e-government and uses IT for disseminating information, simply by posting information or data on websites for constituents to view.

Stage 2 is two-way communication characterized as an interactive mode between government and constituents. In this stage, the government incorporates email systems as well as information and data-transfer technologies into its websites.

In Stage 3, the government allows online services and financial transactions by completely replacing face to face interaction with 'Web-based self-services' (Hiller and Belanger, 2001). This 'transaction-based e-government' can be partially achieved by 'putting live database links to on-line interfaces' (Layne and Lee, 2001, p. 125). Through such online services and financial transactions, for example, constituents can renew licenses, pay fines, and apply for financial aid (Hiller and Belanger, 2001 Layne and Lee, 2001).

In Stage 4, the government attempts to integrate various government services vertically (inter-governmental integration) and horizontally (intra-governmental integration) for the enhancement of efficiency, user friendliness, and effectiveness. This stage is a highly challenging task for governments because it requires a tremendous amount of time and resources to integrate online and back-office systems (Hiller and Belanger, 2001). Hiller and Belanger (2001) suggest three good examples: Australia's state of Victoria (http://www.maxi.com.au), Singapore's e-Citizen Center (http://www.ecitizen.gov.sg), and the US government's portal site (http://www.firstgov.gov). Both vertical and horizontal integrations push information and data sharing among different functional units and levels of governments for better online public services (Layne and Lee, 2001).

Stage 5 involves the promotion of Web-based political participation, in which government websites include online voting, online public forums, and online opinion surveys for more direct and wider interaction with the public. While the previous four stages are related to Web-based public services in the administrative arena, the fifth stage highlights Web-based political activities by citizens.

It should be noted that the five stages are just a conceptual tool to examine the evolution of e-government. The adoption of e-government practices may not follow a true linear progression. Many studies of technological innovation also indicate that the diffusion and adoption of technology may even follow a curvilinear path. For example, a government may initiate Stage 5 of e-government (political participation) without full practice of Stage 4 (integration). It is also possible that government can pursue various components of e-government simultaneously. Like other stage models of growth (Nolan, 1979; Quinn and Cameron, 1983), the framework simply provides an exploratory conceptual tool that helps one understand the evolutionary nature of e-government.

B2C AND B2B E-COMMERCE

The Internet has spawned the creation of a massive industry collectively called e-commerce, which is still young. Some of the key milestone dates in the development of the Internet include the announcement of Java in mid-1995, a programming language allowing sophisticated user functionality to be deployed over the Internet.

Within the overall e-commerce industry, there are two major branches: business-to-consumer (B2C) and business-to-business (B2B). Independent research firms such as Forrester Research have predicted that B2B will become by far the bigger branch, with the total value of commerce conducted electronically in the US B2B segment reaching US$2.7 trillion by 2004; and by that time US$746 billion in commerce will be traded using dynamic pricing mechanisms. The term 'B2G' has been recently introduced to refer to 'business-to-government' commerce.

The stakes are enormously high for businesses. McKinsey & Company has estimated that purchase and supply management costs for automotive businesses equal 80 percent of total cost. Thus, the impact of achieving savings in purchasing activities flows rapidly through total business performance and to the bottom line.

Business-to-Consumer Internet commerce was the first to develop, because the marketplace is comparatively simple. Business-to-Consumer commerce typically emulates catalog retailing, where consumers order standard products from producers or retailers. An Internet website substitutes for the traditional paper catalog. As there was an existing catalog retail segment that was already well developed, substituting the Internet for the catalog was readily understood by consumers. Advantages of B2C included the convenience of 24-hour shopping and real-time availability of information such as promotional sale prices or stock-outs. Business-to-Consumer pioneers, such as Amazon.com, spent enormous sums in consumer advertising to establish their brand names and, in doing so, lifted the entire tide of retail commerce over the Internet.

Business-to-Business commerce was slower to develop because of the vastly more complex market structures involved but has attracted attention because of the comparatively larger value of potential commerce. Business-to-Business is so large because products often stop at many places along the supply chain, with companies adding their unique value at every step of the way. This creates a multiplier effect where products change hands many steps along the way. In addition, there are huge markets for products whose end users are businesses, such as machinery, trucks, aircraft, and ships. The market for B2B solutions accelerated as the B2C companies began going public, and people started to extrapolate the potential success of B2C to the business marketplace.

Industrial and business purchasing is far more complex than consumer purchasing, which slowed the adoption of e-commerce for business as compared to e-commerce for consumers. Some of the complexities of industrial purchasing include: (1) professional purchasing discipline, (2) derived demand, (3) team decision-making, and (4) trade credit.

Professional Purcasing Discipline

Whereas consumers typically act as their own purchasing agents, corporations employ professional purchasing agents. These agents often spend years learning about the product categories that they purchase. They often specialize by product. It is, therefore, not unusual to find different buyers purchasing plastics, metals, and electronics within the same company. Their full-time job is to make sure that their company purchases the best products on time and at the best prices. They are paid to analyze, compare, negotiate, and monitor results. Simple consumer-like marketing techniques and functionality offered by websites fail to impress this group of disciplined and informed users.

Derived Demand

Most consumers choose what to buy and when. They select brands and they shop for bargains. Industrial buyers are typically buying the products that they're required to buy, when they're required to buy them. Expensive software programs called Materials Requirements Planning (MRP) or Enterprise Resource Planning (ERP) programs keep track of the products that the company must buy in order to meet production schedules. In addition, commercial purchasing is often accomplished by forwarding from buyer to supplier documents called 'purchase orders'. A purchase order (PO) represents to the seller that the buyer has duly authorized a purchase and stands ready to take delivery and make payment. Buyers use their ERP/MRP systems to issue POs. Websites that expect industrial buyers to fill in order screens are doomed to fail, by failing to integrate with the legacy systems and the underlying purchasing process used by buyers. Many of the products purchased by industrial companies are custom-made, rather than standard products. These products are not displayed in catalogs by suppliers but are made only after a buyer and supplier agree to make them. For custom-made products, the typical consumer 'shopping cart' metaphor for Web shopping breaks down. Buyers cannot surf the Web looking for the custom materials that they need but rather must open a relationship with a supplier first and subsequently have the parts made.

Team Decision-making

Often, an entire team of design engineers, buyers, production engineers, and quality assurance staff is involved in making a particular decision, especially for larger purchases. Team-based decision-making reduces the chances that industrial buyers could surf to websites and simply order goods. In addition, purchases are often made on different terms for different products. These contracts invariably require negotiation, rather than adoption of standard terms. This further reduces the likelihood that buyers could conduct commerce passively at websites, as consumers are able to do.

Trade Credit

Most industrial purchases are purchased on trade credit. Sellers must do credit reviews and elect to whom they'll extend credit. While companies such as American Express offer corporate purchasing cards (P-cards), these tools have achieved only partial penetration. Once again, the absence of a simple payment infrastructure reduces the chance for passive Web-based relationships in favor of more complex, negotiated relationships between parties. Almost any manufacturing operation consumes a very wide variety of raw materials, components, and supplies. Few buyers have the luxury of buying a narrow range of materials. This complexity requires any given buying organization to adapt to the underlying structure of many different markets simultaneously, rather than optimizing on a few.

The complexities described above eliminate the possibility that simple B2C business models could be successfully applied to business purchases. A further complication of B2B is that businesses purchase a wide variety of items to serve many different needs. Different types of purchases have different characteristics that determine the attributes of successful solutions.

The impact of improved purchasing can be huge, due to the high proportion of costs spent on outside purchases. Major trends include (1) supplier consolidation, (2) cross-division buying, (3) supply chain optimization, (4) outsourcing, (5) consortium purchasing, and (6) global sourcing.

EXISTING AND EMERGING EC TECHNOLOGIES

As with the private sector, both client/vendor e-commerce and consumer/ agent e-commerce are possible. While government has been slower to embrace e-commerce than has the private sector as a whole, government applications for using e-commerce have incredible potential.

The potential for consumer-oriented e-commerce is huge because of the size of markets that can be served. Consumer-to-Business and/or governmental entities are using the existing technologies of Touch-Tone access, fax backs, voice, and network connections to provide self-service options for the customers. The World Wide Web will likely be used extensively for facilitating transactions involving consumers, businesses, and governmental entities. Requests for proposals are being placed on the Internet today, reaching original and new vendors. E-commerce government applications should promote Internet solutions.

Local, state, and federal agencies and departments offer Web pages for information and online requests of application materials through the Internet's World Wide Web. One example would be listing of employment opportunities on the Internet. Another example would be the Social Security Administration's program that allows individuals to access their earnings record and estimates of future benefits from Social Security.

Electronic benefits transfer (EBT) involves the issuance of government benefits (ie Aid to Families with Dependent Children [AFDC], Women, Infant and Children [WIC], or Food Stamps) using a magnetic strip debit card and automated teller machines (ATMs) or point-of-sale terminals in retail establishments. Electronic funds transfer (EFT) is a commonly used form of e-commerce. Direct deposit of paychecks is the most common use of EFT. A number of government agencies also pay unemployment insurance benefits by EFT. Other uses include insurance and retirement payments, travel reimbursements, health and dependent care spending accounts, and financial aid distribution to students.

A smart card is another example of consumer-oriented e-commerce. There are three types of smart cards: non-refillable memory cards, microcontroller cards, and shared-key and signature transporting cards. Memory cards have a limited purpose, a short life, and little security. Microcontroller cards can be used for a variety of simultaneous purposes and have a longer life. Shared-key or signature transporting cards have additional, coded-in security features. One example of smart card technology is universities' providing students, staff, and faculty with a card allowing access to various university services and for making purchases.

Electronic-cash (E-cash) is an emerging digital version of physical cash that performs all the same functions. E-cash can move through a variety of networks including the Internet and be stored on personal computers, in smart cards, or in 'electronic wallets'. Like physical money, e-cash is expected to be widely accepted in the near future and is more suitable for small transactions than credit cards. The advantages of e-cash are expected to be speed, cost savings, and convenience and simplicity for the consumer.

Existing technologies (PCs, telephone, fax-back) allow customers to focus their resources and make decisions through a series of self-service interactions with government. The potential for growth in e-commerce is very large and very rapid. According to several studies, early adopters of e-commerce will tend to be better-educated, higher-income consumers. Medium-size businesses in the US now regularly use the Internet for business purposes, and many of them are either online now or plan to be in the future. Providing goods, services, and information through e-commerce will become more commonplace as businesses, individuals, and governmental entities become better educated on how e-commerce will improve customer service, reduce costs, and save time. The demand for e-commerce activities is growing quickly. Current e-commerce providers are, by and large, companies with large infrastructures or merchants who are satisfied with building market share instead of generating revenue. Exceptions are hard to find, especially as e-commerce setup costs increase annually.

As mentioned earlier, e-commerce is Internet-enabled technology that facilitates transactions of money and information in the course of doing business. And while there is no single, secure e-commerce system, and costs are high, technology isn't the main hurdle for developers. While companies quibble over definitions, customers sit and wait. Customers wait for dynamically generated pages to download, for products to appear, for inventories to be checked, and for packages to arrive in the mail. While customers wait, some companies still ponder e-commerce as a concept, a way of redefining their businesses. For others, e-commerce translates into controlling the sale and distribution of goods and services through Web-based technologies. Customers don't understand or care about these distinctions. They want to know what the 'e' means to them, and they're getting tired of the wait.

For customers to engage in e-commerce, they must experience a radical shift in their relationships with websites. They must develop trust that does not yet exist. Developers and their clients must learn to craft an experience that will persuade and engage customers, and that will deliver rich media at the right time, in the appropriate context, in harmony with highly usable functionality. They must understand that while convenience, price, and the novelty of shopping online will draw customers to a site for the first time, the brand will keep them there.

While security is a concern for shoppers, it has not deterred customers from shopping. Other factors take precedence. The Internet is still slow. Customers are ready to bolt at the slightest indication of technical failure. Beyond technology, customers want accountability. They want to deal with a known entity. They want to shop at brand-name merchants and buy brand-name products, even when it means sacrificing convenience or a lower price.

In order for a business to successfully conduct e-commerce, developers and merchants have to understand what motivates people to make transactions. It's more than security, more than the fact that the plumbing is working. It's consumer trust. It's about creating a balance between functionality, brand benefits and a positive consumer experience – experience that has to be built, maintained and nurtured over time.

Only with this understanding can we start to talk about e-commerce in a meaningful way. E-commerce is not about technology. It's about customers.

E-COMMERCE IN DEVELOPING ECONOMIES

E-commerce diffusion includes diffusion of Internet technologies, telecommunications and the traditional commercial infrastructure. A number of researchers such as Travica (2002) and Wolcott et al (2001) have studied the impact of e-commerce adoption and diffusion of Internet technologies, telecommunications, and traditional commercial infrastructure. The impacts of e-commerce adoption at the firm level have been investigated empirically and theoretically by Garicano and Kaplan (2000), Kumar and Crook (1999), Premkumar et al. (1994), and Santarelli and D'Altri (2003). In evaluating these studies, one cannot help but notice that none have evaluated the social and economic impact of e-commerce diffusion. However, the growth of e-commerce and e-governance is starting to create fundamental changes in the governmental, social, economic and political fabrics of societies all around the world. As a result, while these advances present a number of opportunities, they do constitute a number of threats with wide ranging negative implications across numerous areas of society. The spheres affected by e-commerce include economic productivity, intellectual property rights, privacy protection, and affordability of and access to information (Karake Shalhoub, 2002; Sharma and Gupta, 2003).

As the adoption and diffusion of e-commerce continues to grow in developing economies around the world, it could have significant consequences on the social and economic structures of these countries. The economic, social and political effects cannot be ignored and should be examined closely. In many developing countries, the Internet is quickly displacing older media such as television and newspapers as the prime source of important information for young people. As increasing numbers of young people in the urban cities go online at home and at school, interactive technologies like Internet, CD-ROMs, and video games have begun to supplant television's dominance. They are becoming integrated into the daily lives of many children and youths in developing countries who are no longer passive media recipients. Instead, they are creating websites, participating in chat rooms, e-mail, and instant messaging, and coming up with innovative uses for new media – especially the Internet. However, a large segment of the population in semi-urban and rural areas is still far away from Internet revolution. The digital divide creates a gap between those who have and those who have not, and it is an important policy issue for government and policymakers to address because it creates a class system based on access to information and communication technologies.

Compared with developed countries, e-commerce adoption in developing countries has been relatively slow due to obstacles in the on-line authorization of credit cards, inadequate marketing strategies, and small online population. The lack of interest in e-commerce adoption by several consumer groups is also due to unclear price advantages and a poor supply in this shopping mode. E-commerce in the majority of developing economies is currently afflicted by impediments such as low bandwidth, lack of independent gateways for Internet service providers (ISPs), an inadequate telecommunications infrastructure, a low rate of PC penetration and low tele-density, among others. However, with the expected higher PC or Internet access device penetration levels, current trend of entry of private ISPs, availability of greater bandwidth and the coming together of e-commerce infrastructure will lead to an explosive growth in the number of Internet and e-commerce users in developing countries.

Assessing the socio-economic influences of an e-commerce adoption is difficult because it requires the use of methods capable of revealing often complex and unpredictable community values. However, the growth of e-commerce has created enormous influence on services, market structure, competition and restructuring of industry and markets. These changes are transforming all areas of society, work, business, and government. The use of ICTs for e-commerce deepens and intensifies the socio-economic divisions among people, businesses and nations. It is often reported that there is a complicated patchwork of varying levels of ICT access, basic ICT usage, and ICT applications among socio-economic groups; many disparities are getting even larger. Disparities in the location and quality of Internet infrastructure, even the quality of phone lines, have created gaps in access. Gaps exist in the adoption of digital technologies among different social groups and firms, depending on income levels, education, gender and, for firms, depending on industry structure, business size (large firms versus small and medium-sized enterprises (SMEs)) and location.

The rural-urban divide is caused in part by the inherent difficulty of providing network access, let alone electricity, in extremely rural regions. Poverty remains the greatest barrier to Internet growth and e-government implementation in many developing countries. The monthly connection cost for the Internet in India, for instance, exceeds the monthly income of a significant portion of the population. Stalled by poverty and a poor telecommunications infrastructure, the gap between haves and have nots is widening further and therefore, 'have nots' suffer from a greater disparity in wealth. Regional disparities in technical training exist on the basis of long-standing divisions on investment in education, and such other factors as staff development programs, technical training in schools, and secondary and tertiary enrollment. Most disparities in ICT access are based on socio-economic factors such as income, geographical location, education, age, gender etc.

In addition to the digital divide within a developing country, e-commerce diffusion has led to the problem of marginalization where a group of people are excluded from the mainstream activity, deliberately or otherwise. With the use of the Internet to conduct business, fewer people are required as jobs are automated or made obsolete (*World Employment Report*, 2002, 2003). Therefore, marginalization may be a likely social consequence of e-commerce adoption in a country. The e-commerce technologies need different kind of skills and those who want to become part of the e-commerce bandwagon require greater skills and knowledge. On one hand, this has created opportunities for many unemployed persons to find employment through various training institutes that teach these technical skills. On the other hand, it has also segmented the society further on socio-economic lines; the ones who are able to afford the training and others who are not. People who do not have access to ICTs or are not able to train themselves with new skills are left out of the mainstream activities. Therefore, the poor, on socio-economic lines, are pushed to the periphery due to their inappropriate education or skills. They are further marginalized as the gap in the knowledge attained between themselves and those who join the e-commerce bandwagon grows. Similar sentiments are echoed by the *World Employment Report* (2002), which indicates that the use of technologies such as e-commerce is positively correlated with economic growth – both on a national and organizational level.

A somewhat innovative approach to evaluating e-commerce diffusion comes from a more holistic evaluation of a country or region's infrastructural preparedness to engage in Internet and e-commerce activities. Theories on technology transfer, adoption, and diffusion have emerged that are helpful in understanding how ICTs can stretch in a country (Fichman, 2000). Since 1997, the Mosaic Group has undertaken the Global Diffusion of the Internet (GDI) Project, an extensive investigation of the spread of the Internet into countries all around the world (Wolcott et al. 2001). One of the primary products of GDI has been a framework for assessing the most pertinent dimensions of Internet diffusion at the national level. This GDI Framework is similar in concept to several of the e-readiness assessment tools created and gathered by non-governmental organizations such as Bridges.org and InfoDev, the World Bank's Information for Development program. However, the GDI framework has been rigorously developed and refined over a long time, and has been applied to almost 30 countries, representing every continent and every major socio-economic group of countries. The GDI Framework has six dimensions that it uses to describe the state of Internet diffusion in a country (Information for Development, 2003):

1. **Connectivity Infrastructure**
   This dimension 'assesses the extent and robustness of the physical structure of the network' that supports the Internet (Wolcott et al, 2001, p. 14). It includes the domestic backbone, international links, Internet exchanges, and methods of accessing the Internet.
2. **Geographical Dispersion**
   A measure of the extent to which Internet use is spread throughout a country, ranging from being accessible in just a few major cities to being accessible in rural areas.
3. **Organization Infrastructure**
   This refers to the market environment for ISPs, including the extent and nature of privatization of national telecommunications.
4. **Pervasiveness**
   A measure of Internet use among individuals per capita).
5. **Sector Absorption**
   This dimension captures the commitment to Internet use (as measured by leased lines and Internet servers) in the four major sectors of academia, commerce, healthcare, and government.
6. **Sophistication of Use**
   This last dimension measures the innovative use of the Internet in a country, and to what extent the Internet transforms traditional practices for both individuals and organizations.

Notwithstanding its effectiveness, the GDI has one major deficiency – it exclusively illustrates the state of Internet diffusion without making an effort to diagnose problems or prescribe solutions.

THE DIGITAL DIVIDE

The digital divide is a widely discussed phenomenon where the rich in technology get richer with the rapid move into the information age, while the technologically poor get poorer. It is clear that developed nations with the resources to invest in and develop ICT infrastructure are reaping huge benefits from the information age, while developing nations are moving along at a much slower pace. This difference in rates of technological progress is widening the economic disparity between the socio-economic regions that the development literature commonly refers to as the North and the South, thus creating a digital divide.

Development researchers have acknowledged the Internet as a 'great equalizer' (Smith et al, 2000; Travica, 2002), a ground-breaking technological means that facilitates the efficient transfer of information on a global magnitude. This global information can be used for international trade, online digital libraries, online education, telemedicine, e-government, and many other applications that solve vital problems in the developing world. Another class of solutions that the Internet promises developing countries is the provision of efficient communications within and among developing countries, so that citizens can effectively help each other to solve their own problems.

The distribution of Internet access between developing/emerging and developed/industrial countries is harshly unequal. In addition, the distribution among developing/emerging countries varies dramatically. Despite rapid growth in Internet access in developing/emerging economies, developed/industrial countries still account for the majority of Internet subscribers. More than 70 percent of US residents had access to the Internet in 2002, compared with 1 percent in Sub-Saharan Africa.

E-commerce is also relatively small in most developing countries. In Mexico, for example, e-commerce use is estimated at 3 percent in 2002. Internet access in the developing world varies greatly. Some countries, particularly in East Asia and the Arab Gulf have achieved remarkable penetration rates. For example, the share of Internet subscribers in the UAE has grown rapidly and is estimated at 35 percent of the population in 2002 (Karake Shalhoub and Al Qasimi, 2003), above rates in most European countries. Although per capita subscriber rates in China and India remain low, these countries are so large that they have a critical mass of subscribers ready to benefit from the Internet, a situation that increases the potential for e-commerce transactions.

The budding condition of Internet diffusion in many developing countries reflects the constraints on Internet use, the most important of which is the availability of telecommunications services. A number of studies found strong evidence that the quantity and quality of telecommunications services provided in a country is a significant determinant of the existence of Internet connections and the level of Internet use; to date, almost all Internet users have depended on telephone lines for connection. The trends in 'Internet intensity' – the ratio of Internet subscribers to available telephone lines – are remarkably similar across developing and industrial countries, however. Urban density and the policy environment for private sector development are strongly related to growth in Internet intensity. Many developing countries (including, on average, those in Asia, Latin America, Sub-saharan Africa, and the Gulf countries of the Middle East) are experiencing much more rapid diffusion of the Internet for the given availability of telephone lines than in the US. The digital divide results from a discrepancy in the access to telecommunications, not from the use of the Internet after telecommunications are available. Unfortunately, the gap in telecommunications services between industrial and developing countries is wide, so the digital divide is likely to remain wide for some time. The gap is also large among developing countries, with the least developed countries being specifically deprived. For example, the average OECD country had 70 times, and the average Latin American country had 17 times, the number of telephone mainlines than did countries in Sub-saharan Africa (excluding South Africa) (UNCTAD, 2003). By some statistics, the digital divide is broadening.

Given the massive investments required for telephone lines (and in some countries the continued governance of the telephone system by ineffective monopolies), expectations for reducing the digital divide rest largely on the proliferation of alternative methods of accessing the Internet. The availability of cable, cellular phone, and satellite systems is likely to diminish dependence on telephone lines for access to the Internet during the next few years.

Empirical studies have shown that improving access to the Internet and the use of information have undoubtedly led to increasing the productivity of capital, thus improving its return relative to labor (Odlyzko, 2003). The Internet also increases the demand for skilled labor, particularly in the ICT sector, and will lead to a decreased demand for unskilled labor. The negative effect of the divergence in demand for skilled versus unskilled labor could increase inequality between industrial and developing economies as well as within the developing countries themselves. On the positive side, though, the fall in production costs is likely to increase the demand for all workers, despite the fall in the per unit labor input in production. Although inequality may intensify, the income of the less fortunate may increase. In addition, e-commerce, in all likelihood, will increase market transparency, leading to a reduction in search costs and reliance on intermediaries. These effects will lead to an increase of real incomes of employees, in general.

The occurrence of network externalities, where all stakeholders gain from each addition to the network, implies that market prices may not fully reflect the total benefit to society from increased Internet access. Thus government has an important role in pushing Internet diffusion forward. Incompatible policies and the deficiencies in complementary services, principally in the telecommunications sector, other infrastructure, human capital, and the investment environment negatively limit Internet access in developing countries.

Poor telecommunications is a major limiting factor to the growth of e-commerce and e-governance. Essential telecommunications services include transmission facilities connecting a country's domestic network to the greater Internet, the domestic Internet backbone, and connections from homes and businesses to the backbone. State or privatized monopolies that control international connections impose uneconomical pricing structures and conditions which mean that many ISPs cannot afford to buy enough transmission capacity for e-commerce applications to function without bottleneck. This poor state of domestic backbone networks results in a large volume of domestic Internet traffic being sent to the US before being returned to its region of origin (Cukier, 1999).

A growing number of African Internet sites are hosted on servers in Europe or the US because of poor infrastructure. Hence, even traffic that originates and terminates domestically can cost the same as international transmission. The high cost of Internet access, the lack of local loop infrastructure necessary for basic dial-up modem access, and the poor quality of the local loop infrastructure that does exist all obstruct connections to the domestic backbone. Country comparisons show a strong relationship between usage price and Internet penetration and developing countries face much higher costs relative to incomes than do industrial countries. For many developing countries, the most important issue is the lack of telephone service to homes and businesses. Despite increases in rates of telephone line penetration during the 1990s, more than one-third of the 130 developing countries (excluding small islands) with data for 2003 have fewer than 5 cellular telephone lines per 100 inhabitants (ITU, 2004). The comparable level in the US is 56. The quality of access also is important, as some e-commerce applications that rely on sophisticated technology and high user interactivity require low congestion and high bandwidth transmission between the user's access device and the host server. The most popular alternatives by which developing countries can overcome inadequate local loop infrastructure have been either shared facilities or wireless local loop. Shared facilities, which involve local entrepreneurs selling the use of a computer with Internet access, are a fast and relatively cheap way of increasing Internet use. Wireless and satellite technologies also provide an alternative to the high costs and inefficiencies of many domestic telecommunications systems. Although currently used primarily for voice, mobile phones 'soon will be a much better device for many of the usual Internet applications', according to some technologists. Cellular phones in some developing countries have experienced strong growth rates and relatively high penetration, similar to those in industrial countries. In the UAE for example, mobile phone penetration rate is 67 percent. In Haiti, poor telephone service (0.9 phone lines per 100 people, less than half Africa's average, and huge waiting lists for new lines) has led to the growth of wireless service. In 2002, Ecuador, the Slovak Republic, and Western Samoa had ratios of cellular phone subscriptions to regular phone service similar or higher to those of industrial countries. On average, however, cellular phone penetration remains well below industrial-country levels.

Sub-Saharan Africa averages six cellular phones per 1000 people, compared with 265 cellular phones for every 1000 people in high-income countries (ITU, 2004).

Inadequate infrastructure services (other than telecommunications) are an important restraint on e-commerce. Recurrent and long power disruptions can critically hinder data transmission and systems' performance, so many software firms in developing economies have their own generators. Mail service can be undependable, expensive, and time consuming in many developing countries. For example, the unreliability of postal services in Latin America has meant that more expensive courier services must be used to deliver goods ordered over the Internet, and in response, international courier services are setting up special distribution systems in Miami. The lack of safety measures against sham can severely restrict credit card purchases, the most common means of conducting transactions over the Internet. For example, many consumers in developing countries are unwilling to purchase goods over the Internet because credit card companies will not compensate holders for fraudulent use of cards (in many industrial countries, cardholders have only a limited exposure to loss).

A significant mass of highly skilled labor is needed in developing countries to supply the necessary applications, provide support, and disseminate relevant technical knowledge for e-commerce. The workforce in many developing countries lacks a sufficient supply of these skills, and the demand for this specialized labor from industrial countries has further strained the supply of this labor in developing countries. In the late 1990s and beginning of the twenty-first century North America and Europe had unfilled demand for professionals trained in IT. Employees' salaries in IT industries continue to rise more rapidly than those of employees in other industries. Firms in developed/industrial countries will not be able to fill a fraction the estimated millions of positions open in the first decade of the twenty-first century, and will continue to resort to attracting skilled ICT workers from developing economies. This will lead to more brain drain in developing countries, which is one of the major causes of the digital divide.

Several regulatory obstacles to the widespread adoption of e-commerce exist in many developing countries. Duties and taxes on computer hardware and software and communication equipment increase the expense of connecting to the Internet. The overall environment for private sector activities is a significant determinant of Internet and e-commerce diffusion. An open foreign direct investment regulatory environment helps promote the diffusion of the Internet, which is important to the growth of e-commerce. Foreign direct investment also is one channel that could facilitate the access of local firms to online auctions. Governments also can play an important role in supporting the certification of firms by providing information on certification procedures, promoting access by local and national firms to international organizations and firms that provide certification, and perhaps subsidizing the costs of certification to exhibit the kinds of resources available in the domestic market. This role will be particularly important, at least in the short term, as the intermediaries that formerly helped connect developing-country firms to international markets are replaced by web-based intermediaries and infomediaries that may have less information on developing countries.

Governments must create a supportive legal context for electronic transactions, including recognition of digital signatures; legal acceptability of electronic contracts; intellectual property rights for digital content; privacy and security of personal data; and mechanisms for resolving disputes. The United Nations Commission on International Trade Law has a 'Model Law on Electronic Commerce' that offers national legislatures legal principles and guidelines for dealing with some of these issues (UNCTAD, 2000). Governments also have had direct and significant impact on Internet use through direct interventions. Early examples include the 'Wiring the Border' project, which provides subsidies to small businesses along the Mexico-US border to finance Internet access. The US Department of Defense played a critical role in developing the initial networking technologies for this project (Goodman, 1994). The US government also financed the original Internet backbone until sufficient demand for services led to the creation of commercial backbones; a similar pattern was followed in several other industrial countries (Braga and Fink, 1999). Despite some success stories, however, the high rate in e-commerce technology development greatly increases the risk associated with government involvement to support Internet access. Government investments, however, may jeopardize private sector initiatives that could provide services more efficiently. Finally, government can support the spread of the Internet by switching to online services for its own transactions. Public sector procurement and many governmental functions can often be carried out through the Internet. Decisions on the use of the Internet in public administration should be based on benefit cost analysis, the capability of government personnel, and the level of demand. Nevertheless, greater government use of the Internet can play a role in encouraging public participation.

The fact that most Internet transactions are conducted in English is currently an important constraint for developing economies on using the Internet. Estimates of the share of English used on the Internet range from 70 to 80 percent, but only 57 percent of Internet users have English as their first language (ITU,1999; Vehovar et al, 1999). Per capita Internet use averages about 30 percent in those industrial countries where English is common, compared with about 5 percent in other industrial countries.

Conversely, Internet content is limited in the local language of most developing countries. From a commercial aspect, Schmitt (2000) found that just 37 percent of *Fortune* 100 websites support a language other than English. The amount of non-English material on the web is growing, however. Spanish websites in particular are increasing, in part to serve the large Spanish-speaking community in the US (Vogel and Druckerman, 2000). Improvements in translation services by people and machines, as well as web browsers that recognize characters of different languages should ease language constraints. There is growing recognition that English-only content is insufficient for an international economy.

MODELS OF ELECTRONIC GOVERNMENTS

The drivers of e-commerce and economic digitization include customer expectations and demands, market access and development, efficiency and cost reduction, the emergence of new product or service possibilities, the drive to focus on core competencies and outsource non-core functions, globalization, increasing complexity and regulatory changes.

There are three different themes with which developing countries have viewed economic digitization, including e-commerce and e-government. The leading theme has been one of promoting growth of IT as one of the main sectors of a country's economy. The IT sector offers a massive opportunity for countries to improve economic growth and increase employment, as has been the case in India. According to a recent study, India ranks above many developed countries in terms of software capability. The city of Bangalore alone is a home for more than 50 computer-chip design companies, 170 systems software companies, and 125 communications software companies. At the same time, other regions in India, like Hyderabad, Madras, Delhi, and Kochi have been expanding rapidly, pushing India on a strong path of development.

A second theme that has emerged in the last 6 years is the deployment of IT for delivery of government services, which is covered under the broad term of e-government. Enhancement in delivery of governmental services is an important issue for many developing countries, because electronic delivery can improve efficiency, cut bottleneck for citizens, decrease corruption, and increase transparency. Electronic governments take advantage of information technologies in order to harmonize relations with citizens, businesses, and other government agencies.

The third theme defines the role of electronic and information technology within a society. Within the domain of this view, governments have to deal with issues such as convergence of different technologies, private control over media, and censorship (Bhatnagar, 2003). Electronic government is mainly driven by the private sector push that stands to benefit from increased investments in hardware and consulting. It is also determined by a growing demand for better services from citizens, who now experience greatly enhanced services from the private sector.

In the last decade, many developing and emerging countries have gone through a process of economic liberalization and economic growth under advice from multilateral lending agencies (such as the World Bank or the IMF). Many large countries like India and China have grown at 6 to 10 percent over the last decade (Bhatnagar, 2003). Having completed the first phase of economic policy reform, such countries are now under pressure to move to the next phase of reform, that is governance reform. Since e-government pilots have demonstrated a positive impact on corruption, transparency and quality of service, these countries see this kind of transformation as an effective tool for governance reform.

The experience of many of the developing countries shows that there is considerable intra-governmental competition between government departments that are committed to move forward in implementing e-government initiatives. Brazil, for instance, launched an electronic voting system, which is considered by many to be a better system than that of the US. On another front, proliferation of the Internet in the urban areas of many developing countries is starting to create a critical mass, not as considerable as in most developed countries, but large enough to lead the government to deliver online services, especially in large urbanized areas of Latin America and Asia.

A flourishing IT industry worldwide will also help, of course. It is expected that the next few years could be of particular benefit to developing countries, whose export growth in IT-related products is higher (23.5 percent in the past decade) than in the developed world (10.8 percent). Not only that, but the share of developing countries and emerging economies in IT exports keeps rising, and IT now accounts for a higher proportion of developing country exports than it does in the industrialized countries. This is largely because multinational corporations are increasingly locating hardware production in emerging markets and because developing countries are making efforts to develop the local IT production capacities that attract transnational companies' outsourcing.

Two central developments in the information technology industry are helping developing and emerging economies: (1) The development of open-source software, such as Linux, and (2) the customization and localization of software products and websites, for local and regional markets. Major opportunities, for instance, are created by the greater demand for 'Arabizing' software in the Middle East and a number of UAE, Jordanian and Egyptian-based companies are already transforming themselves from production of media content web hosting.

The UNCTAD 2003 *Electronic Commerce and Development* report finds that, while the above mentioned trends are promising, they all require technological infrastructure and workforce skills beyond the reach of most small-size enterprises in developing countries.

Public sector organizations in developing economies are slowly but surely transforming themselves as a result of the opportunities and threats presented by the development of Internet technologies and the new economic order. Many of these public sector entities are now well beyond web publishing, and have begun to implement transactional capabilities. Individual transaction systems are giving way to Internet-based end-to-end processes, and in the not-too-distant future governments will face a new challenge: the very technologies that deliver enhanced value in public administration will produce new demands for enhanced reflexivity, transparency, and accountability from governments.

One of the noteworthy consequences of the Internet revolution to government is the change in the perception of the citizen. Governmental agencies have a general reputation for being bureaucratic and functionally insular. This refers to the tendency to not integrate services across government departments when responding to citizens' needs. In part, this has been driven by well-established practices and cultures, and by the fact that it was administratively very difficult to integrate systems and practices among various departments. The Internet has been proven to be cost effective for large, private sector bureaucracies, and for a large number of public sector bureaucracies in developed economies.

In the various sources of discussion and debate on questions surrounding the impact of the Internet on governments and public administration, there are serious differences in how the vocabulary is used. There are some authors who make no distinction between e-government and e-governance. With respect to e-government, there is no shortage of articles on the question of how technology generally and the Internet specifically are radically changing the delivery channels of governmental entities, from paying parking tickets to getting climate data on prospective retirement locations. In part, governance involves the appropriate engagement of the citizen at the policy level and technology may significantly influence the shape and size of such engagement (see Toregas, 2001).

There has been substantial discussion around the questions of the digital divides, identifying (1) those who have Internet access versus those who do not; (2) those who have high-speed Internet access versus those with slow speed access that might limit the functional richness of their engagement with e-government, and; (3) those who do not have the necessary experience, training, skills, and comfort to get the maximum benefit from any form of facilities.

One of the alleged advantages of both e-government and e-governance is the way this new communication model can enhance government operational transparency and responsiveness to citizen needs and desires. There are a number of ways in which the word 'transparency' may be used, beginning with the transparency of administrative procedures. In this case, the notion of transparency is more closely related to 'understandability'. When government programs and services are designed for citizen interaction directly online, the designers must make a much greater effort to consider how to make an administrative procedure as simple as possible for the client. This might not be the case when software applications are designed for civil servants, who can be expected to have a better understanding of the background administrative complexities than can citizens at large. In short, the systems designers working in an Internet context have a challenge: a relatively constrained design environment by way of a browser front-end in combination with a public that cannot be expected to have a deep understanding of administrative complexities. Therefore, the only answer is an internal process re-design that hides the inherent complexity of transactions, while at the same time ensuring the ability of the user to successfully achieve his/her objectives. There is also a rising demand for creating processes that hide the complexity of government organizational structure and the machinery of government. This is part of the reason why 'one-stop-shopping' government portals are seen as a critical specification by e-government proponents.

E-government does not stop at the transaction level. There is also what is called, in e-commerce literature, the 'end-to-end process' level. For instance, where there are routine processes in government requiring intermediate considerations and approvals (eg, getting an advance tax ruling), sophisticated e-government applications could provide a citizen the opportunity to determine the progress of his/her request through on-line query. In other words, one could imagine a citizen being able to determine (a) how long each of the steps in a process was taking; (b) who in the administration had responsibility for each step; and (c) who might be contacted to speed things up. The ability to track FedEx and other package deliveries is a rudimentary precursor to such a system. Such capabilities might conceivably affect management practices significantly, while at the same time increasing transparency and accountability.

In all of this change, there is some evidence of institutional push, but even more so of citizen pull. Slevin (2000) has noted that social trends in all developed countries have included rising degrees of reflexivity, that is, the tendency of citizens and customers to react concretely to events on a basis of their own choosing, rather than just accept the explanations of authorities. Chat rooms, instant messaging, and the ability to monitor social and economic outcomes all enable the average citizen to engage more easily and more directly in issues with a public policy component. These technologies mean that individuals can seek out information, opinions, and alternative explanations without the mediation of professionals in the various fields. The Internet has thus exacerbated a loss of deference to doctors, lawyers, civil servants, and all other professionals.

Reflexivity and e-government/e-governance also share the common issue of transparency. Slevin (2000) is careful to note that social reflexivity did not start with the Internet and, presumably, would not have abated had it not been developed. However, it is here and it will contribute to an increase in demands by citizens to participate in the workings of government as capabilities of e-governance develop to allow for it. Indeed, rising levels of citizen reflexivity may themselves be a driving force in the creation of e-governance capabilities.

One place where governments share the same concern as the private sector when it comes to service is the issue of centricity. This concept relates to the orientation or focus of a particular process. Organization centricity implies that the provision of service is focused on the structural characteristics of the organization and the civil servant, rather than on the needs of the citizen. Organization centricity might be entirely appropriate for matters that are of limited concern to the citizen or the customer. Centricity is more often a problem because of departmental 'branding', where citizen desires for a clean and easy approach to government services runs athwart departmental, agency, or ministerial desires for recognition about specifically who is providing the service. This desire for credit is especially problematic where different jurisdictional levels are involved. Federal, provincial, and municipal governments are all involved in taxation, elections, and providing services. This is not a new development, of course. There have been cases of grant program implementations being delayed by months while different jurisdictions debated where to position their respective logos on the envelope in which the grant was mailed. Citizens may not care which level issues passports, drivers' licenses, and water bills, but the providers do care very much and 'one-stop-shop' portals can become a future battlefield.

Dutta (2003) argues that governments can assume three different roles when developing e-government at the national level. They can be producers, facilitators, or leaders. Governments that develop and deploy ICT goods and services and ICT infrastructure are referred to as *producers*. Those that create an enabling environment, including a conduction macroeconomic environment, fiscal policy, regulatory policy, and education policy are referred to as *facilitators*. Those that take the initiative of implementing e-government, addressing digital divides in the country, and making ICT a national priority are referred to as leaders. Based on this classification, leaders include countries such as Singapore, Hong Kong, and the UAE.

Governments play an important role as users of information/ communication technologies. They use IT for reforming government, promoting e-government projects at all levels of government, and enabling online tax payments and online procurement. Examples of developing economies with high e-government capacity include the UAE, the Republic of Korea, Mexico, Kuwait, Argentina, Lebanon, Bahrain, Uruguay and Chile. A good example of developing governments taking an active role as users of e-commerce include the government of Dubai in the UAE, which is using the Internet heavily to purchase materials for state-run companies (up to 75 percent of all purchases were online in 2003).

DELIVERY MODES AND E-READINESS

A number of factors have contributed to the growing popularity of e-government within developing countries, but the prime reason is that there has been a substantial illustration effect of the beneficial and practical difference that e-government has made in advanced economies in the delivery of services, provision of information and internal administration of the public sector. Many developing countries that have developed noteworthy capacity in building IT applications feel that they can 'leapfrog' to take advantage of the new electronic channels that are available for delivering government services. In the last decade, many countries have gone through a process of economic liberalization and economic growth under advice from lending agencies, especially the World Bank and the International Monetary Fund (IMF). Many large developing countries like India and China have grown at 6–10 percent over the last decade. Such countries are now ready to move to the next phase of reform, especially governance reform. Since e-government pilots in a number of countries have proved to have a positive impact on corruption, transparency and quality of service, these countries see e-government as a valuable tool for governance reform.

Applications of e-government can be categorized according to the constituency that is served, from delivery of services to citizens, to delivery of services to business and industry, to delivery of services to other governmental departments. The main objective is to increase efficiency and effectiveness. Significant reduction in costs can result from a paperless environment in which electronic documents flow from workstation to workstation for approval and action. There are one-time costs of hardware/ software and other operating expenses associated with such applications.

Conceivably the ultimate cost reduction takes place in storing paper files. The most important advantage is one of greater effectiveness because the administrative burden on decision-makers is diminished, allowing time for important issues of policy and decision making. In most cases, the data captured by the electronic system enables better control and monitoring of productivity of employees, easy identification of points of delay and corruption, and accumulation of historical data that can be easily mined for policy analysis later. Another significant advantage is the ability to share data across agencies and departments in an electronic form.

Looking at the Middle East, e-government has become a growing priority. By many accounts, the UAE is setting the standard for neighboring countries. Dubai began work on its e-government project in April 2000, when His Highness Sheikh Mohammed Bin Rashed Al Maktoum, who is both the Crown Prince of Dubai and the UAE defense minister, launched a review of how government services had been delivered in the past and how IT and the Internet could be used to improve delivery of services. Dubai's e-government services include the 'e4all' project, which enables citizens to buy and use computers and software programs; the 'e-citizen' program, which helps residents understand how Dubai e-government works; and the 'e-employee' program, which trains government workers. The UAE reached a goal of migrating more than 70 percent of its public services to the Internet by 2005, and plans to migrate more than 90 percent by the year 2007.

Currently, Dubai e-government offers more than 1200 online services through its web portal. According to a new global survey that covered 100 major cities, and which was conducted by the E-Governance Institute at Rutgers University, the State University of New Jersey, in 2003, Dubai has outranked several digitally advanced cities in the world, including Dublin, Paris and Copenhagen, in terms of privacy and security on its official portal. The survey of the official city websites ranked Dubai in the ninth position, along with Auckland, scoring 7.86 out of 20 points, against the average score of 2.85. In addition, the survey ranked Dubai 11th worldwide in the service delivery category, ahead of Dublin, Helsinki and Tokyo. The security and privacy section of the survey examined the availability and quality of privacy policies, and looked at issues related to authentication, encryption, digital signature, data management and use of cookies. According to the findings, only 17 cities showed that they identified the organizations collecting data on their websites and only 14 cities identified the kind of data being collected. Dubai was one of the 12 cities whose privacy policy identified both.

In service delivery, Dubai was ranked eleventh worldwide, with a score of 8.25 (out of 20) against the world average of 4.77. The report also cited Dubai as one of only 10 cities that have websites allowing citizens to pay 'fees' online.

The survey, which used 92 key indicators to evaluate websites under five core parameters, gave weighted scoring of 20 points each – to add up to a total score of 100. Taking all parameters into account, Dubai was ranked eighteenth, ahead of Sydney and Jakarta. The top five cities in digital governance were Seoul, Hong Kong, Singapore, New York and Shanghai.

Dubai was the only city from the Arab world to make the top-20 list. Other Arab cities figuring in the top-100 list were Amman, Manama, Riyadh, Cairo and Beirut, according to the Rutgers University survey.

Developing countries have used three distinct delivery models. These are: (1) Departments going on line, where citizens interact with departmental/ private operators who access data and information from on-line terminals located in the premises of the department. The second model describes conveniently located Service Centers in public places, where multiple services are offered at each location: payment, issue of licenses and certificates. Such counters can quickly move traffic from departmental counters to a service center (as happened in the case of Brazil). Building such centers, which must deal with several departments, requires significant coordination and perhaps setting up a separate agency for the project. The third model describes self-service through a portal which is designed to offer a variety of services and the interface is organized in a fashion that makes it convenient for citizens to access the services (using a life cycle approach as in Singapore). Complete backend computerization is needed and usually there is a middle ware, which directs requests for access to information from different departmental databases/websites. Integration at the back end is needed for data sharing.

There should be policies governing data definitions, structure of data and layered architecture of individual departmental applications. Such self-service delivery naturally presumes a high Internet penetration and the willingness and ability of citizens to use the portals. Adoption rate has to be driven through conscious actions like training and other incentives. Building a portal requires strong centralized leadership for extensive co-ordination. Even then the goal of a joined up government, where a particular service requires approvals from many different departments, is difficult to achieve. For e-government to be successful, governments have to increase their readiness. The e-readiness structure provides a means to help government executives blend business and technology decisions to create focused, flexible, and receptive organizations.

The global economic depression since the year 2000 has undercut IT spending and scaled back public infrastructure initiatives in most of the developed and developing countries. Yet the Internet revolution moves forward. The Internet is reinventing the way that businesses interact with their customers, with other businesses and, increasingly, with governments. Economic might influences, but does not determine, e-readiness. The utility of the Internet is increasingly evident in developed and developing economies alike. Citizens can download government documents, file tax returns and participate in electronic forums with elected officials not only in Singapore, Helsinki, London and Ottawa, but in Cape Town and São Paulo as well. In markets where there are many more mobile phones in hands than PCs on desks – including most of the developing world – wireless devices are becoming delivery mechanisms for Internet services. It is not surprising that mobile banking services are more developed in the Philippines and China than in the US (EIU, 2004). Some government strategies for expanding digital infrastructure and getting people to use it are better than others. Simply putting information online and demonstrating a compassionate attitude towards Internet development is no longer sufficient. To have a strong impact on the day-to-day activities of consumers and businesses, governments must take on their role as early adopter and promote education programs and legislation that make a difference. E-government initiatives are contributing to the steady rise of economies such as Singapore, Hong Kong and Korea.

There are several dimensions to e-government readiness. One aspect of readiness is the maturity of technical infrastructure and back office use in various departments. For example, use of email across government departments, would be indicative of readiness. Readiness also depends on the attitudinal make-up of the civil service. Willingness to re-engineer, share more information, and treat the citizen as a customer indicates high readiness. Attitudinal changes are difficult to bring about, unless there is a champion at the political level and strong leadership within the department. Departmental champions need to be identified and co-ordination committees created at departmental levels. A final aspect of readiness is an aware and demanding citizenry, which understands its rights, is willing to express them and to fight for them in case of laxity and inefficiency. By publishing performance data and citizen charters, e-government can be an instrument in promoting citizen awareness. Delivering e-government services requires a high penetration of Internet in homes or presence of a large number of public kiosks. For handling e-payment and building trust between citizens and government in doing transactions over long distance requires an enabling legal framework. The role that governments have to play in enhancing the readiness for electronic delivery of services encompasses a 'doer's' role – delivering government services electronically – and an enabling role that encourages the private sector to deliver electronic services. Governments need to develop a vision and strategy, create an organization to support and catalyze e-government, build human capacity, and enact policies that will attract private investment in infrastructure and application development.

Public funding of e-commerce initiatives provides another measure of government commitment to Internet business. The Singaporean government subsidizes the cost of e-business consultancy, Internet connections, and hardware and software purchases for qualified companies. Taiwan's Medium-sized and Small Business Administration is offering subsidies over the 2002–2006 period to help 20000 enterprizes in 200 local industries set up Internet databases and online trading systems. With these subsidies, the government hopes to prod companies from original equipment manufacturing into global marketing and logistics. To help companies tap into electronic global supply networks, Malaysia's 2002 budget covered development of RosettaNet, an internationally standardized supply chain management platform, and extended income tax deductions for expenses incurred in its implementation (EIU, 2003).

No government is completely ready on all dimensions. One of the important steps in preparation for e-government is the building of capacity within the government to manage the implementation of projects. States like Andhra Pradesh in India, which is considered as a pioneer in the implementation of e-government, has invested heavily in the training of chief information officers. Andhra Pradesh has trained nearly 100 handpicked officers at the middle and senior levels in intensive residential programs. These trainees are expected to take leadership positions for implementing e-government across 70 departments of the state. The training provided an exposure to technology, so that the trainees could comfortably deal with private sector partners in procuring various products and services. Analysis and design of systems, management for projects, re-engineering of administrative processes and management of change are the other important topics covered in these training programs. Governments also need to create an incentive system so those departments take a lead in implementing electronic service delivery. Policies need to be defined which enable departments to charge a user fee when the quality of delivery is significantly upgraded. If the departments are allowed to retain the user fee and make investments to build new delivery systems, a strong incentive for e-government applications is created.

Systematic evaluation studies need to be conducted to measure benefits during and after implementation. So far the benefits of e-government have been largely anecdotal. Evaluation studies should be carried out by independent agencies. Stakeholders must indicate the benefits that have been delivered and problems that continue to be faced. Serious evaluations can provide feedback for a national strategy, as well as design and implementation of individual projects. Some of the projects that were deemed to be successful (and were awarded prizes by international organizations) have started faltering. A World Bank sponsored evaluation of four projects in India indicates that two projects are moving towards failure. Long-term sustainability can be ensured if the innovation is not championed by just one individual administrator but is owned by the entire department. E-government can advance the agenda on governance and fiscal reform, transparency, anti-corruption, empowerment and poverty reduction. The potential is recognized but implementation is difficult. Pioneers in several countries have shown that gains can be real and projects can be implemented successfully. The challenge is to promote widespread use.

MEASURING READINESS FOR THE DIGITAL ECONOMY

Readiness is measured by evaluating the areas that are most critical for participation in the digital economy. The purpose and intent of each scorecard influences the level of assessment, the factors included and the way the results are used. For example, at the national economy level, the APEC E-Commerce Readiness Assessment Guide (APEC, 2000) was designed for completion at government level. It was developed for use in partnership mode by governments and stakeholders to identify the areas where further development is needed: to develop policies to promote e-commerce or to remove barriers to electronic trade. The assessment includes factors such as the levels of technological infrastructure, Internet access, Internet usage, IT education and the regulatory framework for e-Commerce. The results are intended as an input to the strategic planning processes, rather than as a competitive scoring or ranking system.

Another comprehensive measure of readiness for the digital economy, which also focuses at the national economy level, has been developed by the Economist Intelligence Unit (EIU). The EIU has a proprietary methodology that it uses to rank 60 countries into four levels of e-business preparedness – e-business leaders, e-business contenders, e-business followers and e-business laggards (EIU, 2004). These e-readiness rankings are published on the www. ebusinessforum.com website and are used for evaluating geographic markets and for international benchmarking purposes. Quantitative statistical data and qualitative assessments by country specialists are incorporated into the six weighted categories evaluated for this e-readiness measure:

- Connectivity (30 percent)
- Business Environment (20 percent)
- E-Commerce Consumer and Business Adoption (20 percent)

- Legal and Regulatory Environment (15 percent)
- Supporting e-Services (10 percent)
- Social and Cultural Infrastructure (5 percent)

Assuming successful e-business is not possible without a positive business climate overall, the EIU screen 70 indicators for the business environment scores which provide projections for the next 5 years.

To evaluate the ability of a company to perform and compete in the digital economy requires consideration of a different set of factors to the macro-environmental context or the descriptive measures of current e-business activities. Previous research on the uptake of new technological innovations shows that absorptive capacity depends upon existing knowledge and skills, as well as prior experiences with similar technologies (Cohen and Levinthal, 1990). This suggests that to understand the readiness for, and uptake of, e-business, the competencies, knowledge, skills, abilities, attitudes, and resources involved need to be examined. Following this approach, Hartman et al (2000) conducted an in-depth analysis of Cisco Systems and a series of other net companies. They identified four major drivers of change that are critical for success of an enterprise in the Internet-based economy. Accordingly, their Net Readiness Scorecard incorporates attributes of (1) Leadership; (2) Governance; (3) Competencies; and (4) Technology.

Two versions of this Net Readiness Scorecard, which evaluate factors from each of these four key areas have been developed and published (Hartman et al., 2000). The short version consists of 20 factors that can be evaluated very quickly to provide an approximate measure of net readiness. There is also a more comprehensive version, which is longer and more detailed and managers can complete this scorecard electronically at the www.netreadiness.com website. This measure is designed to profile the company's current state of net readiness, to assess its position relative to others in the same industry and to provide perspective recommendations to improve its competitive positioning.

Aggregate Net Readiness scores are calculated from ratings of the component factors to provide an organization's current level of Net Readiness. Hartman et al, (2000) proposed a series of five levels of Net Readiness for companies as they increase in e-sophistication, which they named: Net Agnostic, Net Aware, Net Savvy, Net Leaders, and Net Visionary.

There is now an established tradition of research within developing and emerging economies connecting characteristics of the institutional environment to the extent and nature of private investment. Some of this work has examined the impact of general characteristics of the nation-state (eg, Murtha and Lenway, 1994; Levy and Spiller, 1996; Henisz and

Zelner, 2000), while others have focused on specific aspects of the legal or regulatory environment (eg, Oxley, 1999). In this work, we attempt to link success of e-commerce in a country to a number of natural and institutional resources the country has. Chapter 4 of this book will cover the development of hypotheses and chapter 5 will present the empirical analysis on the data collected from a sample of developing countries.

ON THE GROUND: WHAT IS HAPPENING?

The effects of Internet-induced changes in the global economy and their implications for developing countries will depend to a significant extent on factors that policy-makers, business players and other stakeholders can influence. Policies must be designed, articulated in coherent e-strategies and implemented in partnership with all the relevant players to ensure that the new opportunities for creating, transforming, applying and exchange information and value are used to improve the productivity of developing economies and their enterprizes. The process of designing the strategies that can make e-commerce a force for development must necessarily include an international component that supports national efforts by ensuring that the developmental perspective is present in a meaningful way in the multiple international discussions of the Internet, ICT and the organization of their economic applications. A close relationship between national e-commerce strategies and international co-operation would be greatly facilitated by the emergence of a common understanding of the fundamental elements of e-commerce strategies for development, especially if, as seems desirable, ICT is to be mainstreamed into official development aid programs.

The names and attributes of the ongoing e-commerce revolution suggest three fundamental and interdependent roles or impacts on the economy:

(1) Accessing information and knowledge, with dramatic increase in the power and speed to access, process, adapt, and organize information. This, in turn, has accelerated learning, innovation, and knowledge creation and dissemination. In this sense, ICT may have the profound impact of the invention of the printing press.

(2) Speeding up and reducing the costs of production and transactions throughout the economy. Information and communication technology is increasingly embedded into all types of production, processes, and transactions. This gives rise to intelligent products and real-time control processes, facilitating trade, outsourcing business-support and back-office services, and enabling complementary organizational innovations. In this sense, ICT may have implications similar to those of the steam

engine, electricity, and the railways in transforming production and transportation systems.

(3) Making connections among people, non-governmental organizations (NGOs), enterprises, and communities. This gives rise to empowerment, participation, co-ordination, decentralization, social learning, connecting communities of practice, mobilizing social capital, and globalizing civil society concerns. Information and communication technologies have been increasingly described as 'technologies of freedom' (Ithiel de Sola Pool, 1983). There may not be a historical parallel to the enabling role of ICT to co-ordinate and empower.

A national development strategy that attempts to position an economy to take advantage of the ongoing revolution must take a comprehensive view of the enabling roles of e-commerce and electronic government. Often, proponents of one framework or another tend to focus on one of the roles of e-commerce at the expense of others. For example, the 'knowledge economy' framework, developed by the OECD, has tended to focus on the role of knowledge in the economy, and thus views the role of ICT mainly in terms of access to knowledge. However, the knowledge lens neglects other equally important roles of ICT: in speeding up and reducing the costs of production and transactions and in empowering people to connect, mobilize, organize, overcome their isolation, and share their experiences and idiosyncratic information. Yet developing countries are characterized by high transactions and logistics costs, and by the isolation of large parts of the population.

Rather than being treated as an isolated sector on its own, ICT should be used as a lens to re-think development strategies, as a tool to enable all sectors, and as a new and powerful means to empower the poor. This does not mean that we believe in ICT as a technology fix, but that an understanding of the full potential and implications of the ongoing technological revolution is necessary to realize its potential for development – far beyond its contribution as a sector. It is also essential to understand what makes ICT different from other technologies or from earlier technological revolutions in order to marshal the specific policies, institutions, and capabilities that must accompany the effective use of ICT as an enabler for development.

In Saudi Arabia, all Internet connections are routed through government hubs that filter 'unsuitable' content. In Turkey, a new media law went into force in mid-2002 that puts the Internet under the same regulations as broadcast media, reducing the freedom of expression that Turkish websites had hitherto enjoyed. A clause in the legislation forbids the media from disseminating pessimism – a term that can be manipulated to include any criticism of the government. Aside from the implications for free speech, the clause will put a damper on local Internet service providers as companies move sites out of the country to avoid run-ins with authorities.

Despite its vigilance about content, the Saudi Government is trying to strengthen Internet usage in what is one of the world's fastest-growing markets for home computers. Saudi Telecommunications Corporation (STC) recently introduced direct subscriber line (DSL) technology in major cities, and has pushed for significant cuts in connection and phone charges, which started in 2003. The STC's intention was to service 3.3 million regular Internet users by 2005, and it reached 2 540 000 by that target date. In North Africa, the Egyptian Government is making an attempt to build up public access by providing free connections (excluding call charges). Under a new system promoted by the Ministry of Communications and involving the state-owned Telecom Egypt (TE), ISPs who claim there has been a rise in usage, collect 70 percent of call revenues from TE, rather than selling subscriptions. TE now plans to promote Internet use in the private sector by cutting fees for integrated services digital network (ISDN) lines.

The picture in East Europe is a bit gloomy. Although IT infrastructure in Eastern Europe continues to be upgraded, it is still insufficient to support a healthy business environment. The Internet is still hindered by high telephony charges relative to average incomes, slow and unreliable connections, and low levels of personal computer ownership. The majority of East Europeans who use the Internet access it from work rather than home. Also, while the educated and members of the middle class make their way online, large segments of the region's population has little or no experience of using the Internet. There are signs of improvement, however. Hungary has made significant progress over the past few years in enhancing the quality of Internet connections and expanding broadband coverage. In the Czech Republic and Poland, increased competition among ISPs is leading to better service and lower prices. The gap between Eastern and Western Europe is even greater with regard to e-commerce development than it is for Internet use and connectivity. Online sales in Hungary account for as little as 0.1 percent of total business revenue compared with an estimated 2 percent in the EU.

Much of the advancement in Internet usage – and even e-business adoption – can be credited to government initiative. The reverse is also true: government inaction and poorly conceived intervention can be blamed for impeding e-readiness in many countries. No government gets everything right, particularly in developing countries, where Internet technology and strategies are still new and experimental. However, the EIU e-readiness rankings suggest that there are clear ways that governments can boost e-readiness in their countries. The obstacles are manifest and some cannot be easily overcome: widespread poverty means a paucity of credit, reduced spending power and less potential for all kinds of business, including e-business. Economic turmoil can repel investment, squeeze consumer and business financing, and put a damper on all kinds of commerce, not only e-commerce. Ingrained consumer preferences – for seeing and touching goods before buying, for example, or paying in hard cash – will not change overnight. Efforts to overhaul a country's entire system of education, law or government, or to build nationwide infrastructure from scratch, also take tremendous reserves of time, money and political will.

However, there are other steps that can be taken immediately. Distrust of on-line payment systems and lack of faith in the delivery of goods can be eradicated with targeted legislation and careful regulation. Where laws and safeguards already exist, but citizens remain unaware or uncertain, governments can focus on 'marketing' the system to reassure the public that transactions are secure. E-business can be given a boost with subsidized consulting services and tax incentives that help smaller entities put their business on line. Governments can improve their countries' business environments by strengthening protections for intellectual property. User-friendly on-line government services that facilitate and transform interactions with other governmental agencies would make business both more efficient and enjoyable and will help all. In addition, governments can improve the technological ability of their operations by devising creative ways to work with the private sector. Internet connections can be made affordable through ingenious government projects that put computers in the public domain and encourage domestic manufacture of PCs and mobile phones.

To be successful, governments should push forward liberalization of the telecommunication sector, lower connection charges, improve technology, and increase access options. Information technology training programs can help countries meet demand for technical expertize. The e-commerce revolution is not led by businesses and consumers alone. Smart government initiatives are boosting the Internet's potential around the world, from the East to the West, and from the North to the South. It is by focusing on these policies that developing and emerging economies can best compete with developed nations on e-commerce.

In Latin America, e-commerce is highly concentrated in four relatively developed Internet markets (Argentina, Brazil, Chile and Mexico). Overall, between 50 and 70 percent of Latin American enterprizes in the formal sector are estimated to have access to the Internet. The Internet is widely used for business contacts and information-gathering, but only a few enterprizes carry out online transactions. Large transnational corporations, such as Ford Argentina, are playing a key role in the development of on-line B2B transactions, especially in Argentina, Brazil and Mexico. Banking is another sector in which B2C providers in the region, particularly in Brazil, have developed a competitive edge. Brazil has also made significant progress in business-related e-government applications (UNCTAD, 2003).

The way to enhance Internet use in Latin America is to find ways to connect people without home computers. With about 6 million mobile phone subscribers in Venezuela, the arrival of Web-enabled mobile phones is a promising development. In Mexico, Internet cafés have helped meet demand. Microsoft has teamed up with the Mexican government to provide universal Internet access in the country by 2006, part of the Vicente Fox administration's 'e-Mexico' project that was officially launched last year. There were 20 200 000 Internet users in the country at June, 2006 (Internet World statistics). The company is to contribute software, consulting and training to 4000 computer operators to manage community-based computer centers. Mexico hopes to put 10 000 free Internet kiosks in place to help provide government services as well as to reduce the country's digital divide (UNCTAD, 2003).

Internet access is still a privilege for the few in Brazil. As part of a government effort to close the digital divide between rich and poor, the country plans to set up at least one Internet-connected PC in each of its 5000 postal offices, with hourly access fees kept low. Another project aims to supply every Brazilian with a free, private e-mail account. In the year 2001, the government passed the Information Technology Law, which became effective from January 1, 2002. These regulations are designed to stimulate the development of national research and development projects and to reduce the importation of IT goods and services. In addition, the law promises to provide incentives to the computer industry and establish free-access Internet stations in many public facilities.

Asia's top-ranked countries have some common characteristics: good infrastructure; high per capita income; substantial (or advancing) telecoms deregulation; low (or falling) transaction costs; strong government commitment to e-commerce; globally competitive companies; good education systems; and openness to trade and ideas.

In this strong field, Singapore has put in place the world's first nationwide broadband network. Hong Kong aims to have 90 percent of its government services online in 2005. However, South Korea appears to be making the fastest progress, where the president of the country launched a crusade for economic transformation based on IT, and the cabinet has established e-commerce as one of the key objectives of social and economic development. The saturation of densely populated urban commercial and residential districts with cheap telephone and broadband networks puts South Korea in a unique position to exploit e-commerce. At the other end of the spectrum, however, poorer Asian countries are held back by telecoms monopolies, widespread poverty, miniscule credit card penetration and unhelpful government intervention. In Thailand, the Communications Authority of Thailand holds a monopoly over international Internet connections; the leasing of Internet lines in Thailand costs six times more than in Hong Kong and four times more than in Japan. Infrastructure initiatives in China are ambitious, but not easy to achieve in a huge country where 70–80 percent of the population lives in the countryside. China's Internet development is also stifled by censorship and competition among government agencies for regulatory control. In India, the rampant theft of user names and passwords has eroded confidence in e-commerce.

State of E-commerce in Africa

With local Internet connection now available in all African capital cities the possibilities (in terms of connectivity) to engage in e-commerce have markedly improved, at least for the minority of Africans who live in the continent's major urban centers. In 18 countries, calls to access the Internet are now charged at local rates. Legal monopolies in Internet service provision have almost disappeared, although *de facto* ISP monopolists still operate in several of the smaller markets. The number of dial-up subscribers grew by 30 percent in 2001 and now stands at about 1.3 million. Incoming Internet traffic represents 1 gigabyte per second, while outgoing traffic is around 800 megabytes per second. According to Intelsat, its data traffic from Africa grew by 30 percent in 2001 and was expected to overtake voice traffic by 2005.

The growth of the internet in West Africa is being held back by the slow pace of liberalization in the market. In 2004, only seven of the 22 West African countries had more than 10 000 dial-up subscribers: Côte D'Ivoire, Cameroon, Ghana, Guinea, Nigeria, Senegal and Togo. The biggest is Nigeria, which is the third largest market on the continent after South Africa and Egypt. In most of the African countries, the number of internet subscribers is growing very slowly or has hit a plateau and without significant changes in the state of the economy (coupled with deregulation) the number will stay the same. Only seven countries of the countries covered have ended the monopoly of the incumbent telephone company (Côte D'Ivoire, Ghana, Guinea-Bissau, Mali, Mauritania, Nigeria and Senegal) if those ending the monopoly in 2004 are all included (Connectivity Africa, 2004).

The success story has been the growth of the number of cyber-cafés. With this explosion in numbers has come a fairly vigorous price war to the point where many businesses are uneconomic. However the prices offered in many countries are now extremely low and it is through these cyber-cafés that most Africans in the countries covered experience the Internet. Although estimating the numbers of Internet users who are using a cyber-café or something other than a dial-up subscription is notoriously unreliable, it is clear that there are now hundreds of thousands of people using cyber-cafés in West Africa's larger Internet markets. In the largest market, Nigeria, there are probably somewhere between 0.5–1 million users and this figure continues to grow rapidly on a year-on-year basis as more cities are connected.

The majority of users tend to go to cyber-cafés to send or collect e mails and this is supported by a survey in Nigeria that shows Yahoo and Hotmail as the most popular sites used. However, there is not yet a large amount of local content and services in most markets and this pattern will change in the next five years.

Although mobile telephony has expanded extremely rapidly across the African continent, it does not yet offer an alternative, for the purpose of connecting to the Internet, to the scarce fixed lines. Cost considerations also remain a very considerable obstacle to access the Internet. The average cost of using a local dial-up account in Africa for 20 hours a month is about US$68 per month, including local call time but not line rental charges. Since the World Bank estimates that the gross income per capita for sub-Saharan Africa in 2000 was US$470, it is clear that for the vast majority of Africa's population it is utterly impossible to pay such access costs.

For the few who can use the Internet, the experience in terms of speed and stability is often very different, and much more inadequate for e-commerce purposes, than that of users in other regions. Given the cost and low speed of connections, email is even more important for African users than in the rest of the world; many turn to Web-based free providers based in developed countries for this service, even if this means longer connection times. The reason for this seems to be concerns about privacy and the long-term survival prospects of local providers.

Very few updated statistics or even estimates of e-commerce volumes in Africa are available, except for South Africa. Some forecasts put total e-commerce in Africa at US$0.5 billion in 2002, concentrated almost exclusively in South Africa, and predict that it will grow to US$6.9 billion by 2006, with South Africa generating US$6.1 billion and Egypt almost all the rest. In this scenario, Africa's share in global e-commerce by 2006 would represent 0.05 percent of global online trade.

Given the comparatively low level of integration of African enterprizes into international trade and the continent's pattern of exports, it is not surprising that B2B outside South Africa remains almost negligible. However, B2B opportunities have been identified in the on-line and off-line services sector. In spite of the extremely low volumes involved, anecdotal evidence of African e-commerce success stories in the B2C sector is amply available. As is to be expected in view of the low levels of income and connectivity on the continent, exports represent the vast majority of online trade in Africa.

Among these, handicrafts and products and services targeting Africans outside their home countries seem to dominate. As for the most mature e-commerce market on the continent, South Africa, retail online sales remain at low levels. According to data released in May 2002, B2C sales in South Africa in 2001 amounted to only US$16 million, which represented 0.1 percent of total retail sales in that country.

In a number of African countries, including South Africa, Uganda, Botswana and Cote d'Ivoire, cellular mobile uptake has been so rapid that mobile phones now outnumber their fixed line counterparts. The pre-paid system has increased accessibility to a point where pre-paid subscribers now account for 50 percent of all cellular users in fast-growing markets such as South Africa and Egypt.

Significantly, the drive by foreign operators to tap into new cellular markets and opportunities is finally helping overturn Africa's chronic shortage of investment funds for telecoms development. At the end of 2000, 18 of the 33 UN-designated 'Least Developed Countries' in Africa had already awarded licenses to cellular operators with one or more foreign investors.

In addition, widespread liberalization of mobile markets across the continent is opening up investment opportunities for fast-moving local operators who can trade on their experience in local markets to expand operations to other countries within the region.

Governments' ability to raise much-needed capital through mobile license fees is also providing a substantial boost to many countries' telecoms expenditure funds, creating a healthy demand for new equipment to upgrade ageing infrastructure and extend services to underserved areas.

Even though Africa is causing little more than a ripple in the Internet pond, waves are in the making: only one of the continent's 56 countries that are members of the UN International Trade Centre are not directly connected to the Internet superhighway. Penetration figures for Africa are, however, skewed strongly in favor of wealthier nations like Seychelles (6.3 percent), Mauritius (4.6 percent), South Africa (4.2 percent) and Cape Verde (1.25 percent) with uptake in lower income countries such as Sudan, Niger, Benin and Chad at tinier fractions.

Currently, the biggest hurdles to faster connectivity are money and the lack of infrastructure. Service costs around US$50 a month, a month's income in many African countries. A number of initiatives, like the ITU's Electronic Commerce for Developing Countries and the US Agency for International Development's Leland Initiative Africa Global Information Infrastructure Project are working to help alleviate these and other problems through resource-pooling, network capacity sharing and the fostering of a competitive environment for Internet service provision.

State of E-commerce in Asia and the Pacific Region

Demographic weight alone could be enough to explain the leading position of the Asia/Pacific region in the spread of e-commerce in developing countries: at current rates, the region is adding close to 50 million new Internet users a year. This is more in absolute terms, and relatively faster than any other region of the world. However, other factors come into play besides sheer demographics. Enterprizes, particularly in the manufacturing sector, are more integrated into intra regional and global trade flows than those of other developing regions. This means that they are more exposed to pressures from their customers in developed countries to adopt e-business methods and are investing to be able to do so. New broadband technologies are being deployed faster in some middle- and high-income countries in the region than anywhere else. For example, the world's top three markets as regards the number of digital subscriber lines (DSL) per 100 people are the Republic of Korea (10.95), Hong Kong, and China (5.56). In all, 46 percent of all DSL in the world at the end of 2001 were in the Asia-Pacific region. Finally, governments across the region, both at the national level and in the context of regional forums such as the ASEAN and the APEC, have taken a proactive role in the promotion of e-commerce, adapting the legal and regulatory framework, embracing e-government and implementing e-awareness and education plans.

Given its massive size and potential, the evolution of e-commerce in China will determine the region's and, in the medium term, for global e-commerce volumes. A report by the China Internet Network Information Center (CNNIC) released in January 2002 confirms the recent rapid growth of the Chinese Internet population (almost at the rate of 50 percent in 2001), the concentration of users in the major urban centers and in the coastal provinces (while the Internet penetration rate is 10.4 percent in the Guangdong region, it is as low as 0.2 percent in Quinghai province), and an improvement in the number of women and people with lower education levels who access the Internet. China's Internet population, already the world's third largest, is well placed to become the largest online population in the region in the near future, even if infrastructure problems and per capita income levels will keep penetration rates low. The transformation of this large potential into an actual e-commerce market may not happen at the same pace. According to CNNIC (2002), more than two-thirds of Chinese Internet users have yet to make their first online purchase. Of those who have done so, only about one third said they were 'quite satisfied' or 'satisfied' with the experience.

Logistical difficulties such as insufficient transport networks represent a serious obstacle to B2B development, as they make it difficult for companies to realize the potential gains of increased efficiency in their supply chains. Another commonly cited obstacle to B2B in mainland China is the emphasis that the traditional business culture places on strong personal relationships. However, this does not seem to have prevented other Chinese-culture markets from adopting e-business practices. Whatever the case may be, forecasts of B2B volumes diverge significantly. While some sources put it at as much as US$6 billion for 2002 and point to strong growth bringing the figure to nearly US$46 billion by 2005, other estimates paint a much less optimistic picture – for them, from a low base of US$600 million, B2B e-commerce in China would amount to only US$9.6 billion in 2006.

Japan, which for the time being still ranks as the country with the largest Internet population in Asia, experienced strong growth in e-commerce sales in 2001 despite the poor overall performance of the economy. According to data from the Electronic Commerce Promotion Council of Japan, on-line sales grew by 58.4 percent in 2001 and reached a total value of US$264.5 billion, of which 96 percent was in the B2B sector.

Other estimates put the total e-commerce volume in Japan at a more modest level, predicting that it will amount to only US$186 billion in 2002. Recent growth in e-commerce in Japan seems to have been strongest in sectors such as chemical and industrial machinery and paper and office goods, although IT goods and the automotive industry remain predominant. In the B2C sector, growth was strongest in clothing, leisure and travel services, and real estate.

Overall, however, e-commerce volumes remain comparatively low considering the high levels of disposable income, the exception being Japan's lead in the adoption by consumers of some mobile Internet services. Broadband access is also growing at a rate of about 300,000 new subscribers per month (1.5 million subscribers were reported as of January 2002), which should bring the total number to 5 million at the end of 2002. The rapid growth of DSL service may have been stimulated by the government's 'e-Japan strategy', launched in 2001, which aims at providing high-speed access for at least 30 million households and ultra high-speed for another 4 million in the next 5 years.

Although absolute volumes remain modest, e-commerce growth in 2001 and in the first quarter of 2002 in South Korea was dramatic. The most recent data available for 2002 from the National Statistical Office show year-on-year increases in e-commerce sales of 83.4 percent (April), 89.2 (March), 84.9 (February) and 89.8 (January). This would represent total on-line sales of US$1.04 billion in the first quarter of 2002. These figures do not capture most of B2B trade in the country. In contrast, other forecasts go as high as US$29 billion for total e-commerce in 2002, rising to about ten times that amount by 2006. Contributing to this will be the fact that the Republic of Korea has the world's highest penetration of broadband technologies (as of May 2002 there were over 8.5 million DSL subscribers or 18 percent of the population). A number of factors seem to be playing an important role in the rapid deployment of this technology, including proactive government policies supporting the laying of a dense optic fiber network in the major urban centers, the high density of the Republic of Korea's residential patterns which facilitated the establishment of 'last mile connections', and intense competition between operators, resulting in affordable subscription costs.

India, whose Internet population is expected to be second only to China's by 2006, remains a small e-commerce market, which is estimated at half the volume of China's, or about a total of US$300 million for 2002. As in most other countries, email is the favorite application of India's 7 million Internet users, who are worried about the security of on-line payments and do very little on-line shopping. As in other developing countries, PC and telephone penetration rates are very low and competition among ISPs is limited. Business-to-business volumes are concentrated in the automotive sector and in banking and financial services. However, India has developed a successful industry in IT and in the IT-enabled services sector, whose potential annual e-commerce sales have been estimated at US$10 billion.

State of E-commerce in Latin America

E-commerce in the Latin American region is highly concentrated in four relatively developed Internet markets (Argentina, Brazil, Chile and Mexico), which together account for more than two-thirds of the number of Internet users in the region and, according to some estimates, 85 percent of all paid dial-up Internet accounts. While Internet access providers in these markets are starting to introduce satellite services and broadband access, the problems faced by the majority of the other countries in the region remain very basic and relate to problems such as low fixed-line penetration.

In the four countries mentioned above (and in other smaller markets, especially in the Caribbean area), enterprises, or at least those in the formal sector, are reasonably e-commerce aware, and the situation is improving rapidly in other countries in the region (Colombia and Peru).

Overall, between 50–70 percent of Latin American enterprises are estimated to have access to the Internet, and by the end of 2001 virtually all companies with 200 or more employees were expected to have a website. However, for most enterprises being aware of e-commerce does not immediately lead to their actually engaging in it. Email is widely used for business contacts and market information is gathered through web services, but only a minority of enterprises carries out on-line transactions. The use of e-business applications for customer relationship management, supply chain management or enterprize resource management is not widespread. In January 2001, it was estimated that B2B transactions in Latin America had reached US$2.85 billion in 2000. Given the relatively large volume of intra-industry trade in the region, B2B e-commerce is expected to continue to expand rapidly. The same study forecast US$67 billion in B2B e-commerce revenue in the region in 2004; Forrester (2001) predicts that by 2006 the figure will have grown to US$215.7 billion (1.8 percent of global B2B e-commerce), up from US$18.1 billion in 2002.

Large transnational corporations, notably in the automotive sector, are playing a key role in the development of online B2B transactions, especially in Brazil and Mexico. In Brazil, the largest e-commerce market in the region by far, the adoption of both B2B and B2C practices has been spearheaded not by dot.com start-ups but by traditional players seeking to diversify their distribution channels and to improve the efficiency of their supply chain operation. For instance, in 2000 Volkswagen's Brazilian subsidiary reported US$5 billion in purchases made through its on-line procurement system, which links it with over 500 suppliers directly involved in production activities and some 3,000 in all.

Locally owned Brazilian players, especially banks and retail chains, are also keen adopters and promoters of B2B e-commerce. Finance and government-related e-commerce applications such as tax collection, information gathering and procurement are among the other major e-commerce sectors in Brazil. According to the Boston Consulting Group, retail sales in Latin America reached US$1.28 billion in 2001, more than doubling the US$540 million estimated for 2000. Of the total retail e-commerce in the region, 54 percent (US$906 million) would be accounted for by Brazil; Mexico's online retail sales would amount to US$134 million, Argentina's to US$119 million and Chile's to US$45 million. Strong growth was expected for almost all these markets in 2001 and 2002, the exception being Argentina, where retail e-commerce is expected to have very little, if any growth at all, in 2002.

Some aspects of B2C e-commerce in Latin America differ from the patterns observed in more consolidated markets. For instance, online car sales, which have not taken off elsewhere, represent the largest e-retail item in Latin America at an estimated US$504 million in 2001 with the Brazilian subsidiary of the French car-maker Renault expecting to sell 15 000 cars (20 percent of its total sales) online in 2002. Consumer auctions (US$203 million), travel (US$140 million) and computer hardware and software (US$139) are the other individual items each amounting to over US$100 million per year. As a curiosity, online groceries sales, at US$79 million, are the only sector in which the share of on-line sales in total sales in Latin America (especially in

Argentina and Brazil) is similar to that of the US. Another sector in which B2C providers in the region, particularly in Brazil, have developed a competitive edge is banking. For instance, Brazil's largest private bank, Bradesco, was among the first five banks in the world to offer Internet services. Another Brazilian bank, Unibanco, was the first to introduce the first virtual credit card in the world, in cooperation with Mastercard.

There are no surprizes as to the major obstacles to the expansion of retail e-commerce in the region, which are the same as in other developing regions: low Internet penetration rates, inadequate payment systems, poor fulfillment systems and low-quality customer service. On the other hand, significant progress has been made in the region in terms of awareness creation as evidenced by the large proportion of formal sector enterprizes with Internet access and the development of a legal framework for e-commerce as illustrated by the fact that all major economies in the region have undertaken legal changes to accommodate e-commerce.

As in other developing regions of the world the effect of widespread access to mobile telephony is an issue whose implications for the future of e-commerce are not yet clear. In several Latin American markets, mobile telephony users already outnumber fixed-line subscribers. Some analysts believe that Internet access through handheld devices could reach the same levels as PC-based access by 2005 and thus make up for the region's low fixed-line penetration. Whether this would be feasible and would have an impact on e-commerce volumes without changes in the technological basis and the business models remains unclear.

The evolution of e-commerce has been characterized by a very positive phenomenon in Latin America. In most countries the awareness on the subject and the potential market that it represents, have resulted in good initiatives to make as much change as possible, from an 'e-business readiness' point of view, to participate as important market players in the new e-economy.

Among the countries in Latin America implementing regulatory and legal infrastructure changes are Argentina, Brazil and Mexico.

THE CASE OF THE UAE

During the past 10 years, the UAE has made great progress in liberalizing its economy; according to the '2003 Index of Economic Freedom', released on November 12, 2002, the UAE ranks twenty-fourth worldwide, the second Arab country after Bahrain (with a rank of sixteenth). *The Index of Economic Freedom*, which is a joint project by the Heritage Foundation and the *Wall Street Journal*, measures how well a country scores on a list of 50 variables divided into 10 areas of economic freedom. These include trade policy, banking regulations, fiscal burden, foreign investment codes, monetary policy, and black market.[1]

While oil revenue continues to be the mainstay of the UAE economy, the country is pressing ahead with efforts to accelerate diversification and economic reform, and continues to seek new foreign direct investment (FDI) inflows. The UAE has the most diversified economy of the Gulf countries, with its percentage of the total oil exports at 44 percent (compared to Saudi Arabia: 78 percent, Kuwait 90 percent, Bahrain 70 percent, Oman 77 percent and Qatar 55 percent). In addition, FDI reached US$16.4b in 2001 (UAE Ministry of Planning, 2002).

Some of the seven Emirates pursue a policy of openness more than others, with Dubai remaining at the forefront of most new initiatives. Dubai, in particular, continues to seek investors in high technology, tourism and other service industries to compensate for the declining oil in its economy.

In terms of movement towards an information/knowledge society, the UAE has emerged as the forerunner in the Arab region and is among the 30 top IT users in the world, based on the classification issued by the International Data Corporation. In its global Information Society Index (ISI) for 2002,[2] the World Times/IDC ISI ranks the UAE 27th overall, out of 55 countries,[3] by evaluating 23 indicators measuring the capacity of a nation's citizenry to exchange information internally and externally. These 23 indicators are classified into four different categories: (1) Computer Infrastructure; (2) Internet Infrastructure; (3) Information Infrastructure; and, (4) Social Infrastructure (World Times and International Data Corporation, 2002).

The ISI measures the country's achievements in IT and related fields, the level of use and its readiness to cope with IT developments. Only four Arab countries are listed among the top 55 countries in IT readiness. The index shows that the UAE is classified among the runners in 2002 and is given 3,526 points. Although Saudi Arabia is second in the Arab world, it lags far behind the UAE, receiving 1,854 points and ranking 44th in the list. Jordan is ranked at 50 and gets 1,664 points while Egypt is awarded the 51st rank and 1,478 points. The perfect score would likely be close to 9,000.

The ISI establishes a standard by which all nations are measured according to their ability to access and absorb information and IT. While GDP measures economic wealth, ISI measures information capacity and wealth. The ISI is designed to help countries assess their position relative to other countries and to guide companies to future market opportunities.

The countries of the Gulf Cooperation Council (GCC) display the highest penetration rates in mobile phones, fixed-lines and Internet users.

Mobile phone penetration in the GCC stands at 26.16 percent, while average Arab world penetration stands at 7.92 percent. Gulf Cooperation Council mobile phone penetration is also well above the world average, at 17 percent. While fixed-line penetration in the Arab world stands at 7.95 percent and Internet penetration at 2.69 percent, the GCC enjoys a much higher fixed-line penetration (16.52 percent) and Internet penetration (9.48 percent) (Karake Shalhoub and Al Qasimi, 2003).

The GCC countries account for 38.17 percent of Arab mobile phone subscribers, and lay claim to 23.6 percent of fixed lines. In August 2002, GCC Internet users made up 42 percent of all Arab Internet users, but currently account for 40.78 percent, indicating a considerable increase in users in the rest of the Arab world. This is mainly due to measures undertaken to reduce Internet connection and subscription rates or eliminate them altogether, as is the case in Egypt. Heading the Arab telecommunication drive is the UAE, which boasts a 62.97 percent mobile phone penetration rate, a figure on par with many Western European nations. Similarly, a 29.19 percent fixed-line penetration rate and 24.86 percent Internet penetration rate place the country squarely at the top of the list, and among leading nations worldwide in telecommunications.

Contrary to common belief, the UAE has a number of supercomputers deployed in several states, mainly in the oil and gas sector. Supercomputing capabilities in the UAE were, and still are, mainly used in geophysical analysis related to oil and gas exploration activities. Abu Dhabi National Oil Company (ADNOC) has an SGI Origin 2000 (64 processors, 32 GB of memory and one terabyte of disk space) that enables the company to carry out large high-definition, full field reservoir simulations with great speed and accuracy. Abu Dhabi Company for Onshore Oil Operations (ADCO) has two SGI Origin 3000s – highly specialized 32-CPU parallel processing supercomputers used for reservoir simulation. These provide 3D seismic interpretation to assist in the optimum placement of wells, thus maximizing oil and gas output. ADCO has also created the UAE's first Virtual Reality Environment Center, powered by a 4-CPU, 8 GB SGI ONYX supercomputer designed specifically for heavy-duty graphical output. Finally, a third UAE oil company, Zakum Development Company (ZADCO) at Abu Dhabi, has one 16-CPU SGI Origin 2000 supercomputer and a multiprocessor SGI Onyx 3200.

Policies and Strategies

The UAE received a full score in an assessment of its role in creating an environment conducive to ICT. The leadership will of the UAE has met eight performance criteria set by the *Global Information Technology*

Report 2002–2003, under the title *Readiness for the Networked World*, which was recently published by the World Economic Forum (WEF). These criteria include a 'Clearly Spelled out ICT Strategy', 'ICT Implementation Plan Clearly Articulated', and 'Technology Incubators'. This report is a joint effort between WEF and the Institute Européen d'Administration des Affaires (INSEAD) of France.

The report indicates that the UAE is clearly moving steadily in the right direction of creating a growing information/knowledge society. On March 26, 2003, for instance, the UAE Ministry of Finance and IBM Middle East announced the signing of a contract for the implementation of the first phase of the federal e-government project. This project is integral to a number of transformation initiatives launched by the UAE Federal Government in order to achieve rapid and significant transformation in the provision and efficiency of federal government services within the UAE. During the first phase of the project, IBM was responsible for evaluating the readiness of various ministries for the introduction and implementation of e-Government services covering people, process and technology, as well as studying the functions of these ministries and identifying initiatives or e-government projects to be implemented.

The work team was also responsible for prioritizing various initiatives, including the identification of specific target performance measures for the successful implementation of various phases of the project; evaluation of technical infrastructure requirements required to support the e-government initiatives; defining essential policies and procedures required to support the e-government initiative and developing a comprehensive blueprint which will allow the Federal E-Government Steering Committee to monitor the successful implementation of various phases of the e-government project.

The first phase of the Federal E-government Project will be followed by subsequent implementation phases, which will cover the provision of the required infrastructure, as well as the development and implementation of systems identified within the UAE Federal E-government blueprint, and the Federal Government IT Strategy.

Legal and Regulatory Frameworks

The Government of the UAE has been a leader in creating the *right* and *appropriate* soft infrastructure, including the legal and regulatory environments, in order to ensure success for its IT initiatives. A number of laws were enacted and passed during the past decade, with the objective of fostering a safe environment for businesses and investors.

In 1992, the UAE federal government passed three laws in regards to intellectual property – a copyright law, a trademark law, and a patent law. These three pieces of legislation have made the UAE largely free of selling pirated computer software because of a strong enforcement policy. In addition, the UAE is a member of the World Intellectual Property Organization (WIPO) and has joined the Paris Convention for the Protection of Industrial Property. Also, the UAE has fully ratified the Agreement on Trade-Related Aspects of Intellectual Property Rights (TRIPS Agreement), which is one of the main agreements of the WTO. The primary difference for the UAE in terms of copyright law as compared to other nations is that any published material must have a registered copyright before being commercialized in the country.

The UAE Copyright Law No. 7 of 2002, repealing the old Copyright Law No. 40 of 1992, came into force on 14 July 2002, upon its publication in the UAE Official Gazette No. 383. The UAE Copyright Law No. 7 of 2002 is a Federal Law and protects: 'Any original work in the areas of literature, arts or science, whatever its description, form of expression and conveyance, significance or purpose'.

As elsewhere, registration is not required to achieve protection. Registration is possible through an application to the Ministry of Information and Culture, but it is not a pre-requisite for the material in question to achieve protection.

Copyright piracy of software has dropped in the UAE from 86 percent in 1995 to 41 percent in 2001, according to an independent research company report. This was a result of the introduction of the UAE Copyright Law No. 40 of 1992, and strict enforcement thereof. Introduction of this and other intellectual property laws in the UAE in 1992, combined with political will, made the UAE the leader in the protection of intellectual property rights in the region, as well as illustrated an example for other GCC and Arab countries to follow.

Public telecommunications services in the UAE are provided under monopoly conditions by the Emirates Telecommunications Corporation (Etisalat), headquartered in the federal capital, Abu Dhabi. Etisalat is a quasi-state company, with 60 percent ownership by the UAE Government and 40 percent by individual UAE nationals.

Most recently, and in an effort to regulate electronic transactions and boost users' confidence, a law was issued for the state of Dubai, Law No. 2 of 2002 concerning electronic transactions and commerce. The Electronic Transactions and Commerce Law abides by international principles associated with e-commerce and dealings and is the latest development in this field. The law has 39 articles that are a combination of the United Nations (UN) guidelines and local qualifications and is intended to: (1)

smooth the progress of e-correspondence through trusty e-books; (2) eliminate any impediments to e-commerce and other e-transactions; (3) smooth the submission of e-documents to government departments and institutions; (4) trim down the number of submissions of e-correspondence and amendments thereto; (5) set standardized criteria for certification and security of e-correspondence; (6) raise the public's confidence in security and soundness of e-books and correspondence; and (7) improve the development of e-commerce and other transactions, locally and internationally, through using electronic signatures (e-signatures).

The proposed federal laws governing Internet-based transactions and related issues are in their second draft, prior to being passed to the higher authorities for approval. A special committee under the Ministry of Justice and Islamic Affairs and Awqaf is overseeing the project with the General Information Authority providing the technical support.

Recently, a new law was issued in Dubai relevant to the use of computers in criminal procedures. Pursuant to this new law, Dubai Law No. 5 of 2001, documents with e-signatures will be admissible as evidence in criminal investigations. The provisions of the law acknowledge signatures of individuals acquired through the use of computers and other means of IT for purposes of proof in criminal cases.

A draft of the 'Cybercrime' Law is currently being reviewed at the federal level on e-signatures, along with direct reference to the Singapore Electronic Transactions Act. According to a Ministry of Justice official, the law would contain two categories to deal with crimes committed on the Internet. One category would be a set of laws on digital signatures and issues related to signing and forgery of electronic documents. The other category would address crimes such as hacking, stealing credit card numbers, invasion of privacy, copyright violations and on-line theft.

Legislation covering the Dubai Technology, Electronic Commerce and Media Free Zone (the Law) was passed by decree in February 2000. The Law creates a business and regulatory environment in which technology, e-commerce, and Internet and media companies will be able to operate globally out of Dubai with significant competitive advantages over local and regional competitors. More specifically, the Law creates a free zone officially known as the Dubai Technology, Electronic Commerce and Media Free Zone (the 'Free Zone'). The Technology Free Zones are many, but we will concentrate on the main three initiatives within those free zones; these are: (1) Dubai Internet City, (2) Dubai Media City, and (3) Knowledge Village.

To attract technology and media companies, the Free Zone will allow entities operating out of the Free Zone to be 100 percent foreign owned, with no need for any sort of national services agent. Furthermore, Free Zone entities will be able to obtain leases on ready-to-operate-from offices or plots of land on a 50-year renewable basis where they may build structures appropriate to their line of business. To facilitate business operations in the Free Zone, there will be a 'single-window' for all governmental approvals, including those pertaining to trade licenses, visas and work permits. Companies based in the Free Zone will be able to sell goods and services throughout the UAE. Dubai Internet City and Media City have already begun to issue licenses to qualified companies.

In order to operate in the Free Zone, the rule of law requires a business entity to be licensed by the Free Zone Authority and to be set up either as a branch of a UAE or foreign company or be locally incorporated as a Free Zone limited liability company (FZ-LLC). The regulations regarding FZ-LLCs, have not yet been promulgated. However, the Free Zone Authority recently promulgated a specimen article and memorandum of association for all FZ-LLCs.[4]

Free Zone entities and their employees are excluded from any restrictions on repatriation and transfer of capital, profits and wages in any currency to any place outside the Free Zone for at least 50 years. It is anticipated that Free Zone entities will have minimal restrictions with respect to visas, ie they will not be restricted with respect to the type and number of workers they need to sponsor. This makes the Free Zone an ideal location from which to access a skilled talent pool from nearby countries such as India, Egypt, and Jordan. The Law specifically states that assets or activities of Free Zone entities shall not be subject to nationalization or any measures restricting private ownership. The Law makes provision for the creation of a court and/or arbitration tribunal with the jurisdiction to hear claims and suits arising out of, or in connection with, activities carried out by Free Zone entities within the Free Zone including suits between Free Zone entities and parties outside the Free Zone.

Recently, and in December 2002, Sheikh Abdalla Bin Zayed Al Nahyan, UAE Minister of Information and Culture, issued a ministerial decree annulling fees on computer programs in a move to help promote the spread of computer software especially in the field of education and to keep abreast of the global advances in IT sectors. The new resolution amended Decree No. 6 of (2000) on imposing fees on business-oriented media licenses. In addition, Sheikh Abdalla called during the Arab Information and Communication Technology Summit in Dubai in October 2004 for free entry of IT to the UAE, providing it with reasonable charges for education and training purposes, and securing easy access to information.

To summarize, then, the regulatory environment and the soft infrastructure in the UAE has lowered the barriers to navigate into a information/knowledge based society, where the enacted laws and regulations act as lubricants and facilitators in the transition phase. It is worth mentioning here that Dubai is rated fifth in the Asia Pacific Universe 2002 index of Economic Freedoms survey in terms of business friendly regulation.

As the UAE is a signatory to the WTO, its provisions relating to intellectual property as stated in the TRIPS Agreement, including reciprocity, are applicable to the UAE.

ICT Infrastructure

To describe the technical infrastructure in the UAE, we will be looking at five main indicators: (1) fixed lines; (2) wireless technology; (3) Internet hosts; (4) Internet users; and, (5) computerization.

Public telecommunications services in the UAE are provided under monopoly conditions by the Etisalat, headquartered in the federal capital, Abu Dhabi. Etisalat is a quasi-state company, with 60 percent ownership by the UAE Government and 40 percent by individual UAE nationals, and is the second most valuable quoted company in the Middle East. Revenues in 2001 increased by 9 percent over 2000 to US$2053 million and profit in 2001 was US$680 million, which represents a 27 percent return on capital employed.

Incorporated in 1976, Etisalat is the sole provider of telecommunication services to individuals and institutions in the UAE. To diversify its sources of revenue, the corporation has also invested in Thuraya Satellite, Zanzibar Telecom, Qatar Telecom, and Sudan Telecom. For the year 2001, Etisalat's silver jubilee year, the company surpassed targets and serviced a million customers in each of the fixed-line as well as Global System for Mobile communications (GSM) businesses. In an effort to provide seamless communication around the globe, the corporation now offers connectivity to 258 international digital codes (IDD) destinations and 213 GSM roaming partners in 96 countries.[5]

The only networks independent of Etisalat are those operated by government departments with special needs such as the Ministry of Interior and Armed Forces/General Head Quarters. The oil companies such as the Abu Dhabi National Oil Company (ADNOC) now use Etisalat facilities but retain their own independent telecommunications facilities as a back-up. Although Etisalat is a monopoly today, this might change in the future due to internal and external environmental pressures.

During 2001, Etisalat launched nine new services and enhancements, including Short Message Service (SMS) for prepaid mobile phones and a prepaid service for fixed lines. Etisalat is also employing a proactive approach to ready itself for opportunities that will arise through the convergence of Internet and mobile phones, namely wireless Internet. To achieve this, the corporation engaged in the development of infrastructure and value-added services. A cable TV and multimedia subsidiary, E-vision, offers interactive services through a fiber/coax network to subscribers. High speed Internet asymmetric digital subscriber line (ADSL) and wireless application protocol Internet services (WAP) have also been introduced. The Thuraya Satellite has been launched and the services will soon be introduced to the target market. Implementation of WAP and general packet radio service (GPRS) technologies is expected to naturally lead to migration to the third generation protocol (3G) broadband mobile network.

Etisalat has the second highest capitalization of any public company in the Middle East. It has a capital expenditure program expected to equal US$1.6 billion over the next 3 years. Its wealth enables it to constantly expand its programs and implement technologies ahead of others in the region (see www.austrade.gov.au).

To summarize, the UAE has a modern telecommunications infrastructure, especially compared to other countries in the region. It has frequently been referred to as the 'most wired' state in the Middle East. The UAE residents have relatively unhindered access to the same modes of communication as Western nations.

The topic of telecommunications is wide ranging in nature, given that it covers both the physical networks over which information is carried, as well as the means to accessing those networks. For this study we have interpreted the term 'telecommunications' very broadly to include all the networks (cable, mobile, Internet, as well as copper wire) over which all types of information (voice, data, sound, image) are carried. So, although we concentrate on telephony networks, we also look at computer networks, the Internet, cable (television as well as telephony), and wireless forms of transmission.

Within the UAE, Etisalat has a fixed exchange line capacity of 1.4 million telephone lines – 100 percent digital – of which around 50 000 are ISDN in addition to the leased circuits. The number of telephone connections increased from 1 020 097 lines in 2000 to 1 052 930 in 2001, which represents a penetration of 34 lines per 100 inhabitants. The number for 2002 is estimated at 1 120 000,[6] placing the country squarely at the top of the list in the Arab World and among leading nations worldwide in telecommunications (Table 2.1).

During the year 2001, Etisalat announced a substantial reduction in its tariffs. The ISDN–tariffs were reduced by a large 34 percent on overage for 225 countries including some reduction of up to 79 percent. The proliferation of mobiles has decreased the dependency on payphones for many subscribers. Consequently, the number of payphones decreased from 28 839 to 28 623 over 2001.

Table 2.1   Fixed telephone lines

Year	Subscribers (1000s)
1997	835
1998	915
1999	975
2000	1020
2001	1053
2002[a]	1120
2003[a]	1195
2004[a]	1277
2005[a]	1362
2006[a]	1461

Note: [a] estimates from Etisalat

Etisalat was one of the first providers to introduce mobile telephones in the Middle East in 1982 and launched the GSM Service in September 1994. The subscriber base of 130000 at the end of 1996 exceeded 2.3 million. The GSM Service incorporates advanced digital communication technology with full roaming facility in countries where there is a reciprocal agreement. The unique feature of the GSM cellular service is the subscriber's identity module (SIM) card, which is used to activate GSM handsets and provides unprecedented levels of security and privacy combined with high quality transmission. Etisalat offers a portfolio of rich services and is considered one of the most advanced countries in the application of wireless technology. Following is a description of applications offered to UAE residents.

GSM International Roaming Service (GIRS) is a facility that allows subscribers to use mobile phones when they travel outside the UAE. This is possible because of roaming agreements between Etisalat and countries around the world.

GSM Ishaar Package is a combination of three GSM value added services: GSM Call Waiting Facility; GSM Call Conference; and Email Notification on GSM handsets via SMS Text. In addition, Etisalat's GSM Fax and Data Service allows GSM customers (excluding the WASEL service) to send and receive fax and data using their mobile phones over the GSM Network at speeds of up to 9600 bps within the UAE or while roaming. The service enables GSM users to work from home, hotels or airport lobbies and to constantly keep in touch with the office, colleagues or information sources. All GSM users are able to send and retrieve fax and data from GSM, anywhere at any time. Conventional fax modem and plug-in telephone are not required. The service is excellent for business travelers, executives, entrepreneurs, transport, courier and computer companies.

Etisalat's Prepaid GSM Service, WASEL, ensures cost-effective and instant communication. The service is ideal for people who wish to keep in touch with their friends and relatives. International Roaming is also available for WASEL customers. Furthermore, Etisalat's messaging service AL MERSAL for GSM, and WASEL customers, is a combination of voice mail, fax mail and short message service that includes SMS notification and SMS mail.

RISALA (SMS mail) is a service that allows GSM and WASEL customers to send a short text message of up to 160 characters from their GSM handsets to other GSM subscribers within the UAE.

Etisalat's SMS Breaking News Service provides the latest breaking news in politics, business, sport or entertainment as it happens around the world. News content is provided as SMS alerts on GSM handsets. The service is available to GSM and WASEL customers.

Etisalat's EWAP Service and a WAP-enabled handset helped people in the UAE to have a more organized life. They can have the latest news, sports scores or stock positions. They can check out airline schedules, make a booking, pay their bills and carry out their banking all from their WAP enabled handset.

General Packet Radio Service (GPRS), is an innovative mobile data technology utilized for accessing information via GPRS enabled mobile phones. Etisalat has also launched prepaid GPRS, following the successful launch of postpaid GPRS at the start of 2002, which has so far attracted over 7000 subscribers.

SMS 2 Fax and SMS 2 Email are unique and convenient ways to send SMS text messages to a fax number and to an email address. The facility allows GSM customers (postpaid and prepaid) to send a text message from their mobile to a fax number and to an email address with a maximum of 160 characters.

Mobile telephony has made giant strides in the UAE in a relatively short time, beating fixed-line telephony. The telecommunications sector in the UAE has undergone extensive development. At the end of 2001, there were 1.9 million GSM users indicating 62 percent penetration rate, which is compatible to the most advanced countries in the world. At the end of October 2002, the number of mobile phone users rose to 2.33 million, or at 62.97 percent penetration rate. Compared to other countries of the GCC, which has a mobile penetration rate of 26.16 percent, the UAE penetration rate is more than double and stands on par with many Western European nations. Similarly, a 29.19 percent fixed line penetration rate and 24.86

percent Internet penetration rate place the country squarely at the top of the list, and among leading nations worldwide in telecommunications. In absolute numbers, the UAE, at 2.33 million mobile phones, accounts for slightly more than 10 percent of mobile phones in the Arab World (23.1 million phones.) In addition, the UAE mobile phone penetration rate is well above that of the world average, which stands at 17 percent.[7]

Currently, Etisalat is focusing on enhancing its service offerings for mobiles. EW@P, the Etisalat brand name for its wireless applications protocol (WAP) service, was launched at the beginning of 2001. Wireless applications protocol is essentially a technology that puts a micro browser on the handset and a WAP gateway on the GSM network, allowing the mobile subscriber to browse the Web in a text format. EW@P enables a vast range of value added services such as email access, latest news, entertainment, financial information and location-based services. By the end of 2001, nearly 150 000 customers had started using EW@P. Responding to this popularity, Etisalat has also launched the Arabic language WAP service (see Table 2.2).

Table 2.2 Mobile subscribers

Year	Mobile Subscribers (1000s)
1997	313
1998	492
1999	830
2000	1428
2001	1909
2002[a]	2361
2003[a]	2770
2004[a]	3150
2005[a]	3522
2006[a]	3854

Note: [a] estimates from Etisalat.

In order to cater for the substantial growth in telephone and mobile users, the volume of traffic and product offerings for the support network have been suitably enhanced. The Intelligent Network (IN) capacity has been increased to cater to 2.4 million accounts. The SMS platform has been increased to cater to 1242 messages per second and a new voice mail platform has been contracted to serve one million accounts.[8]

In a report issued in July 2000, *The Economist* ranked the UAE 18th in the world in terms of its Internet infrastructure. While the UAE fixed line subscription grew at an average of 5.2 percent in the 5 years 1997–2001, and mobile telephony grew at an average rate of 101 percent for the same period, Internet users swelled by 169.6 percent on average during the same period. This was due to many factors, including the proliferation of Internet cafés, lower subscription and connection fees, and the introduction of the Internet to all universities and many schools in the countries. At the outset, it must be noted here that individuals who accessed the Internet at least once (regardless of subscription and connection method) are defined as users, while mobile phone penetration is an indication of the number of individuals possessing a mobile phone subscription (an individual might possess more than one phone).

The history of the Internet in the UAE goes back to the year 1995, when Etisalat started providing Internet services to all categories of users, including academic, business, industry, and home users. Since 1995, the number of Internet users in the UAE has grown exponentially and had reached 256 000 subscribers by the end of 2001.

In March 2000, Emirates Internet and Multimedia (EIM)[9] was established as a Strategic Business Unit within Etisalat to be the first ISP in the UAE. Even though a newly established unit, EIM has been playing a strategic role in quickly responding to the needs of Internet users, gaining a competitive edge by acquiring state-of-the-art Internet backbone and infrastructures, and enabling people of all walks of life to have access to the Internet.

The UAE is the most wired nation in the Arab world and one of the top nations of the online world. With a customer base of about quarter a million, EIM has around 25 percent of Internet users in the Arab world. While the number of Internet subscribers is 256 000, the actual number of Internet users in the UAE is about 900 000 users, with 29 percent penetration, putting the UAE among the top 18 most wired countries in the world, even ahead of some Western European countries (Etisalat, Yearbook 2001). In addition to the dial up customers, Internet is also used by 427 leased line customers, 600 local area network (LAN) connected subscribers and 7511 Al Shamil subscribers. There were also almost 1000 Business One customers and 4500 Web-hosting customers. Business One is a DSL service from Emirates Internet & Multimedia specifically developed for small- and medium-sized businesses. Its objective is to provide high speed Internet access and Web presence quickly, easily and cost effectively.

Dial up services grew during the year 2001 to 46 688 subscribers. The recent trends show a decline in the rate of growth because the market is perhaps approaching the saturation stage, and because the launch of prepaid cards and the sprouting of Internet cafés give residents the option to dial up access without having subscription to the service (Table 2.3).

Table 2.3   Internet dial-up subscribers

Year	Subscribers (1000s)
1997	27
1998	66
1999	127
2000	209
2001	256
2002[a]	286
2003[a]	316
2004[a]	335
2005[a]	345

Notes: [a] estimates from Etisalat

As mentioned earlier, the number of Internet leased lines was 427 at the end of 2001; this number is estimated to be at 567 lines for 2002 and, based on Etisalat's estimates, is expected to top 1280 lines by the end of 2005.

Etisalat is upgrading Internet access for home users by launching high-speed access to enable them to enjoy speeds of up to 2Mb/s. The service went live in 2003, offering customers the choice of 1Mb/s or 2Mb/s, up to six times faster than the existing Al Shamil service. The new Al Shamil 1Mb/s and 2Mb/s packages are targeted at domestic Internet users who use the Web extensively. These subscribers will have superior use of high bandwidth applications from video streaming to online gaming, while dramatically speeding up download times of large documents.

Al Shamil Cable will utilize Etisalat's HFC cable infrastructure, which is presently used to deliver E-Vision's digital cable television services. It will complement the existing DSL infrastructure, which currently delivers high-speed Internet access to homes over copper telephone lines. The experience of Al Shamil Cable will be identical to the existing DSL package, but will utilize a separate network to the current copper telephone lines. The key benefit of offering high-speed Internet over the cable is that the service is not limited by distance, while it is not always possible to transmit high-speed Internet over very long distances via the current telephone network.

In addition, EIM and E-Vision are working on a bundled package (Al Shamil Cable plus E-Vision's Basic Package). Although the pricing of the new service has yet to be confirmed, subscribers to the bundled E-Vision and Al Shamil Cable package will benefit from a discounted rate.

Al Shamil Internet allows users to access the Internet at speeds up to 10 times faster than the normal dial-up connection. With downstream speeds of up to 384 kbps and an upstream speed of 128 kbps, the user is able to effectively use a range of hi-bandwidth applications, from video streaming to online gaming, that are generally slower to download on a dial-up connection. In addition, Al Shamil gives users unlimited Internet usage with a fixed monthly subscription.

Business One is an ADSL service from Emirates Internet & Multimedia specifically developed for small and medium-sized businesses. Its objective is to provide high speed internet access and web presence quickly, easily and cost effectively.

Digital Subscriber Line, or DSL, is a new technology that transforms ordinary telephone lines into high-speed digital lines for Internet access and other broadband applications. It can support downstream speeds of up to 8 mbps and up to 1 mbps upstream, depending upon line length and conditions, and allows access to corporate networks for telecommuters, as well as exciting new on-demand multimedia applications such as software, video, music and games.

There are two types of general DSL applications: (1) high-speed data communication, such as Internet access, telecommuting (remote LAN access), and specialized network access; and (2) interactive multimedia, such as on-demand games, software, news, music and video.

At the year end of 2001 the total number of subscribers for this service was 946. Small and medium business customers of the Etisalat Dial Up service, its LAN Connect subscribers and Leased Circuit subscribers who require economical 'Always On' Internet connections are switching over to Business One. Etisalat estimates the number for 2002 to be 3260 subscribers. This number was expected to exceed 10 700 subscribers by the end of 2005.

At the end of 2001, the UAE had 4500 web hosting customers. Estimates for 2002 and 2003 are 8094 and 13 741, respectively. The number was expected to top 31 000 customers by the end of 2005.

In October 2001, E-SHOP, an online virtual business center, was launched by Etisalat and is available free of charge to customers who can, following a registration process, access and view their bills online and settle outstanding amounts using their credit cards. In addition, they can subscribe to Star Services and track the status of their applications. E-SHOP is a practical demonstration of a successful implementation of e-commerce applications provided by Comtrust, Etisalat's business unit.

The development of the telecommunication sector is a government priority and it is one of the fastest growing areas in the economy. The telecommunications market remains highly competitive, being dominated by government procurement.

Currently, there is only one ISP in the UAE, but this is changing in 2006. Emirates Internet has been the Middle East's first and foremost Internet service since 1995, from Etisalat – the premier ISP in the Middle East. Its state-of-the-art technology, commitment to the customer, and constant improvement of its services has won it a rapidly growing subscriber base. While its ICT infrastructure is available, reliable and secure, with respect to affordability, the UAE is listed among the most expensive countries in the Middle East in terms of cost of ICT services.

Computer utilization is on the rise with current computer users moving toward upgraded and higher capacity computers. Recent industry reports indicate that the UAE ICT sector has experienced a ten-fold increase since 1997. Combined ICT spending by the GCC countries (including UAE) in 2001 was US$6.194 billion (WITSA, 2002). As of December 2002, the PC installed base in the UAE amounted to 490000 units, with a penetration rate of 13.24 percent. The number of PC units purchasable per GDP per capita amounted to 18.19 percent in 2002.

Statistics recently released by Madar Research indicate that in the six GCC states, there are 121 users per 100 PCs, a ratio that appears to be set to change dramatically in view of the high computer literacy in the GCC region. The positive growth forecast has generated great interest among PC vendors operating in the region, as they can now look forward to expanding their customer base and increased IT spending. The Internet has been a driving force for many people to buy PCs, laptops and notebooks. The excitement surrounding the Internet has become all-pervasive and is reflected in the general trend for individuals to own a PC and in the mushrooming of Internet cafés. Sooner or later, these new converts are going to become PC owners, slowly bridging the gap between PC penetration and Internet usage.

According to early forecasts by International Data Corporation, the UAE should cross the 200000 PCs a year mark for the first time in 2003. In value terms, this would be around US$320 million, out of which the portable PCs would account for US$130 million. In 2002, the corresponding figures were US$280 million and just over US$100 million respectively. The growth predicted for 2003 belies the increasingly worst-case scenarios that have been painted in recent times for PC growth in the country (*Gulf News*, December 19, 2002).

The UAE packaged software market is estimated at US$190 million, and if combined with the market for customized packages it could be as high as US$550 million. Growth areas include a range of online services including tele-banking, financial and trading services, federal and local administration services, health care, insurance, e-commerce, multimedia publishing, as well as services to the oil and telecommunications sectors. Additionally, the UAE Government is embarking on ambitious e-Government initiatives aimed at improving government processes and service offerings by employing internet and other technological solutions.

The launch of tablet PCs, while still a niche product, holds the promise of firmer margins for vendors in the short-term. Already, notebooks represent the highest growth category, and is expected to expand by more than 25 percent in 2003. Of the overall tally, notebook shipments in the UAE are expected to reach nearly 60 000 in 2002 for a total value exceeding US$100 million, according to IDC.

Supercomputing capacity in the Arab world was, and still is, primarily used in geophysical analysis associated with oil and gas exploration activities. The UAE is one of four Arab countries owning supercomputers. The Abu Dhabi National Oil Company (ADNOC) has an SGI Origin 2000 (64 processors, 32 GB of memory and one terabyte of disk space) that enables the company to carry out large high-definition, comprehensive field reservoir simulations with great speed and precision. The Abu Dhabi Company for Onshore Oil Operations (ADCO) has two SGI Origin 3000s, with 32-CPU parallel processing supercomputers used for reservoir simulations. These offer 3D seismic explanation to aid in the most advantageous placement of wells, thus maximizing oil and gas output. ADCO has also created the first Virtual Reality Environment Center, which is powered by a 4-CPU, 8 GB SGI ONXY supercomputer designed specifically for heavy duty graphical output. Finally, Zakum Development Corporation (ZADCO), another oil company in Abu Dhabi, has one 16-CPU SGI Origin 2000 supercomputer machine and a multiprocessor SGI ONYX 3200.

In general, the UAE has one of the most advanced automated systems in the private and public sectors, whereby all financial institutions, academic entities, governmental agencies, and public service departments are equipped with technology from Web fiber optics all the way to PCs, minicomputers, databases and office tools.

Capacity Building

The UAE takes a leading place in terms of ICT awareness and the dissemination of the ICT culture. To facilitate the dissemination process, several initiatives have been undertaken to contribute to ICT capacity building. To raise ICT awareness and increase ICT dissemination, for instance, the Emirates Internet Association (EIA) was established in June 2000. The Association is the first of its kind in the UAE and supports and co-ordinates the use of the Internet for personal and corporate IT developments.

Emirates Internet and Multimedia, recognized as the best ISP by the Middle East Information Technology Award for 2001, is dedicated to providing state of the art and best of class services. During 2001, EIM launched Al Mawrood Internet Surfing Centers, M-Player Arabia and re-launched the high-speed Al Shamil service and bilingual portal Al Bahhar.[10]

- Al Bahhar, the new value-packed bilingual portal, provides Arabic users with their essential information needs covering news and current affairs, business and sports, over one million pages of Arabic literature, history and philosophy, text-based Arabic discussion forums and English language news content. The launch of Al Bahhar has been immensely popular, with more than one million hits per month.[11]
- Al Mawrood Internet Surfing centers facilitate access to the Internet for users of all ages. There are currently 100 such centers all over the UAE and the number is growing. In January 2002, and in collaboration with Galaxy kids, EIM launched ALEFON, the interactive Web learning channel for children and parents. ALEFON provides an introduction to reading, writing and mathematics through animated stories and makes learning fun. The launch of www.alefon.albahhar.com is the latest in a line of recent UAE initiatives aimed at facilitating and popularizing Internet usage in the country.
- In October 2001, EIM launched M-Player.Arabia.com, the region's first multiplayer games community site with over 20,000 registered users. This facility provides a wide range of classic games, support for popular PC games and allows users to play against one or more players over the Internet.

Future plans of EIM include the launch of several interesting applications such as TV-based Video on Demand, Online Distance Learning and Education, Online Travel, Business News and Financial Information Center, Internet Kiosks, Internet Executive Workstations, Web Design Centers, Online Games and Entertainment and Internet Home banking.

Economic Diversification

One of the primary goals of the UAE Government is economic diversification into the non-oil sector. Therefore, the government has implemented policies and programs to encourage citizens to pursue higher education – specifically training in engineering and IT. Primary, secondary, and higher education is provided gratis to all Emirati citizens. To meet the challenge of the evolving telecommunications and computer industries in the UAE the government places a strong emphasis on education.

Education

Computer and information technology is being taught as a subject in UAE schools at all levels – starting with primary schools and going all the way through high schools. Currently, a number of committees established by the UAE Ministry of Education and Youth are in the process of developing a computer-based integrated curriculum where computers are taught as a subject, in addition to integrating computer-based education in other subjects.

The Elementary and Secondary Education Development Committee at the Ministry of Education and Youth has mapped out a plan to reorganize the Resources Centers at government schools for the benefit of students with special needs.

The step comes in line with a comprehensive vision laid down by the committee to improve special education services at government schools, along with introducing e-learning projects and other electronic plans into the UAE's educational sector.

Training

Emphasizing technical education/vocational training to bridge the gap between the skills possessed by college and high-school graduates and skills required by the labor market, with particular attention to engineering and sciences qualifications, is a requirement for a successful ICT strategy. In addition, developing human resources is fundamental to putting the country on the right ICT track. There is a broad consensus that schools and the education system are the basic tools needed to provide gradual greater comfort with the digital environment.

Hundreds of students who leave schools before finishing their secondary education are taking courses in institutions such as the Abu Dhabi National Oil Company's Career Development Center, whose aim is to train them for technical positions within the oil industry.

The Emirates Institute for Banking and Financial Studies focuses on providing training for personnel within the financial sector. The Higher Colleges of Technology are also involved in the provision of vocational education.

Early on, the UAE government realized the importance of technical and vocational training for its citizens – both male and female – so that they could help in meeting the demands of the local job market. To help meet these demands, in 1988 a system of Higher Colleges of Technology was set up. These offer a more technically oriented course of study. As in the university and the government schools, tuition at the Colleges is free and the curriculum has been produced in consultation with potential employers such as banks, airlines and the local oil industry. In 1992, when the first group of students graduated, they had little or no difficulty in finding jobs.

A new Certificate and Diploma program was introduced in 1995–96 which offers a year-long course of basic studies for those who lack adequate preparation to enter the 4-year Higher Colleges course.

Additional technical education and training is also available in institutions such as the Dubai Aviation College, the Emirates Banking Training Institute or the Career Development Centre of the Abu Dhabi National Oil Company.

Outside the government sector, there exists a wide range of private vocational training schools with an enrolment of thousands of students. A number of these schools teach in the language of one of the expatriate communities living in the UAE and follow the curriculum of their countries. For example, there are English, French, German and Urdu schools preparing children for life in their home countries.

In the last few years, a number of universities and colleges from overseas have begun to offer partial or full degree courses through affiliates in the UAE. This means that a full range of education is available for both citizens and expatriates.

The UAE authorities officially recognize only six universities, even though there are 33 private universities in the country. UAE students comprise only about 10–15 percent of enrolment. Higher education is provided free to all citizens. In addition to these higher education institutions, Etisalat has placed great importance on the development of engineering education and training facilities, particularly in the field of communications, in order to encourage the reliance on indigenous sources. Also, the Etisalat College of Engineering, has remained dedicated to the engineering education of national citizens and has already produced more than 200 graduates. This institution has served as an important source of 'home-grown' engineers who are appointed in management cadres in the Corporation, and some are sent abroad for postgraduate specialization

Table 2.4 shows the number of students graduating in the various IT fields, from the major universities and colleges in the UAE.

Building the ICT Sector

As stated earlier, country readiness is defined as 'initiatives facilitating the change in the transformation process' into an information/knowledge

Table 2.4　ICT Graduates in the UAE

		Number of Graduating Students in a Certain Major						
Graduation Year	University	MIS	Computer Science	Computer Engineering	IT	Higher Diploma	Diploma	Certificate Program
1997–1998	Higher Colleges of Technology (HCT)					70		249
	UAE University		2					
1998–1999	HCT					141	171	525
	UAE University		95					
1999–2000	HCT					176	201	305
	UAE University		131					
2000–2001	Sharjah University	50	20					
	HCT	17		1	28	171	314	593
	UAE University		174					
2001–2002	Sharjah University	61	24	35				
	HCT	23	13	27	61	222	330	856
	UAE University		139					
2002–2003 (Fall 2002)	Sharjah University	74	28	33				
	HCT	13		7	13			

Source:　Collected by authors.

Table 2.5　Distribution of companies in the UAE by sector

Sector	Percentage of Total Companies
Web-based companies	34
IT support	22
Software development	17
Application Service Providers	6
Back office	8
Consultancy	6
Others	7

Source:　Collected by authors.

society. In this section, a number of initiatives are presented and their impacts are discussed.

A large number of ICT firms operate in the UAE, including major multinationals such as Microsoft, Oracle, HP, Sun Microsystems and Cisco. The distribution of companies by sector appears in Table 2.5.

INVESTMENTS IN ICTS

The UAE ICT investment witnessed a host of healthy activities in the past 4–5 years. This has manifested itself in terms of major contracts and projects, both in numbers and values. Among the Arab countries, the UAE market comes only second to Saudi Arabia in terms of investment in ICT and amounts to US$1.245 billion in 2002, which constitutes 1.77 percent of the GDP, and US$336 per capita in 2002.

Dubai Internet City

Dubai Internet City's (known as DIC or City) objective is to nurture the growth of the new economy and the IT industry as a whole, by providing a cutting-edge, high bandwidth, Internet services and telecommunications, intelligent infrastructure, real estate, company registration and facilitation, to support any level of service a client might wish to use for efficient operations. The DIC, which completed its first phase (in 2001) in a record 364 days, gives tenants a technology platform fit for the twenty-first century. It also fulfils the vision of the government of the UAE to provide the e-world with a world-class ground base for every virtual company.

Dubai Internet City has already attracted more than 450 firms,[12] mostly international companies operating in various IT industry sectors. The number of companies applying to work in the City has run well beyond preliminary expectations. The interest of the international IT industry in the City culminated in decisions by many leading firms, such as Oracle, Cisco, Microsoft, Siemens and IBM, to set up their facilities there. The City is well equipped to play a pivotal role in supporting and promoting IT related activities within a vast geographical area covering the Gulf, Middle East, the Indian Subcontinent, Central Asia, North and South African countries.

The City is also keen on creating an ideal environment for growth and flourishing of IT projects. An environment wherein software and multimedia developers, IT firms, communications companies, service providers and suppliers all work side by side, thereby providing a solid base, not only for the growth of operations of each company within the City, but also for the creation of new business opportunities.

Companies operating within the City enjoy a set of investment promotion incentives including 100 percent foreign ownership of projects, corporate tax exemptions, streamlined government procedures, 50 years land lease contracts, competitive prices for rendered services, cost effective business sites, in addition to facilities for financing, training, education and research.

The initial DIC complex was established at an estimated cost of US$272 million, provided by the Dubai Government in the form of land in a prime area of Dubai. In addition, the Dubai government is the guarantor of a US$500 million loan, put together by a consortium of banks for the purpose of completing the infrastructural support for the project;[13] this will ultimately act as an 'incubator' for e-commerce in the region. It is estimated that private investors, representing 450 firms, some of them from American, European, Asian, and Australian business communities, would spend three times the amount contributed by the Dubai Government to set up their own businesses at the complex. In terms of eligibility, all ICT companies who would like to expand their operations to cover the foot print of DIC can locate there.[14]

Benefits from the DIC project have many spillover effects; for partners,[15] it enhances the chances of success, raises credibility, helps improve skills, creates synergy among client-firms, facilitates access to mentors, information and seed capital. In addition, DIC offers more than 1000 different services to their partners starting from a pick-up at the airport and issuing of visas, to providing cleaning service of their facilities! DIC is most beneficial in offering businesses opportunities for acquiring innovations and interacting with other businesses that might support, complement, or even compete with them in the same geographical area. From the Government perspective, DIC helps promote regional development, generate jobs[16] and incomes, and becomes a demonstration of the political commitment to SMEs. As for the local community, in addition to job creation, DIC has created an entrepreneurial culture, especially among young university graduates.

His Highness Sheikh Maktoum bin Rashid Al Maktoum, Vice President and Prime Minister, recently issued, in his capacity as Ruler of Dubai, Law No. 6 for 2002 on the establishment and protection of the Dubai Internet City's telecommunications network. Issued on November 10, the 12-article legislation has set out missions that the DIC should carry out in cooperation with other concerned authorities to provide telecommunications services to individuals and companies via a fiber optic network, and land and air stations.

Technology Parks

Technology parks may be part of the urban development plan and encompass: a university; research laboratories, which may be associated with firms or research institutes; new technology firms, including start-up SMEs; testing and analytical facilities; a variety of services for technology transfer; financing association and governmental agencies. The first of its kind in the Gulf region (announced in October 2002) was the Sheikh Mohammad Technology Park (the Park). The Park's purpose is to support its tenants by playing two main roles. First, it provides tenants with technological support, involving ready access to relevant and up-to-date technological knowledge through contact with a university research center. This is what we call 'technology brokering'. Secondly, the Park will support its tenants by establishing and providing business links, advice and services, as well as general assistance. The latter function, in particular, could cover a wide range of contacts, ranging from basic building refurbishment and maintenance, secretarial and administrative services, advanced business and financial counseling to accessing sophisticated research equipment and instrumentation.

The Park is envisioned simultaneously as an effective instrument for local development and technology transfer, stimulators of innovation and seedbeds for new business enterprizes. It is hoped it will create enormous success in employment creation, new technology generation, and as catalyst for enterprizes.

The Park has been designed and developed after years of extensive research, and as part of phase one it will be located in Jebel Ali Free Zone, covering a land area of 3 square kilometers. The Park is a clear indication of the UAE's, in general, and Dubai's, in particular, strategic focus on its role as an international information technology center. Through the Park, the country will utilize the gains made in both technology and knowledge-based systems in a specific and focused way, which when channeled and applied to industry will benefit the region as a whole. The Park will enhance the development of the knowledge-based economy, providing a wide range of opportunities for technology companies.

The Park is designed to develop industrially based knowledge economy 'clusters'. These clusters are developed in strategic industrial sectors that will stimulate economic growth and ultimately boost the competitive edge in the region. Clusters will include a range of R&D and product development companies, laboratories, incubators, training institutes, technology transfer and technology acceleration organizations. The focus of the Park will center on 'demand-driven' industrial technologies, such as desalination.

Companies providing services associated with industrial technology, from Korea, Japan, Switzerland, the United Kingdom, and the US, have also expressed interest, and will potentially bring with them a range of activities that include laboratory services, renovation services for industrial plants, university research and technical services and engineering and R&D projects. The Park will also focus on attracting business accelerators, consultancy firms and venture capital groups in addition to manufacturing and industrial companies. High-tech services such as design, consultancy, prototype production of incubated innovations, industry and the spin-offs will also hold viable positions in the Park. In addition, environmental management companies will focus on water resource management, biosaline products and technology, pollution management and control systems, recycling industries and 'clean energy' industries such as solar and wind technology. Health technology businesses will concentrate on biotech products and processes, pharmaceuticals and medical devices and equipment.

The Park is in the process of forming strategic alliances with a number of local universities and research institutes. International organizations such as the International High Technologies Consortium from Russia have indicated their interest. The Park is also in the process of forming strategic ties with potential investment organizations and banks.

The renowned services sector in the country is also expected to see business increase as the Park develops. Furthermore, the type of industrial companies in the Technology Park will potentially provide benefits to both the UAE and the region in terms of the study of pollution, improved safety automation (with tailor-made intelligent control systems) and an improved supply of components through central warehouses for desalination and other industries and components.

Especially important for long-term development of the country and the region are the employment opportunities that the Park will offer. In line with Dubai's focus as a proponent of the high-tech and new education strategy, and with the cooperation of universities locally and throughout the region, skilled national graduates in specialized industries will be able to find lucrative employment in the Park's industries. The Park will not only raise the expectations, skills and abilities of the region's workforce, utilizing local talent as a source of long-term competitive advantage, it will also bridge the gap between industrial viability and the application of knowledge.

Dubai Silicon Oasis

On December 29, 2002, General Sheikh Mohammed bin Rashid Al Maktoum, Dubai Crown Prince and UAE Defense Minister, announced the establishment of the Dubai Silicon Oasis (DSO) for the global semiconductor industry. Spread across 6.5 million square meters, the DSO will also encompass the US$1.7 billion Dubai factory of Communicant, the joint venture between Intel, the Dubai Government and the German government of Brandenburg State. Germany's project cost US$1.35 billion, and the

DSO construction will begin within six months after finalizing the designs by experts (including designers of other silicon parks). Construction of the Dubai-based Communicant plant will start within 2 years and production should commence by 2007.

In collaboration with the German IHP technological center, an Institute of Technology will be set up at DSO to train and develop local technical expertise. The DSO will offer several programs, with an initial focus on communication and system-on-chip design complimented by technology management. Dubai Silicon Incubation Centre (DSIC) at DSO will provide a facility for broadband and wireless incubation for the development and commercialization of intellectual property and will help create regional enterprizes at the top end of the technology spectrum.

The incubation center will partner with several high-end global research and development centers and educational institutions. A portal will be based at DSO to provide career management and recruitment services to the global semiconductor industry professionals. Around 320 companies will be able to access it.

As for the agreements with Communicant project partners, it is reported that 240 UAE nationals will be provided with masters studies in microelectronics within 10 years and another 250 nationals will be trained over a period of 12 years in IHP and the Germany-based Communicant on 2-year contracts (*Gulf News*, December 30, 2002).

Government Facilitation

Since 2000, the UAE has made great progress in liberalizing its economy; according to the '2003 Index of Economic Freedom', released on November 12, 2002, the UAE ranks twenty-fourth worldwide, and is the second Arab country after Bahrain (which has a rank of sixteenth). The Index of Economic Freedom measures how well a country scores on a list of 50 variables divided into 10 areas of economic freedom. These include trade policy, banking regulations, fiscal burden, foreign investment codes, monetary policy, and black market.[17]

With respect to the ICT sector, the government of the UAE has developed a number of policies in order to attract ICT firms and facilitate their ways of doing business in the UAE. Dubai Internet City, for instance, is the first complete IT and Telecommunication Center to be built inside a free zone. Companies are exempt from income tax. In addition, companies in the DIC can take advantage of special terms not previously available for free zone companies in the emirates. The key special terms are: (1) 100 percent foreign ownership of companies is allowed, without a local sponsor; (2) 100 percent tax free; and (3) companies may obtain 50-year renewable land leases.

Currently, the newly established Dubai Development Investment Authority is assuming the role of attracting investments to the UAE and encouraging the development of local SMEs. It does not provide capital allowances to support investment by SMEs in ICT; however, it acts as an incubator for ICT SMEs. In addition, the country does not have any provision for tax breaks or credits for ICT training by businesses, something that should be encouraged.

Recently and in December 2002, Sheikh Abdalla bin Zayed AL Nahyan, Minister of Information and Culture, issued a ministerial decree annulling fees on computer programs in a move to help promote the spread of computer software especially in the field of education and to keep abreast of the global advances in IT sectors.

Applications in Commerce and Business

The UAE has perhaps the best developed physical and IT infrastructure in the region. The continued rapid development of its e-infrastructure through initiatives like the DIC and Technology Parks will further increase the UAE's attractiveness to overseas companies.

The popularity of credit and debit cards is steadily gaining ground as evidenced by double digit growth rates in the number of cards in circulation and the level of spending using electronic mediums, reported by various card companies in the UAE. This is clearly contributing to growth in e-commerce transactions.

While the dot.com bubble may have burst, the digitization of the economy and commercial transactions is slowly but surely gaining momentum. As businesses face increasing competition, they are forced to enhance the quality of service to improve response time and curtail costs. E-commerce helps to achieve all this. Comtrust is Etisalat's brand name for the Business Unit dedicated to the development of e-commerce in the UAE. Against all odds and global depression in this sector, Comtrust has enjoyed a year of substantial growth, developing new alliances and establishing networks to lay the foundation for future growth. In August 2001, the Central Bank of the UAE decided to link Comtrust's e-commerce systems with its UAE exchange network. This link helped facilitate payments for goods and services through direct debit requests processed in a secured environment and transmitted over the Internet. Online payment services are at the heart of Comtrust's activities with more and more organizations opting for these services to support their online business. Financial transactions made through Comtrust have seen a six-fold increase during 2001 (see www. etisalat.co.ae).

Some of the services that are currently in place are: website developments, electronic mail, Business-to-Business, financial applications, eDirham and electronic transactions.

Website development

This is the first step towards being a customer-focused government. Information and services pertaining to each Ministry is posted in the UAE Government website. The general public or businesses can interact and transact their needs over these websites. This website is developed maintained and hosted by the Information Systems Department of the Ministry of Finance.

The introduction of these websites became the catalyst for the integration of various government services offered by various Ministries. By just clicking to a single website (www.uae.gov.ae) the public can navigate through the entire Federal Government and also understand what various services are offered by the different Ministries. Important information is always updated and this website itself has undergone major improvements.

E-mail

Electronic mail (email) was introduced to improve communication between employees and also to reduce paperwork. Almost all employees have an e-mail account and this has tremendously improved the cycle time for making decisions. In some Ministries e-mail has replaced the normal 'internal memo' as a formal tool for information dissemination throughout the Ministry.

The introduction of email has also created much needed awareness on the importance of 'information technology' in creating an effective government. This mind set change has become one of the most important impetus for introducing government-wide e-government initiatives.

Business-2-Business

On 20 June 2000, a major Business-to-Business Marketplace was established by the Dubai government – Tejari.com. This service is for all business-to-business (B2B) e-commerce transactions in the UAE. It is a private venture owned at this time by Ports, Customs and Free Zone Corporation. Tejari has quickly become the premier digital marketplace in the Middle East and has proven a success story for e-commerce implementation in the region.

Tejari.com   As part of Dubai's drive to embrace the knowledge economy, Tejari.com was established in June 2000, based on the directives and vision of his His Royal Highness Sheikh Mohammed bin Rashid Al Maktoum, with the aim of facilitating B2B e-commerce in the region. Tejari Marketplace was incubated at the Jebel Ali Free Zone Authority to be the electronic gateway for 1,200 Free Zone companies that serve the region in many different trade commodities. The project was then spun off to cater for the government procurement as a priority for the following reasons:

- Dubai government is the biggest buying power and it is technology ready.
- Another initiative launched close to this timing was e-government, and one area of collaboration with the trade community was G2B; since the government buys from these traders it was obvious that the marketplace will affect the G2B part of the e-government initiative.
- This approach will create the critical mass once proof of the concept was demonstrated by the government purchasing through this marketplace.

Tejari's mission is to maximize the business potential of regional customers by providing them with innovative, reliable, and versatile B2B and e-marketplace services that extend their reach and enhance their competitive standing in the new global economy. It provides an online meeting point for buyers and sellers of goods and services. Procuring products through Tejari.com allows buyers to access a global base of suppliers, while reducing paper-based administrative costs. Companies that sell goods and services through Tejari.com instantly reach new markets and customers online.

Based on the Oracle technology platform, Tejari.com allows organizations to search online catalogues, create auctions, perform spot-buys, and participate in reverse auctioning. Tejari.com uniquely enables companies to reap the benefits of e-business: improved efficiency, faster time to market, better customer awareness, and increased profitability.

Tejari's target market includes business and government organizations that actively trade in goods and services within the region, which including Turkey, the Indian sub-continent, North and East Africa, has a combined foreign trade volume of US$590 Billion and a total GDP of approximately US$1,190 billion (in 1998). Tejari's market is segmented into:

- Government and semi-government organizations (eg ministries, public services departments, municipalities and national companies);
- Large businesses (eg global companies, manufacturers, producers, agents and financial institutions);
- Trading companies (eg business groups, and commodity traders operating on a local or regional level);
- Small businesses (eg business organizations with smaller trade requirements).

During a challenging business climate for the B2B industry, Tejari has come out as a clear winner. The Tejari workforce has more than doubled in the last 2 years to reach 42, the number of auctions being conducted on Tejari is doubling every month, and the value of the transactions and auctions had reached more than US$100 million by the end of 2001. Tejari's total transaction value since its inception had exceeded US$500 million as of quarter one 2003 for 8000 auctions and 4000 spot purchases. Tejari now has over 1500 trading partners transacting. Tejari, which started in the UAE, is now aggressively expanding into the rest of the Middle East and Africa, through local partnerships with influential private and public sector groups. In June 2002, Tejari signed its first partnership with Jordan. Tejari has also moved significantly in covering the different commodity types on the marketplace.

Currently there are regular auctions and transactions for computers, IT and office equipment, stationery, automotive and spare parts, pharmaceutical products, fast moving consumer goods, office furniture and building and construction materials. Other commodities are rapidly being catalogued and uploaded on the Tejari Marketplace by eGlobal and Cataloga, two catalog management partners. The Supplier Adoption rate of Tejari has been one of the highest in the world according to the catalog management partners.

Tejari enables its customers to extract the full benefits of business-to-business transactions from spot-buying to auctions/tenders and requests for quotes. Tejari is also adding new functionality to enable logistics support, supply chain management, project management and design collaboration to provide a comprehensive suite of services to its customers. By providing an online medium to connect, communicate, and collaborate with suppliers, buyers and trade partners, Tejari aims to create value for customers by helping them streamline business processes, reduce costs and ultimately increase revenues.

The success of Tejari in the Middle East can be attributed to many factors. A firm commitment and backing by the Government of Dubai for its procurement needs; a strong and experienced management team led by an accomplished and charismatic Chief Executive Officer; a well-orchestrated marketing campaign to establish a strong and well-known brand around the region; and a successful business model which leveraged existing trading partner relationships and demonstrated immediate savings.

The tyrannies of geography, culture and language are significant barriers to a company's international trading objectives in the Middle East – Tejari removes these obstacles, saving time for suppliers and dramatically reducing procurement costs for buying organizations. Tejari provides a host of benefits for both suppliers and buyers – in fact anyone involved in the procurement process.

Tejari provides the most technically advanced electronic procurement environment available today, including features such as:

1. Catalog management, hosting and search facilities

    *   Tejari enables manufacturers/suppliers to post their products and services they sell on the marketplace.
    *   Suppliers can easily load their catalogs through online HTML authoring screens, spreadsheet loaders and XML interfaces.
    *   In Tejari, they can even load pricing that is applicable to all marketplace members or, optionally, load buyer specific pricing for one or more of their customers.
    *   Suppliers can review, approve and audit their catalog data in the marketplace.
    *   Products and services listed in the catalogs can be searched by: product type, brand, supplier, country etc.

2. Spot buying

    *   Buyers can source products using the powerful search features of Tejari or through its Trading Partner Directory.
    *   Buyers can even compare product prices online.

3. Contract purchases

    *   Both buyers and suppliers have access to a full suite of HTML queries to check order status, history and related information.
    *   Tejari will also support payment via P-card or on account.

4. Auctions and Tendering (reverse auctions)

    *   Tejari supports both seller and buyer auctions.
    *   Other features include: auto extension, multiple bidding, open/sealed auctions etc.

5. Supply chain management

    *   Tejari allows trading partners to view inventory levels, in order to rapidly fulfill purchase needs.

- Using Tejari, buyers and suppliers can improve their forecast accuracy by enabling collaborative demand buying.
- Tejari members can improve end-customer service levels across a 'virtual supply chain' by instituting collaborative order promising processes.

Together with the creation of the Dubai Internet City and the formation of the Dubai E-Government initiative, Tejari.com aims to sustain a viable e-business strategy for organizations in the Middle East. Furthermore, it was believed that Tejari would break even by the end of 2003.

Financial applications

As any other government all over the world, the traditional accountability on 'control and measure' lies with the Ministry of Finance. Thus, this became one of the important applications introduced to automate financial services provided by the Ministry. The Ministry is currently using a central financial system through the WAN using NCR UNIX Platform.

This system is now undergoing major changes as the Ministry of Finance is introducing the new 'Performance Base Budgeting System' where accountability is now decentralized. All financial processes will be re-engineered and 'financial personnel' 're-trained' on how to operate this new system. This is a classic example where 'IT' is used as a tool for re-inventing the way the Ministry works. It will be moving from a centralized accountability to decentralized accountability.

It has re-engineered all financial processes and is now reviewing the right IT application to be implemented. The system became operational in early 2004.

eDirham

The eDirham (https://edirham.uae.gov.ae) is a payment tool devized by the Ministry of Finance and Industry in order to facilitate the collection of federal revenues. It provides the government with a secure payment method and the public with a convenient payment tool. The eDirham card, which is readily available all over the UAE, not only improves financial transactions but also provide 'in-situ' transfers of payments between the public and government agencies. Front service government employees do not have to burden themselves with the security of 'physical money', and with this system the government could balance the revenue by the end of the day without looking at the physical books.

The eDirham has its own secure payment system guaranteed by the government, and the payment card can be used for any government services. This project has been very successful and has received inquiries from many other countries in this region interested in implementing a similar system.

Electronic transactions

Since the UAE government is moving toward implementing the e-Government project (see https://egov.uae.gov.ae), the Ministry of Finance and Industry has started to offer online services to its customers and the public through new electronic services (called e-Procurement and eSinaee). Here the customer can register, select the service and apply, complete the forms, upload the documents and pay online using the eDirham card – and finally receive the services. The e-Procurement provides a mechanism for government agencies and businesses to transact electronically. This is the first step towards government e-commerce. The government is in the midst of further reviewing the 'supply-chain process'. By re-engineering the supply chain systems it is hoped to eventually create a total 'Electronic Procurement' where this application will be linked to the financial and asset management system.

The eSinaee service is an application specially introduced to factories within the UAE. Factory owners not only have the latest information regarding industrial promotion but can also apply for tax exemption and other industrial services.

The introduction of all these services has created an awareness of the importance of IT in easing government administrative services. More importantly, this has paved the path for the introduction of the overall e-government implementation. Much has been learned from the initial application implemented, especially the importance of having an overall e-government strategy in place.

Given the commitment from the highest authority to e-government, a steering committee has been formed to drive the project. One item was clear to the members of this committee – that 'Information Technology' should be used as a tool to re-invent and reform current 'management' of the government.

The e-government project will improve the convenience, accessibility and quality of interactions between the federal government, business and the people residing in the UAE. More importantly, e-government will improve information flows and processes within all government Ministries.

The systems and processes of government will be re-engineered to capitalize on the potential benefits of new ICT applications. This process of re-engineering will redefine the way each government department performs its tasks in the new ICT environment. It is hoped that the introduction of e-Government will provide:

- innovative services;
- managed government information as a strategic resource;
- a government that is closer and more transparent to the people and businesses;
- functional integration within the government;
- effective information flow to facilitate policy development and implementation.

To manage this project effectively the UAE has planned this initiative as three phases:

Phase 1: Creating an e-government strategy (completed in 2003);
Phase 2: Contracting out the chosen e-government application; and
Phase 3: Implementation of the chosen e-government application.

The e-government initiatives will eventually be the central catalyst that will integrate all government entities towards realizing a single vision.

Applications in Healthcare

At present the UAE Government finances 81 percent of the cost of healthcare. The federal government and the Abu Dhabi emirate have taken steps to begin the privatization of healthcare, and several initiatives are taking place as a joint effort between the Ministry of Health and the UAE Offsets Group (UOG).

In February 2003, the Dubai Municipality, one of the key units of Dubai government, selected MEDICOM to provide an 'e-Medical Certification System' at the Dubai Municipality Clinic, as part of its ongoing process to establish e-governance.

Established more than half a century ago, Dubai Municipality is the principal body of the Dubai Emirate to provide civic services, currently with more than 10,000 staff working in over 20 departments. It serves companies in Dubai that apply for occupational health cards and medical certificates. With the Dubai Government opting for 'e-Governance', the Municipality has put in place expansion plans to enhance the efficiency of the current resources and to manage the large volume of applications and clinical services through the use of IT services. MEDICOM will provide a Web-enabled software application to aid the business processes of Dubai Municipality. Use of Web-based technology would mean that Dubai Municipality could e-enable the services offered to residents. MEDICOM's implementation will help the process of issue and renewal of medical certificates, occupational health cards and medical examination certificates by tracking the clinical procedures at the Municipality Clinic. It will also provide clinic treatment and consultation activities for the Dubai Municipality staff, patients and dependents. MEDICOM targets the implementation at the Clinic in a record time of 6 months to cater to the overall objectives laid down by the Dubai Municipality.

In line with its policy to adopt the latest in medical technology, a wide-ranging telemedicine service has recently opened at Al Mafraq Hospital (in Abu Dhabi) to improve patient care and reduce the cost of foreign travel for patients. The system links Al Mafraq Hospital to the Mayo Clinic in Minnesota (US) and enables the exchange of digitized data and high-resolution, diagnostic video images. The Al Mafraq Hospital is also purchasing an electronic medical records system which will make it possible to establish physician-to-physician contact via the telemedicine link.

The telemedicine system will enable physicians at Al Mafraq Hospital to consult 1,600 physicians and scientists at the Mayo Clinic and its associates in Minnesota, Arizona and Florida. Consultations will initially focus on cardiovascular diseases, but the scope will quickly be broadened to cover microsurgery, orthopedics, dermatology, oncology and other disciplines. The Mayo Clinic will also establish similar links with Al Jazeirah Hospital in Abu Dhabi and Tawam Hospital in Al Ain. The Ministry for Health also plans similar links at other hospitals including the Al Qasimi Hospital in Sharjah, the Al Baraha Hospital in Dubai and the Al Ain Hospital.

In 1999, and fully aware that IT can be of major assistance in improving efficiency, the Ministry of Health engaged in a project to develop a central database at its premises in Abu Dhabi linking all hospitals, health centers and medical zones in the country. The initial cost of the project was Dh120 million. In addition, the Ministry also implemented a Dh70 million plan for modernizing its computer network and a Dh4 million project to replace medical equipment incompatible with the new platform. It has also modernized medical registration services, particularly in Al Ain hospitals, laboratory testing and administrative services at a cost of Dh40 million. The Ministry also prepared a database on psychiatric services in all medical zones in preparation for the development of these services.

Digital Arabic Content

Arabs account for less than 1 percent of the world's 500 million Internet users. In the UAE, 28 percent of the population use the Internet. Recent research on the ICT sectors in the region sounds the alarm that Arab nations still endure a serious digital divide with their international counterparts. This is not due to being less well educated or computer literate, but the increasing rates of people who lack the ability to own a PC.

While the spoken dialect of the people of the UAE is Arabic, given the fact that more than 80 percent of UAE residents are expatriates, English is spoken and understood by the majority of the people of the UAE. Nevertheless, Arabic remains the language of written communication, including newspapers and educational material. However, the complexity of Arabic has yet to come to terms with IT, a lingo-centric technology favoring English and other Latin alphabet-based Indo-European languages. Arabization of network interfaces and software still slows new product appearances. The lack of enforced standards in Arabization and keyboard layout persists, causing further delays in product integration, despite the 1985 recommendations of the Arab Standards and Metrology Organization (ASMO).

A common concern, and the focus of much effort in the UAE, has naturally been the Arabization of software. The large regional population and the localized utility of Arabic guarantees a substantial amount of work and a market for Arabized software products. An Arabic computer standardized code (ASMO-449) was established in 1985 by ASMO and the Arabization Coordination Bureau, both specialized organizations under the Arab League. However, both groups died due to political and budgetary problems and the codes have not been updated, resulting in a proliferation of many new codes and additions. (Arabic letters take different written forms depending on their position in a word. Thus Arabic word processors have to be a little smarter than those for European languages because previously typed character may have to change shape, depending on what is typed after it.) Creating an awareness of Internet usage requires efficient initiatives to facilitate people's access to the Web. Lacking an Arabic content is a factor deterring ICT usage in the region. Arabic is the sixth most widely spoken language in the world. However, the share of Arabic content on the Internet remains as low as 1 percent.

CONCLUSION

E-commerce has induced changes that are transforming the rules of competition and giving rise to new types of competitive strategies: innovation-driven competition, time-based competition; mass customization; lean manufacturing, and demand-driven competition. E-governments have drastically cut longstanding obstacles to communication in terms of time and distance. New communication technologies allow economic entities to source inputs independent of location. With costs of transport and information diminishing, countries are forced into the same competitive field. The 'new competition' entails flexible response, customization, networking, and new forms of inter-firm organization (clustering), rather than classic price competition dominated by vertically integrated economic entities.

This chapter has explored the impact of the Internet on governments using a four-cell model that emphasizes the dimensions of focus and centrality. The model helps to identify the issues and depth of complexity that the ICTs have begun to create for public servants and politicians in developed and democratic countries. As governments move beyond relatively simple informational websites, they are and will continue to be confronted by more complex challenges, especially in the area of e-governance. National governments may harbor the notion of 'government as a lead user' in the sense of being a kind of living demonstration project for both the private sector and other levels of government, including internationally. With respect to acting as a model for the private sector, this is unlikely given the pace of technological change. Governments typically have neither the money, the decision speed nor the change capacity to act as a pathfinder for large private sector organizations. The prospect of government success as lead user would depend on what one might describe as lead.

It is necessary to reconsider the approach to e-government. We would recommend rebalancing the investment in outward-facing and inward-facing systems. If we were to examine government promotional material from 1995, or any of the popular culture publications of that date, we would be hard pressed to find a URL. Today they are ubiquitous. There is a clear requirement to look toward the potentially unanticipated impacts of disruptive technologies such as the Internet on governance structures and processes. These disruptive technologies mean significant changes to our view of the prospects for the year 2020, compared to our view of the same date from the vantage point of just 7 years ago. The future simply isn't what it used to be for governments and governance everywhere.

NOTES

1. Refer to *2003 Index of Economic Freedom Report* by the Heritage Foundation and Dow Jones & Co.
2. The *2002 World Times/IDC Information Society Index: Measuring the Global Impact of Information Technology and Internet Adoption* is the fifth installment of the ISI research.
3. The 55 nations account for 98 percent of all IT investments in the world.
4. For more information, refer to www.internetcitylaw.com.
5. Refer to www.etisalat.co.ae.
6. Preliminary estimates from Etisalat headquarters.
7. Source: Madar Research Group, December 2002–January 2003 issue.
8. Numbers are estimated by Etisalat.
9. See www.emirates.net.ae.
10. See www.albahhar.com.

11. Source: www.emirates.net.ae.
12. According to Dr Omar Bin Soleiman, the CEO of DIC, the number of registered partners as of December 15, 2003 is 450.
13. The project is to be completed in seven phases; as of the time of this writing, phases one, two and three have been completed and work on phase four is undergoing.
14. At an early stage in the project, initial investment was set at 500,0000 dirhams; but in an effort to help young entrepreneurs, this requirement was reduced to 1,000 dirhams.
15. The DIC refers to tenants as partners.
16. Dr Omar told the researchers that DIC has created more than 8,500 high tech, professional jobs, in addition to thousands of jobs in support services.
17. Please refer to the 2003 *Index of Economic Freedom Report* by the Heritage Foundation and Dow Jones & Co.

REFERENCES

Anderson, Kim (1999), 'Reengineering public sector organizations using information technology', in R. Heeks (ed.) *Reinventing Government in the Information Age*, New York: Routledge.

Asia-Pacific Cooperation Council (APEC) (2000), *APEC E-commerce Readiness Assessment Guide*, Singapore: APEC.

Bhatnagar, S. (2003), 'E-government and access to information', *Global Corruption Report*, accessed at www.globalcorruptionreport.org.

Braga, Carlos and Carsten Fink (1999), *How Stronger Protection of Intellectual Property Rights Affect International Trade Flows*, Washington, DC: World Bank.

Brown, M. (1999), 'Does pay structure matter? A compaison of flat and hierarchical pay structures', *ACA Journal*, **8** (2), 64–72.

China Internet Network Information Center (CNNIC) (2002), '15th statistical survey report on the internet development in China', accessed January 2002 at www.cannic.net.cn/download/2002/2005012701.pdf.

Clemons, Eric K., Il-Horn, Hann and Lorin M. Hitt (1998), *The nature of competition in electronic markets: an empirical investigation of online travel agent offerings*, Wharton School working paper, the University of Pennsylvania, accessed at http://citeseer.ist.psu.edu/article/clemons99nature.html.

Cohen, W.M. and D. A. Levinthal (1990), 'Absorptive capacity: a new perspective on learning and innovation', *Administrative Science Quarterly* **35**, 128–52.

Connectivity Africa, (2004), 'Slow pace of liberalization holds back internet growth', accessed at www.connectivityafrica.ca/.

Cukier, Kenneth Neil (1999), 'Internet governance and the ancient regime', *The Swiss Review of Political Science*, University of Zurich, Spring.

Davis, B. and Sieb, G. (2000), 'Technology will test a Washington culture born in the industrial age', *Wall Street Journal*, 1 May.

EGI/NCPP, (2003), *Digital Governance in Municipalities Worldwide: An Assessment of Municipal Web Sites Throughout the World*, Newark, NJ: The E-Governance Institute/National Center for Public Productivity, Rutgers, the State University of New Jersey.

Dutta, Soumitra (2003), *The Global Information Technology Report 2002–2003: Readiness for the Networked World*, Oxford University Press.

The Economist (2000), 'No gain without pain. Government and the internet survey', 24 June, p. 7–10.

Economist Intelligence Unit (EIU) (2003), The 2003 E-readiness ranking: a white paper from the Economist Intelligence Unit, accessed at http://graphics.eiu.com/files/ad_pdfs/ERR2003.pdf.

Economist Intelligence Unit, (EIU) (2004), The 2004 E-readiness ranking: a white paper from the Economist Intelligence Unit, accessed at http://graphics.eiu.com/files/ad_pdfs/ERR2004.pdf.

Fichman, R.G. (2000), 'The Diffusion and Assimilation of Information Technology innovations', in R. Zmud (ed.), *Framing the Domains of IT Management Research: Glimpsing the Future through the Past*, Cincinnati, OH: Pinnaflex Educational Resources, Inc.

Fountain, Jane (2001), *Building the Virtual State: Information Technology and Institutional Change*, Washington DC: Brookings Institution.

Garicano, L. and S.N. Kaplan (2000), 'The effects of business-to-business e-commerce on transaction costs', *NBER working paper* no 8017, Cambridge, MA.

Goodman, S.E. (1994), 'The global diffusion of the Internet: patterns and problems', *Communications of the ACM*, **37**(8), 27–31.

Gore, Al (1993), *Creating a Government that Works Better and Costs Less: Reengineering Through Information Technology*, report of the National Performance Review, Washington DC: Government Printing Office.

Gulf News (2002), 'PC trends in the UAE', 19 December.

Gupta, J. and S. Sharma (2000), 'Creating business value through e-commerce', in A. Hartman, J. Sifonis and J. Kador (eds), *Net Ready: Strategies for Success in the E-conomy*, New York: McGraw-Hill.

Hartman, A., J. Sifonis and J. Kador (2000), *Net Ready: Strategies for Success in the E-conomy*, New York: McGraw-Hill.

Henisz, W.J. and B.A. Zelner (2000), 'The institutional environment for telecommunications investment', Wharton School Working Paper, University of Pennsylvania.

Hiller, Janine and France Belanger (2001), *Privacy Strategies for Electronic Government*, E-Government Series, Arlington, VA: PricewaterhouseCoopers Endowment for the Business of Government.

International Labor Organization (ILO) (2002), *World Employment Report*, Geneva: ILO.

ILO (2003), *World Employment Report*, Geneva: ILO.

Information for Develoment project (Infodev) (2003), *ICT Infrastructure and E-Readiness Assessment Initiative*, World Bank, accessed at www.infodev.org/ereadiness/.

International Telecommunications Union (ITU) (1999), *Challenges to the Network— Internet for Development*, February, Geneva: United Nations.

ITU (2004), *Telecommunications Basic Indicators*, Geneva: United Nations.

Karake Shalhoub, Z. (2002), *Trust and Loyalty in Electronic Commerce: An Agency Theory Perspective*, New York: Quorum Publishing.

Karake Shalhoub, Z. and L. Al Qasimi (2003), *The UAE and Information Society*, ESCWA report, Beirut, Lebanon: United Nations.

Kumar, R. and C. Crook (1999), 'A multi-disciplinary framework of the management of interorganizational systems', *Database for Advances in Information Systems* **30**(1), 22–37.

Landsbergen, David, Jr and George Wolken Jr (2001), 'Realizing the promise: government information systems and the fourth generation of information technology', *Public Administration Review* **61**(2), 206–20.

Layne, Karen and Jungwoo Lee (2001), 'Developing fully functional e-government: a four stage model', *Government Information Quarterly* **18**(2), 12–136.

Levy, B. and P. Spiller (1996), *Regulations, Institutions and Commitment*, Cambridge: Cambridge University Press.

Lorack, S. (2000), 'Embracing the electronic economy', *Electronic Business Online*; accessed at www.reed-electronics.com/eb-mag/article.

Moon, M. Jae, and Stuart Bretschneider (2002), 'Does the perception of red tape constrain IT innovativeness in organizations? Unexpected results from simultaneous equation model and implications', *Journal of Public Administration Research and Theory* **12**(2), 273–91.

Mussa, J., C. Weare and M. Hale (2000), 'Designing web technologies for local governance reform: good management or good democracy?', *Political Communication*, **17**(1), 1–19.

Murtha, T. and S.A. Lenway (1994), 'Country capabilities and the strategic state: how national political institutions affect multinational corporations' strategies', *Strategic Management Journal* **15**, 113–29.

Nolan, Richard (1979), 'Managing the crises in data processing', *Harvard Business Review* **57** (March/April) 115–26.

Norris, Pippa (1999), 'Who surfs? New technology, old voters, and virtual democracy', in Elaine Ciulla Kamarck and Joseph S. Nye, Jr (eds), *Democracy. com? Governance in Networked World*, Hollis, NH: Hollis Publishing Company, pp. 71–94.

Nunn, Samuel (2001), 'Police information technology: assessing the effects of computerization on urban police functions', *Public Administration Review* **61**(2), 221–34.

Nye, Jr, Joseph (1999), 'Information technology and democratic governance', in Elaine Ciulla Kamarck and Joseph S. Nye, Jr (eds), *Democracy.com? Governance in Networked World*, Hollis, NH: Hollis Publishing Company, pp. 1–18.

Odlyzko, A. (2003), 'Privacy, economics, and price discrimination on the Internet', University of Minnesota Digital Technology Center, accedded at www.dtc.umn. edu/odlyzko.

Oxley, J.E. (1999), 'Institutional environment and the mechanisms of governance: the impact of intellectual property protection on the structure of inter-firm alliances', *Journal of Economic Behavior and Organization* **38**(3), 283–310.

Peled, A. (2000), 'First-class technology – third rate bureaucracy: the case of Israel', *Information Technology for Development*, **9**(1), 45–58.

Pool, Ithiel de Sola (1983), *Technologies of Freedom on Free Speech in an Electronic Age*, Cambridge, MA: Belknap Press.

Premkumar, G., K. Ramamurthy and Sree Nilakanta (1994), 'Implementation of electronic data interchange: an innovation diffusion perspective', *Journal of Management Information Systems* **11**(2): 157–86.

Quinn, Robert and Kim Cameron (1983), 'Organizational life cycles and shifting criteria of effectiveness: some preliminary evidence', *Management Science* **29**(1), 33–51.

Santerelli, E. and S. D'Altri (2003), 'The diffusion of E-commerce among SMEs: theoretical implications and empirical evidence', *Small Business Economics*, **21**(3): 273–83.

Schmitt, E. (2000), 'The multilighual web sites', accessed at www.forrester.com.
Sharma, S. and J. Gupta (2003), 'Transforming to e-government: a framework', paper presented at Second European Conference on E-government, pp. 383–90.
Slevin, J. (2000), *The Internet and Society*, Malden, MA: Polity Press.
Smith, Michael D., Joseph Bailey and Erik Brynjolfsson. (2000), 'Understanding digital markets: review and assessment', in Erik Brynjolfsson and Kahin (eds), *Understanding the Digital Economy*, Cambridge, MA: MIT Press, pp. 99–136.
Sprecher, Milford (2000), 'Racing to E-government: using the Internet for citizen service delivery', *Government Finance Review* **16**(5), 21–22.
Toregas (2001), 'The politics of E-Gov: the upcoming struggle for redefining civic engagement', *National Civic Review*, **90**(3), 235–40.
Travica, B. (2002), 'Diffusion of electronic commerce in developing countries: the case of Costa Rica', *Journal of Global Information Technology Management* **5**(1), 4–24.
UNCTAD (2000), World Investment Report. 2000 Cross-border Mergers and Acquisitions and Development, New York: United Nations.
UNCTAD (2003), *Building Confidence: Electronic Commerce and Development*, UNCTAD/SDTE/MISC. 11. Geneva: United Nations.
United Nations Conference on Trade and Development (UNCTAD) (1999), *Report of the Pre-UNCTAD-X Workshop on Exchange of Experiences among Enterprises in the Area of Electronic Commerce. TD(X)/pcl3*, Geneva: UNCTAD.
UAE Ministry of Planning (2002), *Direct Foreign Investment in the UAE*, Abu Dhabi: Ministy of Planning.
United Nations and American Society for Public Administration (ASPA) (2001), 'Global survey of e-government', accessed at www.unpan.org/egovernment2.asp.
Vehovar, Vasja, Zenel Batagelj and Katja Lozar (1999), 'Web surveys: revolutionizing the survey industry or (only) enriching its spectrum?', proceedings of the ESOMAR Worldwide Internet Conference Net Effects, 21–23 February, London, pp. 159–76.
Vogel, Thomas T. and Pamela Druckerman (2000), 'Latin Internet craze sets off alarm bells', *Wall Street Journal*, 16 February, pp. 1–24.
Weare, Christopher, Juliet Musso and Matt Hale (1999), 'Electronic democracy and the diffusion of municipal web pages in California', *Administration and Society* **31**(1), 3–27.
Weare, C., J. Musson and M. Hale (1999), 'Electronic democracy and the diffusion of municipal web pages in California', *Administration and Society*, **31**, 3–27.
White House Press Office (2000), 'President Clinton and Vice President Gore: major new e-government initiatives', US Newswire, 24 June, accessed at http://web.lexis-nexis.com/ universe.
Wolcott, P., L. Press, W. McHenry, S.E. Goodman, and W. Foster (2001), 'A framework for assessing the global diffusion of the Internet', *Journal of the Association for Information Systems* **2**(6), 50–55.
World Information Technology and Services Alliance (WITSA) (2002), *Digital Planet*, vol. 3, Vienna: WITSA.
World Times and International Data Corporation (2002), *Information Society Index*, Washington, DC: World Times and International Data Corporation.

3. Resource-based view and theory

INTRODUCTION

One of the fundamental missions of strategic management research is to investigate and explain differences in performance among firms. The reigning incumbent explanation for the heterogeneity of firm economic performance is based on the concept of competitive advantage. More work has focused on the expanded concept of sustained competitive advantage, which, simply put, is the idea that some forms of competitive advantage are very difficult to imitate and can therefore lead to persistent superior economic performance. Popular extant theories of competitive advantage in strategic management research, based on industrial organization economics (Porter 1980, 1985) and the resource-based view (RBV) of the firm (Barney 1991; Conner 1991) predict that the factors that sustain competitive advantages will generate superior economic performance that persist over time. On the other hand, historical economic theories such as those arising from neoclassical economics and the work of the Austrian school of economics (Schumpeter, 1934), as well as the hypercompetitive model (Brown and Eisenhardt 1997, 1998; D'Aveni 1994) of strategy, predict the opposite: that temporal dynamics, resulting from factors such as imitation, entry, and the introduction of substitutes, will erode almost all competitive advantages, and thus prevent superior economic performance from persisting. More recently, Foster and Kaplan (2001) have presented an empirically based, managerial view of the transitory nature of competitive advantage and some of the economic and management mechanisms that generate it.

The central questions addressed by the resource-based view concern why firms differ and how they achieve and sustain competitive advantage. Penrose (1959) argues that heterogeneous capabilities give each firm its unique character and are the essence of competitive advantage. Wernerfelt (1984) suggests that evaluating firms in terms of their resources could lead to insights different from the traditional industrial/organization (I/O) perspective (Porter, 1980). Barney (1986) suggests that strategic resource factors differ in their 'tradability' and that these factors can be specifically identified and their monetary value determined via a 'strategic factor market'. Barney (1991) later established four criteria to more fully explicate the idea of strategic tradability. He suggested that firm resources and capabilities could be differentiated on the basis of value, rareness, inimitability, and substitutability.

The resource-based view of the firm is one of the latest strategic management concepts to be enthusiastically embraced by information technology (IT) and information management scholars. This book and the empirical analysis carried out maintain that the RBV holds much promise as a framework for understanding strategic information/knowledge economy issues but cautions that, before it is adopted, it needs to be fully understood. This chapter charts the development of the RBV from its origins in early economic models of imperfect competition, through the work of evolutionary economists to the contributions of strategy economics scholars over the past two decades. This broad literature base has given rise to a great deal of ambiguity, inconsistent use of nomenclature and several overlapping classification schema. The book seeks to draw together common themes of firm heterogeneity, barriers to duplication, sustainable competitive advantage and Ricardian rents within an overall model of resource-based competitive advantage.

The second part of this chapter describes three aspects of strategic information technology likely to benefit from adoption of the resource-based perspective in developing countries, namely, strategic analysis, positioning of an economy, and globalization through electronic commerce (e-commerce). In terms of the former, it is argued that the RBV helps to overcome some of the frequently cited problems of the strengths, weaknesses, opportunities and threats (SWOT) framework. Similarly, it contends that understanding a firm's resource-base is central to effective positioning, while applications in the area of globalization through e-commerce highlight important differences between firm-specific and country-specific resources. This chapter concludes by noting some important conceptual and methodological issues that need to be addressed by future research adopting the RBV perspective.

PRINCIPLES OF RESOURCE-BASED VIEW THEORY

A central principle of the RBV is that performance is a function of an entity's unique resource bundle. Resources are broadly defined to encompass specific assets as well as human competencies and intangible abilities. Ideally, managers will strive to build up resources that are valuable, rare, without substitutes, and structured in a manner so that the organization's resources are unique and difficult to replicate by competitors. Accumulating such resources requires that significant acquisition barriers be overcome. Thus, managers who overcome these barriers place their organizations in a desirable competitive position. Over time, the most successful organizations may develop such a strong competitive advantage that their competitors will cease their attempts toward imitation through resource accumulation.

The RBV is primarily interested in the extent to which strategies are distinctive. Differences that yield superior organizational performance are determined by the distinct abilities of an organization and its management to accumulate and implement strategic resources. Thus, while generic strategies may be used to label an organization's basic strategic focus, broad generalizations alone are not useful for understanding differences that lead to a sustained competitive advantage. The RBV of the firm posits that, to be competitive and successful, firms should possess and develop valuable, rare, competitively superior resources that are difficult to imitate and substitute (Barney, 1991). According to this view, a high-performing firm is expected to have more unique resources, while a low-performing firm is expected to possess less unique resources.

The RBV theory provides an explanation to understand why firms do obtain strategic advantage and are able to keep it. It has been used previously in IT to explain how information technology could be used to gain competitive advantage. It also gives an interesting framework to assess whether an activity should be kept within the firm or given to a supplier. It focuses on the strategic resources that firms develop and nurture. Even though they are not always readily discernible, these resources are important investments for organizations and should be leveraged for strategic advantage (Barney, 1991).

The key elements on which the resource-based theory is constructed are simple deviations from the perfect market environment. Resource-based theory argues that, in many situations, three hypotheses of a perfect market are not met: (1) the firms are constrained by their past choices (history matters), (2) the resources are not perfectly mobile, and (3) expertise is not easy to reproduce or imitate. These elements are now discussed in sequence and can be applied at the macro level to a country's economy.

Firms are Constrained by their Past Choices

Recent work in the area of resource-based strategy has sought to more clearly explicate the role of resource value in determining firm competitiveness and performance (Barney, 2001; Bowman and Ambrosini, 2000; Priem and Butler, 2001). Bowman and Ambrosini (2000, p. 1) note that, 'a more precise and rounded underpinning theory of value is required to help us identify "valuable resources"'. These authors then proceed to set out a process model that distinguishes between creating new 'use value' and capturing 'exchange value'. We are concerned with both in this chapter, as use value of goods is perceived by potential buyers (eg, managers), and exchange value is a key determinant in the profitability of resource-based strategies. As we focus mostly on managers' perceptions of value in this chapter, we specifically define value to be that (or those) characteristics of a good that makes the firm better off – more capable, more efficient, more effective etc. (Barney, 1991) with than without the good. These characteristics are embodied in the components of our model discussed later. Naturally, there are several ways to define 'value' in this context (Bowman and Ambrosini, 2000; Priem and Butler, 2001). As we are interested in valuation decisions, we agree with Bowman and Ambrosini (2000) that it is the 'use value' perceived by managers that is important, and not value inherent in the good under consideration. Valuable resource bundles are heterogeneous not so much because of inert physical characteristics of the assets, but because of their unique employment in the creation of use value. The uniqueness of such employment arises from the initial perceptual differences upon which our model elaborates.

These perceptual insights cannot be easily transferred across firm boundaries. What implications does this have for price and value? Resource-based scholars suggest that value/price discrepancies form the first step in the development of sustainable competitive advantages, as some firms 'see' opportunities that elude others (Barney, 1986; Bowman and Ambrosini, 2000; Kirzner, 1979). Above normal returns accrued in such scenarios as ultimate values are not fully imputed into the costs of procurement (Rumelt, 1987). Sellers in the resource-based scenario may fail to recognize this value, and thus fail to incorporate true asset value into prices they charge (Barney, 2001); competitors may also fail to grasp these insights and, therefore, will provide less than adequate competition necessary to drive the knowledge rich firm's returns to 'normal' levels. It is this learned, tacit valuation capability that provides the potential for resource-based competitive advantage (Nelson and Winter, 1982; Penrose, 1959).

Viewed from a growth perspective, resource-based theory is concerned with the origin, evolution, and sustainability of firms (Conner, 1991; Peteraf, 1993). Firms experiencing the highest growth have added new competencies sequentially, often over extended periods of time (Hall, 1992, 1993). Although everyone seems to agree that resources are developed in a complex, path-dependent process (Barney and Zajac, 1994; Dierickx and Cool, 1989), no resource-based theorist has explained or predicted this growth path. With the exception of work investigating the direction of firm diversification (Montgomery and Hariharan, 1991), analysis of the sequential development process of a firm's resource base over time is lacking in the literature.

Resource-based sequencing is important for achieving sustainable growth (Heene and Sanchez, 1997; Montgomery, 1995). In a changing environment, firms must continuously invent and upgrade their resources and capabilities if they are to maintain competitive advantage and growth (Argyris, 1996; Robins and Wiersema, 1995; Wernerfelt and Montgomery, 1988). This sequential development of resources and capabilities can make a firm's advantage inimitable (Barney, 1991; Lado et al, 1997). Competitors cannot simply buy these resources and capabilities without acquiring the entire firm. This is because the resources and capabilities are built over time in a path-dependent process that makes them inextricably interwoven into a firm. This facet of resources and capabilities development makes it theoretically impossible for competitors to imitate completely (Dierickx and Cool, 1989; Reed and De Fillippi, 1990).

GROWTH AND DEVELOPMENT IN EMERGING COUNTRIES

Going into the twenty-first century, it seems that almost every country wants to be an active participant in the 'New Economy.' This trend is not hard to understand. Many emerging economies have made technology-led economic development a primary goal. Moving beyond technology parks (ie Egypt), incubation projects (in Singapore) and other real-estate based initiatives (ie Dubai), developing countries now look to promote IT entrepreneurs, increase the amount of venture capital, improve basic and applied research, encourage the development and commercialization capacity of higher educational institutions, and attract and retain talented workers and research personnel.

Whatever the state of the IT and life science industries, no one expects technology to become a minor economic concern any time soon. Skills have become the currency of competitiveness for businesses, people and communities. Information and knowledge-based technology can only help a country so much if its workforce does not have the skills to apply it. Technology tends to create a demand for more highly skilled workers. Much of the labor market research in developed economies shows us that most of the new jobs being created, both now and in the future, requires training beyond a high school level.

To deal with this, some developing economies are looking at ways that universities can partner with industry to provide skills training (ie the American University of Sharjah). Some economies target high school education, using school-to-work and other models to start building twenty-first century skills early on (for example, the UAE), Mexico, Brazil, India).

The key to workforce initiatives is creating business partnerships that can leverage resources and, more importantly, jointly identify skill and training needs for the industry as a whole. A number of developing economies ahead of the learning curve are implementing complete human capital investment strategies (ie India, Singapore, and the UAE).

Michael Porter and numerous other gurus and researchers have recently been preaching the doctrine of economic 'clusters' that are groupings of economic activity focused on a particular industry within a particular region. These can be high-tech oriented or not; however, as Porter states, there is no such thing as a truly 'low-tech' industry any more. New technological applications can enhance productivity in almost any field, be it agriculture or automobile manufacturing. In a number of developing countries, IT cluster development has been underway, either with government involvement or only at the regional level (ie Bangalore, Dubai).

The dawn of the twenty-first century came with a digital revolution and economic globalization with a New Economy. We are moving towards a global knowledge society where information, skills, and competence become the driving forces of social and economic development. Information technology and greater competition at all levels of business and government are transforming the goals and practice of economic development. Beginning in the 1980s, private/public partnerships helped revitalize key industries. Now, a new generation of such partnerships is being formed to focus on technology innovation. These twenty-first century partnerships link technology based economic development to an area's competitive advantage, providing important models for economic development in the coming years. As we navigate the new millennium, IT is driving the key economic development challenges. At the same time, competition has become a daily fact of life at every level of business and government. Consequently, developing countries have realized that to compete in the twenty-first century they must design new ways to turn these dynamics to their advantage. While technology has the power to transform industries, it cannot do so alone. Successful transfer and insertion of new technologies into the workplace are tremendously dependent on other factors, especially an exceptionally skilled workforce willing to suspend conventional practices and recalibrate its skills for new technologies.

Various viewpoints on the development process have been advanced by the many development economy scholars and observers. The leading work of Sen (1999) singles out freedom as both the primary end and principal means of development. Others have paid more attention to poverty reduction and the empowerment of poor people. All approaches regard economic growth as a critical component of the development process and stress that development is about more than growth. Growth in real income is a significant determinant of development but it is not the basic objective. The means and ends of the development process should not be mystified. As a matter of fact, it may thus be possible to improve the human condition without requiring significant growth in real incomes. Eventually the development process is about providing people with real opportunities. Closely linked to this broader definition of development is the importance of poverty reduction in the development process. It is estimated that of the world's 6 billion people, 2.8 billion live on less than US$2 a day, and 1.2 billion live on less than US$1 a day (World Bank, 2000).

Poverty not only includes material insufficiency but it is also coupled with low levels of education and health, greater weaknesses, possible ill treatment by institutions of the state and society, and powerlessness to influence key decisions. A major objective of poverty alleviation is to enable people to take greater control of their own future. Empowerment requires that people have access to information, can participate in decisions that affect them, hold public and private institutions accountable, and develop organizational abilities; IT and the digital economy make all of these possible.

In the 1960s and early 1970s, concern about the impact of economic growth on the environment came to the fore. As a consequence, the concept of sustainable development gained ground. Sustainable development means that the needs of the present should be met without jeopardizing the ability of future generations to meet their own needs. The eight Millennium Development Goals (MDGs), adopted by the United Nations (UN) Millennium Summit held in September 2000, exemplify the holistic approach to development. The MDGs are a set of time-bound and measurable goals for combating poverty, hunger, disease, illiteracy, discrimination against women and environmental degradation. The fact that economic growth is not listed as a goal reflects the accepted view that has been described above, namely that growth is a means to achieve development goals, not an end in itself. The MDGs involve eight goals and 18 targets. Economic growth can generate the resources necessary to meet these development challenges. In addition, these goals tie human and economic development together. The MDGs are based on the premise that human and economic development often move in concert. The interdependence of human and economic development suggests that human development is unlikely to be sustained in the face of enduring economic stagnation. Economic growth is driven by two major forces: finding new and better ways of utilizing existing resources, and generating new productive resources through investment. Better utilization of existing resources (especially IT resources) appears to be the most important of the two factors. Countries utilize resources differently because they have different histories, institutions, cultures, and geographical circumstances.

Early research on economic growth focused on the accumulation of capital, such as investment in machinery, equipment and infrastructure. That is why during the 1950s and 1960s the development strategy in newly independent countries and other struggling countries stressed investment and speedy industrialization. Other factors and resources have been proven to be major determinants of growth and development. Human capital is one of these factors. Human capital acquired through education and work experience is clearly required in order to operate efficiently and effectively. A better educated labor force makes investment in physical capital more profitable and therefore attracts more of it. However, not all countries with a well educated labor force and a high investment rate grow. The Eastern European countries during the 1980s are a case in point and again illustrate that it is not the accumulation of capital (human and physical) that is most important, but the way it is utilized. In short, high-yielding investment opportunities become exhausted if not complemented by other factors such as education and research and development (R&D).

Knowledge has two characteristics which make it a significant contributor to the development process. The first is its permanence, implying that it can be used over and over again. The second is its non-exclusive nature. More than one person can take advantage of knowledge without lessening its value to others. Yet there are huge technology gaps between developed and developing countries. The key questions for understanding the linkage between knowledge and growth are how far ideas spread; how ideas affect behavior and technology; and to what extent a large stock of knowledge makes it easier to discover or create new ideas. When individuals, firms and governments are able to act upon new ideas in terms of changing behavior, improving technologies or changing policy respectively, ideas affect economic growth. From the R&D side, common knowledge of technologies – for example how a computer works – can be used by all producers of computers once the innovation has been made. Obviously reproducing what has already been invented is less costly than inventing the product. New innovations create new investment opportunities while the prospect of capitalizing on new inventions motivates further R&D. Capital investment and R&D thus feed on each other in much the same way as investment in human and physical capital feed on each other. Furthermore, R&D prevents investment from running into diminishing returns, as new technologies are more productive than the ones they replace, and new products often fetch higher prices than comparable existing products.

Economic activities are not equally distributed among countries and regions, but tend to cluster in certain areas. In these clusters each activity benefits from access to inputs produced by others located in the same area and to a pool of skills, infrastructure and business services. A sufficiently large market allows for extensive specialization while each company is still able to exploit economies of scale. Furthermore, when manufacturers have access to a broad variety of specialized inputs their productivity improves, their costs are reduced and they can expand sales. As the market expands, room for more specialized producers is created with a further lowering of costs. It is entirely possible for this process to create a self-sustained virtuous cycle.

The forces driving growth and development operate within a social, cultural, geographical and institutional context. The notion of an institution embodies several elements – formal and informal rules of behavior, ways and means of enforcing these rules, procedures for mediation of conflicts, and sanctions in the case of breach of the rules. Institutions are more or less developed, depending on how well these different features operate. Institutions can create or destroy incentives for individuals to invest in human and physical capital, and the incentives to engage in R&D and work effort.

One feature of institutions that is of particular relevance for economic development and growth is the treatment of property rights. In addition the rule of law, the enforcement of contracts and payments of debts are important. Property rights, combined with access to credit and education, grow in importance with the degree of complexity of the industrial and technological environment. An industrial society, for instance, requires entrepreneurship and creativity. The distribution of such talents in the population is independent of the distribution of income. Limiting economic opportunities to a small percentage of the population represents a huge waste of resources. Conversely, when entrepreneurs have access to funding and can expect to receive a return on their investments, society will be better able to benefit from new technologies and continue to upgrade their industrial base as new technologies arrive. Transparent and efficient institutions that facilitate the establishment and enforcement of contracts therefore become more important as development proceeds. This does not mean that institutions are not important in developing countries. To the contrary, the rule of law and the enforcement of contracts are equally important in developing countries. It is, however, important that the complexity of regulations matches the institutional capacity to enforce the regulation.

A current issue in the development debate is the relative role of institutions and geography in explaining the fact that poor countries tend to be located near the equator. The question is whether a tropical climate *per se* is detrimental to growth, or whether countries in the tropical climate zone tend to have less development-friendly institutions. The direct impact of the tropical climate on development goes through agriculture and health. While tropical conditions were favorable to agriculture in the very early history of mankind, the invention of heavy ploughs, systems of crop rotation and the introduction of new crops favored temperate zones. Tropical diseases are found to have both a direct and an indirect impact on development. They represent higher health risks, and consequently a lower stock of human capital. Furthermore, the demographic transformation towards lower mortality and fertility rates has been slower in tropical areas due to higher health risks. This transformation is part of the development process towards sustained growth. The suggested linkage from climate to institutions is that the prevalence of tropical diseases prevented Europeans from settling, but not from exploiting, the natural resources in tropical areas. They therefore imposed institutions with the exclusive purpose of extracting resources. These institutions concentrated wealth and power within a small elite and the associated structures have tended to prevail after independence. A number of empirical analyses suggest that institutions are indeed important determinants of the growth and development process.

The concept of institutions is, at present, rather abstract and the discussion of their role in growth and development has much in common with the discussion in the 1980s of the role of technology, following the first publications on endogenous growth. An understanding of how economic agents and the institutional framework interact in the growth process, and how geography benefits or impedes the process, is emerging. However, there are still gaps in our knowledge about what aspects of the institutional framework are the most relevant for growth, to what extent and how the optimal institutional framework depends on geography, culture, religion and the level of development in each case, and how far and how quickly 'getting institutions right' would generate growth and development. We do know, however, that corruption, severe impediments to trade and unclear and non-transparent regulations are detrimental to growth and development. Yet the brief discussion above has illustrated the sheer complexity of the growth and development process. No quick fixes have been identified. Nevertheless, in the section that follows, we discuss fairly well-established propositions about the circumstances in which engagement in the world economy can contribute to improved economic performance (UNCTAD 2003).

RESOURCE-BASED VIEW AND ECONOMIC GROWTH

The resource-based view is very insightful and, originally, is centered on the economic entity itself (Porter, 1991). It argues that the origins of competitive advantage are core competencies (valuable resources) that the entity possesses. Most of these resources tend to be intangible assets such as skills, customer and supplier relationships, and reputations and are viewed as relatively immobile (Khosrow-Pour, 2004). The literature further suggests that successful entities are successful because they are unique resources and they count on these resources to be successful. Furthermore, resources are not valuable unless they allow firms to perform activities that create advantages in particular markets. The competitive value of the resource can be improved or wiped out by changes in technology, competitive behavior or buyer needs (Porter, 1996).

Ansoff (1965) was one of the first scholars to address sequential stages of firm growth. Ansoff's product-market expansion grid identified stages that a firm would follow to generate growth. The firm would first attempt to gain more market share from its existing products in existing markets (market penetration). Next, its leaders would consider whether the firm could find new markets for its current products (market development). Third, the firm would develop new products for its existing markets (product development). Fourth, the firm would develop new products for new markets. Since Wernerfelt (1984) viewed products and resources 'as two sides of the same coin', it is possible to substitute resources for products in Ansoff's original matrix. This substitution implies the following resource based arguments:

1. Firms are collections of unused productive services (Penrose, 1959).
2. These unused productive services provide excess capacity. This excess capacity provides an internal mechanism for growth that allows the firm to better utilize the excess capacity to service existing markets (Penrose, 1959). This utilization of excess capacity may be especially relevant when a firm experiences a transition from an environment of regulation to one of deregulation.

In a regulated environment, a regulatory agency controls the scale and scope of firm operating authority (Hambrick and Finkelstein, 1987; Smith and Grimm, 1987). Thus, firms may be constrained from achieving maximum efficiency from their resource base. For example, Johnson et al (1989) showed that prior to the deregulation of the airline industry, airlines did not pursue strategies that would enhance their efficiency. Upon deregulation, these firms had the option of more fully and creatively using their existing resource bases (Gruca and Nath, 1994). Kelly and Amburgey (1991) empirically demonstrated this change in firm behavior in their study of the deregulation of the airline industry. Utilization of excess capacity increases in a deregulated environment. The use of excess capacity gives the firm an internal mechanism for growth and an opportunity to extract the maximum leverage that its existing resource base can provide (Penrose, 1959).

Firms would be expected to utilize excess capacity as their first resource response to deregulation.

Resource-based theory suggests the existence of 'focus effects' (Montgomery and Wernerfelt, 1988). Montgomery and Wernerfelt argued that a given resource will lose more value when transferred to markets that are dissimilar to that in which the resource originated. In their 1988 study, they found that narrowly diversified firms received higher rents (measured as Tobin's Q) than widely diversified firms. This result supports the resource-based hypothesis that expansion by firms into activities in which they have comparative advantages is likely to yield rents (Penrose, 1959). As Wernerfelt pointed out, 'It is better to develop the resource in one market and then enter other markets from a position of strength' (Wernerfelt, 1984, p. 176).

Wernerfelt also asserted that firms will follow a path of sequential entry, first fully using their resource bases in existing domestic markets and then leveraging these existing resources in international markets. Specifically, Wernerfelt discussed the fact that production capacity can be used to support both domestic and international markets. Resources that can be 'dualutilized' to service international markets provide increasing economies of scale. So firms would tend to focus on using existing resources in international markets (gaining international economies of scale) the second resource-sequencing phase after deregulation.

A fundamental idea in resource-based theory is that a firm must continually enhance its resources and capabilities to take advantage of changing conditions (Barney, 1991; Kraatz and Zajac, 1997). Optimal growth involves a balance between the exploitation of existing resource positions and the development of new resource positions (Chatterjee and Wernerfelt, 1991; Ghemawat and Costa, 1993; Hansen and Wernerfelt, 1989; Itami and Numagami, 1992; Rubin, 1973). Thus, a firm would be expected to develop new resources after its existing resource base has been fully utilized. Building new resource positions is important if the firm is to achieve sustained growth. When unused productive resources are coupled with changing managerial knowledge, unique opportunities for growth are created (Castanias and Helfat, 1991; Cohen and Levinthal, 1990; Henderson, 1994; Henderson and Cockburn, 1994; Teece et al, 1997).

Only recently have scholars begun to focus on how firms first develop firm-specific resources and then renew these to respond to shifts in the business environment (Henderson, 1994; Iansiti and Clark, 1994; Teece et al, 1997). Firms, in essence, develop dynamic capabilities to adapt to changing environments (Chandler, 1990; Dierickx and Cool, 1989; Teece and Pisano, 1994). The term 'dynamic' refers 'to the capacity to renew resource positions to achieve congruence with changing environmental conditions' (Teece et al, 1997, p. 515). A 'capability' refers to 'the key role of strategic management in appropriately adapting, integrating, and reconfiguring internal and external organizational skills, resources, and functional capabilities to match the requirements of a changing environment' (Teece et al, p. 1997: 515).

When a firm has extracted the maximum value it can from its existing resource base, then it must develop dynamic capabilities to maintain growth in a dynamically changing environment. From a dynamic capability perspective, the firm continually replaces previously defined sources of competitive advantage with new sources of advantage to provide for dynamic firm growth (Bogner and Thomas, 1994; Hamel and Heene, 1994).

If firms are to develop dynamic capabilities, learning is crucial. Change is costly; therefore, the ability of firms to make necessary adjustments depends upon their ability to scan the environment to evaluate markets and competitors and to quickly accomplish reconfiguration and transformation ahead of competition (Teece et al., 1997). However, 'history matters' (Nelson and Winter, 1982). Thus, opportunities for growth will involve dynamic capabilities closely related to existing capabilities (Teece and Pisano, 1994). As such, opportunities will be most effective when they are close to previous resource use (Teece et al, 1997). Firms would develop dynamic capabilities within existing markets in the third resource-sequence phase.

After dynamic capabilities have been developed, resource-based theory suggests, there are managerial limits to the rate of firm expansion (Penrose, 1959). Existing managers must train new managers, in the so-called Penrose effect (Morris, 1964; Shen, 1970; Slater, 1980). Penrose stated that: 'Managerial resources with experience within the firm are necessary for the efficient absorption of managers from outside the firm. Thus, the availability of inherited managers with such experience limits the amount of expansion that can be planned and undertaken in any period of time' (Penrose, 1959, p. 49). Empirical evidence shows that firms that have grown rapidly in one period typically regress to the average growth rate in the next time period (Ijiri and Simon, 1977; Shen, 1970). On the basis of the Penrose effect, we would expect firms to utilize the excess capacity provided by the dynamic capabilities as the fourth resource-sequencing phase.

Responding to environmental change is not sufficient to generate long-term growth. As Penrose pointed out, 'The environment is not something out there, fixed and immutable, but can itself be manipulated by the firm to serve its own purposes' (Penrose, 1985, p. xiii). Building new resource sets to service emerging markets is one way of generating long-term firm growth (Hamel and Heene, 1994; Hamel and Prahalad, 1994; Sanchez et al, 1996). This view of firms as being able to interpret and lead environmental change extends the traditional position of the firm beyond responding to environmental change ex post. By acquiring new resources to service new markets, a firm can shape environmental change that may alter the competitive environment in its favor to provide for long-term growth (Hamel and Heene, 1994). The capability to lead environmental change is related to the concept of 'creative destruction'.

Schumpeter (1942) first developed this concept, stating that '[gales of creative destruction] revolutionized the economic structure by destroying the old and creating a new one' (Schumpeter, 1942, p. 83). The new focus of the resource-based view is firms' ability to create the 'rules of the game' by developing new resources to service new markets (Hamel and Prahalad, 1994; Levinthal and Myatt, 1994; Sanchez et al, 1996). This is a core competence perspective. It extends the traditional notion of the fit of a firm's capabilities to its environment to embrace the idea that a firm can change to acquire new competencies that can shift the competitive environment in its favor (Collis, 1991, 1994; Hamel and Heene, 1994). This ability of the firm to lead environmental change depends upon its managerial resources (Penrose, 1959).

The resource-based view of organizations can be used as a theoretical perspective to explain how IT infrastructure and electronic government (e-government) may be viewed as a source of competitive advantage. According to this theory, the internal resources of any economy can be one source of sustained competitive advantage. If one country has a particular resource not easily created, bought, substituted, or imitated by others, then this resource confers some degree of sustained competitive advantage on the economy that possesses it. The speed of change in the competitive landscape coupled with increasing hyper-competition necessitates the development of global dynamic capabilities, which is the creation of difficult-to-imitate combinations of resources on a global basis that provide a competitive advantage (D'Aveni, 1999; Eisenhardt and Martin, 2000; Teece et al, 1997). The RBV of the firm has traditionally focused on firm – level resources (ie, internal factors semi-permanently linked to the organization) providing a firm with a unique competitive posture (Barney, 1991; Dierickx and Cool, 1989; Wernerfelt, 1984). However recently, researchers have demonstrated that a RBV of idiosyncratic inter-firm linkages can be a source of relational rents and competitive advantage (Dyer and Singh, 1998), thus extending the RBV.

Powerful forces for change are re-mapping the economic and business environment but they have also led to a key alteration in organizational processes. The fundamental drivers of change comprise globalization, higher degrees of complexity, new technology, intense competition, volatile customer demands, and movements in the economic and political structure. These evolutions mean companies must strive to learn quickly, respond faster, and proactively adapt and shape their organizations. Firms are beginning to perceive that the conventional product-based competitive advantages are transient and that the only sustainable competitive advantages they possess are their resources (Barney, 1991). This means a greater focus, in practice, on intangible assets. To maintain competitive momentum and to endure over time in a competitive market, organizations need to measure, assess and manage their strategic potential with incomparable efficacy.

Country-specific Factors

Evaluating country-specific factors such as the political system, the regulatory framework and the cultural variables, will help us assess the level of economic growth. Supposedly, the level of economic development of the country will be associated with a higher interest in strategic issues in IT management, and therefore investment and management of e-governments. Among the strategic issues in IT we can mention IT-based business process redesign, planning and managing telecommunications networks, improving information systems (IS) strategic planning, etc (Brancheau et al, 1996). On the other hand, issues such as the scarcity of qualified human resources and obsolescence of computing equipment are still of a great importance in under-developed countries (Palvia et al, 1992). Few countries, unlike the UAE, have developed very useful policies and adopted strategies to: (1) develop their indigenous workforce through training and education, and (2) attract talent from neighboring countries by facilitating the movement of skills into the country (Karake Shalhoub and Qasimi, 2003).

Political and regulatory factors in different countries also have an effect on key IT management issues such as the transformation into e-government. Chepaitis (1996) accentuates the problems caused by the effect of a political system that includes control and pressure by the authorities, poor public data stores and a lack of competitive market experience. The political and governance philosophy (socialism, capitalism, communism, democracy and dictatorship) affects therefore the conditions in which e-government is managed and developed (Palvia et al, 2002).

Differences in national cultures also play an important role in the success or failure of e-government initiatives. Hofstede (1980) has provided the basis for analyzing the cultural impact on key IT issues *including electronic governments*.[1] Hofstede defined four dimensions of national culture: individualism/collectivism, power distance, uncertainty avoidance, and masculinity-femininity. There are important precedents in the study of the effect of national culture on IT management. Nelson and Clark (1994) proposed a research agenda of the cross-cultural impact on managing information systems. Shore and Venkachalam (1995) analyzed differences in systems analysis and design related to culture. In other cases, the relationship between culture and technology acceptance (Kwon and Chidambaran, 1998) and between culture and group support systems adoption (Davison and Jordan, 1998) has been the object of analysis. This question is still a very open line of investigation, because other studies do not find a direct relationship between different national cultures and IS management issues.

Firm-specific Factors

The firm specific factors can also impose upon key IT management issues including the management of e-governments. Most information technology research has considered the type of industry a firm competes in as an independent variable (Palvia et al, 2002). The level of development, the composition and the objective of the IT portfolio can differ depending on the type of industry. Niederman et al (1991) studied the differences in IT management in manufacturing, service and non-profit organizations. Service and manufacturing firms seem to manage in a different manner some IS issues as has been suggested by Deans et al (1991). They found that computer integrated manufacturing, local cultural constraints and vendor support in foreign subsidiaries were more important for manufacturing companies. On the other hand, data security, data utilization, currency restrictions and exchange rate volatility were more important for service firms (Palvia et al, 2002).

Global strategies is the second firm specific element included in the study of Palvia et al (2002). Based on the model of Bartlett and Ghoshal (1989), it is possible to analyze the relationship between the four basic strategies of internationalization (multinational, global, international and transnational) and IT architecture. As Palvia et al (2002) point out, most previous work suggests aligning IT architectures strategies with each type of global business strategies is a critical success factor for global firms.

Global business and IT strategy is the fourth firm specific factor that can affect key IT issues. Several IT management issues may have an important impact on the firm strategy definition and implementation. The utilization of IT as a driver of the firm's strategy has been a topic in business management since the early 1980s (Parsons, 1983; Porter and Millar, 1985) and has been revisited in the 1990s (eg Henderson and Venkatraman, 1993). Given that IT can delimit the firm strategy, the global strategy of the firm can also be shaped by IT issues. The means of introduction and expansion in new markets or the defense strategies against external competitive pressures can be interrelated to IT utilization and development choices. As an example, some multinational firms use new logistics and commercialization electronic devices to quickly cut costs and therefore to oust national, non-technological competitors, from the markets in which they enter/participate.

Country-specific variables and firm-specific variables will be used in the next sections to explain the relationship between global issues and the main theoretical frameworks developed in IT general management.

RESOURCE-BASED VIEW AND GLOBAL ISSUES

The RBV (Wernerfelt, 1984) has been the dominant view in the development of the strategic approach in recent times (Hoskisson et al, 1999). According to the RBV, a firm that possesses a valuable, rare and difficult to imitate or substitute resource will achieve a sustainable competitive advantage. A large number of studies have related the creation of value by means of IT with the gaining and maintenance of competitive advantage (eg Powell and Dent-Micallef, 1997; Bharadwaj, 2000). The options for further study in this area consist of the identification of new resources complementary to IT, and the description of the conditions under which IT behaves as a valuable resource. Additionally, it would be useful to supplement the RBV with other approaches, such as the above-mentioned institutional theory (Selznick, 1957), or that of the appropriation of value by stakeholders (Coff, 1999). Despite this weakness, the RBV, complemented with the dynamic capabilities framework (Teece et al, 1997), can serve as a basis from which to explain the competitive impact of IT over a time period, an area with little empirical evidence so far.

The RBV has a number of points in common with other theoretical frameworks, like the upper echelon (Hambrick and Mason, 1984; Karake, 1995), knowledge management (Kogut and Zander, 1992; Nonaka, 1994) or the organizational stakeholders approach (Coff, 1999). Apart from the knowledge management view, which has already added significantly to the study of IT, the upper echelon and the stakeholders approach can be further developed in the future. The first (Pinsonneault and Kraemer, 1997; Pinsonneault and Rivard, 1998) may be able to explain the interrelation between the characteristics of management (age, previous experience, technological knowledge, and international experience) and the effective introduction of the new technologies. It should be noted that there is a strong parallel between this approach and the RBV because the personal and career characteristics of the executives can be resources that are valuable, scarce and difficult to imitate, and in combination with IT they may have a positive and lasting effect on competitive position. The second may be able to explain the situations in which IT generates value although the organization cannot take advantage of it in the form of income, benefits, or in general, increase in competitive advantage. In these cases there are certain powerful groups in the organization (stakeholders) that might absorb the resource's capacity for creation of value.

Other research questions arise if we consider approaches related to RBV, such as the knowledge management view (KBV) and the stakeholders view. First, more research is needed to fully understand the relationship between IT utilization and competitive advantage using knowledge management practices by the same firm in different parts of the world. As an example, firms that try to compete in new markets could find difficulties implementing knowledge sharing practices in countries with a high individualistic orientation. Secondly, the stakeholder approach can be used to explain specific situations in which branches of multinational firms that introduce a valuable IT-based system do not achieve better economic results. In these cases, the parent company might be appropriating the economic rents generated by the IT.

To turn the new elements of e-commerce technology and Internet information systems into competitive advantage, the firm must find some way to turn them into an invisible asset that other firms cannot easily copy (Barney, 1991). Yet the very nature of the e-commerce revolution, its openness and the ability of all players to access the new technologies, means that hard aspects alone are not going to be easily transformed into a competitive advantage for the firm. Customers may still benefit from lower costs and increased bargaining power, yet firms will have to find something extra if they are to find competitive advantage in these new technologies and systems. This can be found in the soft aspects of information management. Even if hard elements are easily accessible, two possible sources of competitive advantage remain: effective utilization of these hard technologies within the wider organization of the firm, and unique combinations of the soft organizational and hard systemic aspects of the e-commerce revolution.

When a firm does make use of these organizational skills, the resulting information flows are more likely to be an invisible asset than those based purely on IT or information systems (IS). These flows can be from the firm to its environment, from customers to the firm, and internally in the firm. Competitors cannot easily duplicate the 'experiences of working together'. These assets are not easily purchased in the market, and even when created within the firm, take time to develop. A firm that responds quickly to the challenge of new technologies and systems has an organization with an advantage in dealing with technological change.

Combinations of assets can often be used to set a firm's strategy apart from competitors' strategies (Itami and Roehl, 1987). Firms that might not have a single outstanding technology may still be able to create a portfolio of invisible assets that allows them to be competitive.

International business literature also addresses this issue. Mathews (2002) argues that firms from developing countries can still become multinationals by combining the skills and relationships available globally with a dynamic internal company organization. In the case of e-commerce, it is the combination of hard and soft elements that can produce a portfolio of assets that is hard for competitors to copy easily. Firms that combine the hard elements of e-commerce technology and systems effectively are likely to find themselves strongly positioned in the marketplace (see Globerman et al, 2001, for examples from electronic brokerage).

Systems for knowledge development work best when the firm has created an atmosphere in which organizational innovation can easily take place (Nonaka and Takeuchi, 1995). Thus, a firm that has taken the first step of establishing an organization that is able to create soft elements is also able to create new combinations of assets that further strengthen its position (Brynjolfsson and Hitt, 2000; Itami and Roehl, 1987).

Resource based view theory has shed light on the hidden side of the competitive assets: the soft, invisible, or intangible assets. They are at the heart of the key capabilities of the innovative firm (Christensen and Overdorf, 2000): for example, leadership and change management as resources, new knowledge creation as processes, and reciprocity and information sharing as values. Ideally, these assets should be created in the course of regular operations, since doing so reduces the cost of acquiring the assets and tests them against the day-to-day issues faced by all employees of the firm. Hard resources alone are often easily available to competitors, as Globerman et al (2001) have shown in the case of the electronic brokerage industry.

Nature and Categories of Resources

According to Wernerfelt (1984, p. 172), resources can include 'anything that might be thought of as a strength or weakness of a given firm' and so 'could be defined as those [tangible and intangible assets] which are tied semi permanently to the firm'. Resources are said to confer enduring competitive advantages to a firm to the extent that they are rare or hard to imitate, have no direct substitutes, and enable companies to pursue opportunities or avoid threats (Barney, 1991).

The last attribute is the most obvious: resources must have some value, some capacity to generate profits or prevent losses. However, if all other firms have them, resources will be unable to contribute to superior returns: their general availability will neutralize any special advantage. For the same reason, readily available substitutes for a resource will also nullify its value. Thus, resources must be difficult to create, buy, substitute, or imitate. This last point is central to the arguments of the RBV (Barney, 1991; Lippman and Rumelt, 1982; Peteraf, 1993). Unusual returns cannot be obtained when competitors can copy each other. Thus, the scope of this chapter will be limited strictly to non-imitable resources.

Clearly, there are many resources that may meet these criteria, albeit with differing effectiveness under different circumstances: important patents or copyrights, brand names, prime distribution locations, exclusive contracts for unique factors of production, subtle technical and creative talents, and skills at collaboration or coordination (Black and Boal, 1994).

There are a number of ways in which the resource-based view can be further developed. First, it may be useful to make some basic distinctions among the types of organizational resources that can generate unusual economic returns. By specifying the distinctive advantages of different types of resources, it may be possible to add precision to the research. Such distinctions will help avoid vague inferences that impute value to a firm's resources simply because it has performed well (cf. Black and Boal, 1994; Fiol, 1991).

Secondly, to complement its internal focus, the RBV needs to delineate the external environments in which different kinds of resources would be most productive. Just as contingency theory attempts to relate structures and strategies to the contexts in which they are most appropriate (Burns and Stalker, 1961; Thompson, 1967), so too must the RBV begin to consider the contexts within which various kinds of resources will have the best influence on performance (Amit and Schoemaker, 1993). According to Porter (1991, p. 108), 'Resources are only meaningful in the context of performing certain activities to achieve certain competitive advantages. The competitive value of resources can be enhanced or eliminated by changes in technology, competitor behavior, or buyer needs which an inward focus on resources will overlook'.

Thirdly, there is a need for more systematic empirical studies to examine the conceptual claims of the resource-based scholars. Such studies, although growing in number (cf. Henderson and Cockburn, 1994; McGrath et al, 1995; Montgomery and Wernerfelt,1988; Robins and Wiersema, 1995), remain too rare, perhaps because of the difficulties of pinning down the predictions of the RBV and even of operationally defining the notion of resources (Black and Boal, 1994; Fiol, 1991; Peteraf, 1993).

Several researchers have attempted to derive resource categorization schemes. Barney (1991) suggested that resources could be grouped into physical, human, and capital categories. Grant (1991) added to these financial, technological, and reputation creative resources. Although very useful for the purposes for which they were designed, these categorizations bear no direct relationship to Barney's (1991) initial criteria for utility, namely, value, rarity, difficulty of imitation, and unavailability of substitutes.

In this chapter, therefore, we revisit a pivotal one of these criteria – barriers to imitability – to develop our own typology.

Imitability may be an important predictor of performance as, indeed, it is a central argument of the RBV that a firm can obtain unusual returns only when other firms are unable to imitate its resources (Barney, 1991; Lippman and Rumelt, 1982). Otherwise these resources would be less rare or valuable, and substitutability would become irrelevant.

Property-based Versus Knowledge-based Resources

There appear to be two fundamentally different bases of nonimitability (Amit and Schoemaker, 1993; Hall, 1992, 1993; Lippman and Rumelt, 1982). Some resources cannot be imitated because they are protected by property rights, such as contracts, deeds of ownership, or patents. Other resources are protected by knowledge barriers – by the fact that competitors do not know how to imitate a firm's processes or skills.

Property rights control 'appropriable' resources: those that tie up a specific and well-defined asset (Barney, 1991). When a company has exclusive ownership of a valuable resource that cannot be legally imitated by rivals, it controls that resource. It can thereby obtain superior returns until the market changes to devalue the resource. Any rival wishing to obtain the resource will have to pay the discounted future value of its expected economic returns. Examples of property-based resources are enforceable long-term contracts that monopolize scarce factors of production, embody exclusive rights to a valuable technology, or tie up channels of distribution. Property-based resources apply to a specific product or process. Many such resources buffer an organization from competition by creating and protecting assets that are not available to rivals – at least not under equally favorable terms (Black and Boal, 1994, p. 134). Typically, it is only the fortunate or insightful firms that are able to gain control over valuable property-based resources before their full value is publicly known.

Most competitors will be aware of the value of a rival's property-based resources, and they may even have the knowledge to duplicate these resources. However, they either lack the legal right or the historical endowment to imitate successfully. Indeed, it might be argued that in order for property-based resources to generate unusual economic rents, they require protection from exclusionary legal contracts, trade restrictions, or first-mover pre-emption (Conner, 1991; Grant, 1991).

Many valuable resources are protected from imitation not by property rights but by knowledge barriers. They cannot be imitated by competitors because they are subtle, and hard to understand because they involve talents that are elusive and whose connection with results is difficult to discern

(Lippman and Rumelt, 1982). Knowledge-based resources often take the form of particular skills: technical, creative, and collaborative. For example, some firms have the technical and creative expertize to develop competitive products and market them successfully. Others may have the collaborative or integrative skills that help experts to work and learn together very effectively (Fiol, 1991; Hall, 1993; Itami, 1987; Lado and Wilson, 1994).

Knowledge-based resources allow organizations to succeed not by market control or by precluding competition, but by giving firms the skills to adapt their products to market needs and to deal with competitive challenges. Economic rents accrue to such skills in part because rivals are ignorant of why a firm is so successful. It is often hard to know, for example, what goes into a rival's creativity or teamwork that makes it so effective. Such resources may have what Lippman and Rumelt (1982) called 'uncertain imitability': they are protected from imitation not by legal or financial barriers, but by knowledge barriers. The protection of knowledge barriers is not perfect – it may be possible for competitors to develop similar knowledge and talent. However, this normally takes time, and by then, a firm may have gone on to develop its skills further and to learn to use them in different ways (Lado and Wilson, 1994).

The respective advantages of property-based and knowledge-based resources are quite different. Property rights allow a firm to control the resources it needs to gain a competitive edge. They may, for example, tie up advantageous sources of supply, keeping them out of competitors' hands. Such control of a specific asset, in effect, is the only source of value for property-based resources. Knowledge-based resources typically are better designed to respond and adapt to the challenges facing an organization. Creative skills, for instance, can be used to interpret customer desires and respond to developing market trends. Of course, property and knowledge-based resources are not always independent, as the latter may sometimes be used to develop or procure the former.

A key theme of this chapter is that the benefits of property-based resources are quite specific and fixed and thus, the resources are appropriate mostly for the environment for which they were developed. For example, a process patent ceases to have value when it has been superseded by a new process; a prized location becomes useless when customers move away. In short, a particular property right stops being valuable when the market no longer values the property. As a result, when the environment changes, property-based resources may lose their advantage. This is especially true if the environment alters in ways that could not have been predicted when the property was developed or acquired or when the fixed contract was made (Geroski and Vlassopoulos, 1991). Thus, an uncertain environment – one that is changing and unpredictable – is the enemy of property-based resources.

Knowledge-based resources, on the other hand, often tend to be less specific and more flexible. For example, a creative design team can invent products to meet an assortment of market needs. Such resources can help a firm respond to a larger number of contingencies (Lado and Wilson, 1994). Many knowledge-based resources are, in fact, designed to cope with environmental change. Unfortunately, these resources are not protected by law from imitation, and many are unduly expensive in predictable settings, where more routine but far cheaper response mechanisms can be equally effective. Also, in placid environments, a firm's knowledge may evolve so slowly as to be subject to imitation by rivals. In short, property-based resources will be of the greatest utility in stable or predictable environments, whereas knowledge-based resources will be most useful in uncertain, that is, changing and unpredictable, environments.

Some property-based resources are in the form of systems and their interwoven components; these typically include physical facilities or equipment. By themselves, most concrete facilities are easily imitable: thus, much of their value relies on their role within and their links to an integrated system whose synergy is hard to duplicate (Barney, 1991; Black and Boal, 1994). This is true of some integrated supply, manufacturing, and distribution systems. The units of a distribution network, for example, may be valuable because of their connection with a steady source of supply or with economies of administration and promotion engendered by a well-respected parent company (Barney, 1991; Brumagin, 1994).

In the case of systemic resources, managers do not aim to tie up more and more individual assets, but to enhance the range and comprehensiveness of a pre-existing system. Resources are added not to substitute for existing assets but rather, to strengthen a system or competence that is already in place. For example, one might acquire more distributors or outlets to bolster a distribution system (Lado et al, 1992). The more elaborate the system, the more market penetration it can provide, the more economically it can allocate marketing, administration, and even operating expenses, and the more it can make use of an established brand image or reputation.

Like discrete property-based resources, systemic resources will be more useful in predictable than in uncertain competitive environments. When an environment is predictable, it is easier to appraise the value of systems and to augment them in an orderly way with the aim of increasing the scope of market control. Predictability also allows a firm to determine the steps that it needs to take to fortify its system. Indeed, it is only when the environment is predictable and the existing system is secure, that it makes sense for a firm to develop that system.

When the environment is changing unpredictably, however, managers may be reluctant to build onto a system whose longevity is difficult to estimate or that is at risk of becoming obsolete. For example, if distribution technology changes unpredictably, one cannot build onto existing networks. In an uncertain environment in which clients' demands are ever-changing and hard to anticipate, most property-based systems are threatened with obsolescence (Wernerfelt and Karnani, 1987). Here the useful life of systemic resources may be short and hard to predict, and a firm may find itself controlling assets that generate little revenue (Geroski and Vlassospoulos, 1991).

To parallel our analysis of property-based resources, we examine both discrete and systemic knowledge-based resources (Black and Boal, 1994; Brumagin, 1994). Discrete knowledge-based resources may take the form of specific technical, functional, and creative skills (Itami, 1987; Winter, 1987). Such skills may be valuable because they are subject to uncertain imitability (Lippman and Rumelt, 1982). It is often hard to discern just what it is about these skills that generate economic returns or customer loyalty. Therefore, competitors do not know what to buy or imitate. This advantage is protected precisely because it is in some way ambiguous and mysterious, even to those who possess it (Lado and Wilson, 1994; Reed and De Fillippi, 1990). As with discrete property-based resources, firms can benefit from simultaneously developing as many of these knowledge resources as possible. For example, firms can at the same time pursue expertize in design, production, and marketing. Although unforeseeable changes in markets may render many property-based resources obsolete, knowledge-based resources such as unusual creative and technical skills may remain viable under varying conditions. Indeed, they may actually help a firm adapt its offerings to a changing environment (Wernerfelt and Karnani, 1987). Some creative skills are also quite flexible as they apply to different outputs and environments. This makes them especially useful in a changing, uncertain setting. For example, where the environment is particularly competitive and rivals are introducing many new offerings, the skills of experts who can adapt and create better products will be especially valuable. In a stable or predictable environment, firms may also benefit from discrete skills. However, these afford less effective, less efficient, and less secure advantages than do discrete property-based resources. Where a firm can enforce its legal property rights, it possesses almost perfect protection against imitation. This is not true of the protection given by knowledge, which can be lost, especially in stable settings in which knowledge and its application evolve more slowly and are thus easier to copy. Moreover, the high costs of retaining very talented employees may not produce much net benefit in stable contexts that do not demand the full exploitation of their unusual abilities.

Predictable settings do not typically call for as deep or extensive a set of skills for product or process innovation and adaptation as do uncertain and changing environments (Miller, 1988; Miller and Friesen, 1984).

Systemic knowledge-based resources may take the form of integrative or co-ordinative skills required for multidisciplinary teamwork (Fiol, 1991; Itami, 1987). Some organizations not only have a depth of technical, functional, and creative expertise but are also adept at integrating and co-ordinating that expertise. They invest in team-building and collaborative efforts that promote adaptation and flexibility. Indeed, it is not just skills in any one domain, but rather, the way skills from several domains complement one another in a team, that gives many firms their competitive advantage (Hall, 1993; Itami, 1987; Teece et al, 1990; Winter, 1987).

Collaborative skills are most subject to uncertain imitability (Hall, 1993; Peteraf, 1993, p. 183). According to Reed and De Fillippi (1990, p. 93), 'ambiguity may be derived from the complexity of skills and/or resource interactions within competencies and from interaction between competencies'. There is much subtlety in effective teamwork. The systemic nature of team and co-ordinative skills makes them especially firm-specific – more valuable to a firm than to its competitors (Dierickx and Cool, 1989, p. 1505). Team talents, therefore, are difficult for rivals to steal as they rely on the particular infrastructure, history, and collective experience of a specific organization.

Collaborative skills typically do not develop through programmed or routine activity. Instead, they require nurturing from a history of challenging product development projects. These long-term projects force specialists from different parts of an organization to work together intensively on a complex set of problems. Such interaction broadens both the technical and social knowledge of organizational actors and promotes ever more effective collaboration (Itami, 1987; Schmookler, 1966).

The above arguments suggest that team building is apt to be more necessary, more rewarding, and perhaps even more likely in uncertain than in predictable environments (Hall, 1993; Porter, 1985). Collaborative talents are robust, they apply to a wide variety of situations and products. In contrast with fixed routines, teamwork enables companies to handle complex and changing contingencies (Thompson, 1967). Moreover, 'unlike physical assets, competencies do not deteriorate as they are applied and shared. ... They grow' (Prahalad and Hamel, 1990, p. 82). Collaborative skills not only remain useful under changing environments, they also help firms to adapt and develop new products for evolving markets (Lawrence and Lorsch, 1967; Thompson, 1967). Indeed, the flexibility born of multifunctional collaboration will help firms to respond quickly to market changes and challenges (Mahoney and Pandian, 1992; Wernerfelt and Karnani, 1987).

In stable environments, on the other hand, the returns to collaborative and adaptive skills may be small. Where tasks are unvarying, co-ordination can be routinized very efficiently, and thus co-ordinative or team skills will be less important (Thompson, 1967). Moreover, when customer tastes and rivals' strategies are stable, there is little need to constantly redesign or adapt products. In such contexts, the most benefits of intensive collaboration may not justify the costs.

RESOURCE-BASED VIEW, STRATEGY AND ECONOMICS

The resource-based view approaches the firm as a historically determined collection of assets or resources which are tied semi-permanently to the firm's management (Wernerfelt, 1984). Some users of the resource-based view distinguish fully appropriable resources, such as physical capital or brand names, from less tangible assets, such as organizational routines and capabilities. Similarly, distinctions may be drawn between static and dynamic resources. The former are those that, once in place, may be considered to represent a stock of assets to be utilized as appropriate over a finite life. Dynamic resources may reside in capabilities, for example, such as an organization's capacity for learning, that generate additional opportunities over time. It is worth noting that the crucial requirements of the RBV are that the relevant resources, whatever their nature, are specific to the firm and not capable of easy imitation by rivals (Barney, 1991). Therefore, such resources constitute the source of Ricardian rents that comprize a firm's competitive advantage and, to the extent that their replication by others *is* problematic, imply a sustainable advantage over the longer term. Since each firm's resource bundle is unique, the consequence of its past managerial decisions and subsequent experience, it follows that so is each firm's opportunity set.

Thus it would appear that the RBV directly addresses issues that are of central interest to researchers in strategy and economics alike. Strategy may be considered as the process of determining, exploiting and developing the firm's opportunity set. Here the RBV would appear to offer direct insights. Economics is fundamentally concerned with the efficiency of resource allocation to productive users. This includes, or certainly should include, a consideration of the behavior of the firm, as the principal productive unit in capitalist economies, as well as comparative institutional assessments of alternative configurations of economic activity (eg vertical integration versus out-sourcing, franchising versus ownership, etc). Here we would contend that the RBV offers important insights into the delineation of appropriate boundaries of the firm and hence for firm performance and economic organization. However, when we compare *explicit* interest in the RBV across the disciplines of strategy and economics there is a clear and obvious asymmetry. In strategy the RBV has been highly influential. Hoskisson et al (1999) point out that from the 1960s, until the late 1980s, the subject was dominated by consideration of external (ie product market) sources of competitive advantage. This reflected the influence of structure–conduct performance (SCP) work, in general, and the particular success of Michael Porter (1980, 1985) in synthesizing this in a strategy context. Hoskisson et al (1999) suggest that the growing popularity of the RBV since the late 1980s has refocused attention on internal sources of competitive advantage.

In the economics journals, by contrast, explicit references to the RBV are scarce. A citation search, covering 165 economics journals, revealed that only a very small proportion of cites of the leading RBV papers occurs in the economics literature. For example, in not one of the key papers by Wernerfelt (1984), Barney (1991) and Conner (1991) did the proportion of citations in the economics literature rise above 5 percent. Restricting attention to the ten leading 'core' influential economics journals, following Stigler et al (1995), produces an even bleaker picture with a total of three citations.

However, a concentration on the lack of explicit attention given to the RBV in economics conceals the very considerable influence that has been achieved by many of the ideas that underpin it. The same contributions that informed the architects of the RBV, particularly those of Penrose (1959), Richardson (1972) and Teece (1980) who at the time of these publications would have been considered mainstream economists, have received much greater attention in the economics literature than the subsequent RBV papers. Papers published by these authors appear to have helped economists trained in the neo-classical tradition to accept the importance of path-dependency in firm evolution. The result is that over the last decade or so, a period corresponding to the diffusion of the RBV in strategy, there has been a very substantial output of applied economics research that has sought to explain firm decision-making and firm performance in a context in which history matters. Firm behavior is typically modeled as a consequence of existing firm-level attributes, many of which (eg size, diversification, vertical integration, market and technological experience, etc) may be considered as proxies for the firm-specific assets discussed by proponents of the RBV.

This growing economic literature on the importance of path-dependency in firm development is reviewed below. That it has largely bypassed any explicit consideration of the RBV does not, in our opinion, invalidate the conclusion that its findings provide a systematic body of evidence that is both largely supportive of the predictions of the RBV and, as such, worthy of the interest of strategy scholars. That is not to say, of course, that many of the papers reviewed would not have benefited from insights drawn from the RBV. This point is developed below.

RESOURCE-BASED VIEW AND NEW INSTITUTIONAL ECONOMICS

As stated by North (1990), the new institutional economics is an attempt to incorporate a theory of institutions into economics. However, in contrast to the many earlier attempts to topple or take the place of neo-classical theory, the new institutional economics builds on, amends, and broadens neo-classical theory to allow it to come to grips and deal with an entire range of issues beyond its domain. What it maintains and builds on is the fundamental assumption of scarcity and hence competition. What it leaves behind is instrumental rationality – the assumption of neo-classical economics that has made it an institution-free theory. Institutions are formed to reduce uncertainty in human exchange. Together with the technology utilized they determine the costs of transacting. Coase (1937) made the central connection between institutions, transaction costs and neo-classical theory. As he stated, 'the neo-classical result of efficient markets only obtains when it is costless to transact; when it is costly to transact, institutions matter'. As a large part of an economy's income is devoted to transacting, institutions and specifically property rights are crucial determinants of the efficiency of markets.

Practically, there is still a tendency for resource-based theory and the branches of 'new institutional economics' to be used in isolation from one another. For example, much research in financial economics still assumes away firm heterogeneity, except perhaps for industry membership, and concentrates upon the agency problem, while some strategy research ignores agency considerations as belonging to a lower level or strategy implementation dimension. This division is far from universal and it was seen above that the analysis of corporate refocusing issues has drawn liberally upon both traditions. However, one consequence of the bifurcation is the relative neglect of governance-RBV interactions. It was noted earlier that the internal governance devices adopted by the firm (the composition of its board, the control systems covering its divisional management, etc) do not merely have implications for the level of agency costs, but have implication for the optimal configuration of the firm's activities.

The firm's governance mechanisms (both internal and external) are to be considered as a relevant resource. For example, in the United States or in the United Kingdom these could include the skills of the non-executive directors, and in Germany could include the firm's interlocking directorships with suppliers and customers and its banker relationships (Cable and Dirrheimer, 1983). Similarly, the firm's set of transactional arrangements with suppliers and customers is not simply a cost-minimizing device, in terms of transaction cost economics (TCE), but a resource that may yield competitive advantage. In general, this suggests that firms may need to secure an appropriate fit between the set of activities undertaken and the governance mechanisms and transactional arrangements in place. For example, external factors, such as the debt-equity funding mix and the extent of equity ownership concentration may influence the optimal mix of activities (Demsetz and Lehn, 1985). Similarly, internal factors, including the choice between strategic and financial control systems, may determine the appropriate extent of diversification.

The authors share the view that in the beginning stages of market development, institutional theory is unmatched in illuminating the impact on government strategies. This is because government and societal pressures are stronger in developing economies than in developed countries. Institutional theory underlines the influences of the social and organizational behavior of organizations. These systems might be internal or external to the company, and they do affect organization's processes and decision making. Perspectives derived to examine these institutional pressures have both an economic orientation and a sociological orientation. This new theory focuses on the interaction of institutions and organizations resulting from market imperfections (Harris et. al, 1995). North (1990) maintains that institutions provide the rules of the game that shape interactions in societies and that economic entities are the players constrained by those rules (formal and informal). The role of institutions in an economy is to reduce information costs and information asymmetry through minimizing uncertainty and crafting a stable structure that facilitates interactions. Palmer et al (1993) examined the institutional constraints on American corporations in developing countries.

The authors tested the institutional, political, and economic accounts of adoption of the multidivisional form (MDF) among large US industrial corporations in the 1960s, most notably by elaborating the institutional account. Their results suggested that institutional processes, including coercive and normative dynamics, substantially underpinned the MDF's diffusion during the 1960s. Firms producing in industries that shunned the MDF earlier in the twentieth century were slow to adopt this form in the 1960s, an effect mediated by the percentage of firms in a corporation's sector using the MDF at the time. Firms with high debt-to-equity ratios, whose chief executives had elite business school degrees, and whose directors had non-directional corporate board contracts with the directors of MDF firms adopted the MDF more frequently than other firms. Peng and Heath (1996) argued that the internal growth of transition economies is limited by institutional constraints. As a result, it was concluded that a network-based growth strategy was more appropriate in developing economies. Child and Lu (1996) maintained that economic reform of large state-owned enterprises was moving very slowly because of relational and cultural constraints. Following the same rationale, Suhomlinova (1999) found that government institutions had a negative impact on Russian enterprize reform. In a study of Chinese enterprises, Lau (1998) concluded that market and political forces were the institutional constraints that hindered the effective functioning of chief executive officers in these enterprises. Many firms in developing and emerging economies are influenced by existing institutional mechanisms and realities.

From a strategic perspective, institutions can also facilitate the process of strategy formulation, alignment, and implementation. Enterprizes can play a more active role in an institutional environment when these institutional mechanisms allow them to manoeuvre and move beyond imposed constraints. A number of studies dealing with institutional effects on developing countries focus mostly on state-owned enterprises.

In 1996, Lee and Miller studied the changes of institutional mechanisms and their impact on firms in various industries in Korea. They found that firms benefited to various degrees from a number of institutional and cultural changes in the country. Soulsby and Clark (1996) showed how institutional changes in the Czech Republic have led to a revamping of how managers think about and do their jobs in terms of acquiring new strategic thinking skills and other managerial techniques which are more appropriate to their new semi-open market environment. In an earlier article, Jefferson and Rawski (1995) concluded that the success of industrial reform in China was attributed to relaxing institutional constraints, market-leaning institutional change, development of property rights, and gradual relaxation of state ownership and control. In the case of China, these institutional changes provided appropriate incentives and the necessary changes in corporate culture that motivated firms and enabled them to take steps forward.

The number of studies using resource-based and institutional perspectives in developing economies is scarce, even though some theorists have argued that these perspectives are the most applicable for explaining economic behavior in developing economies. Characterized by trends towards market liberalization and privatization but still heavily regulated, developing and emerging economies provide the necessary institutional and resource influences in testing the theories.

THE RESOURCE-BASED VIEW AND DEVELOPING ECONOMIES

Until recently, little research using a RBV framework has examined strategy differences in the social context of developing economies. As with most resources that create competitive advantage, resources for competitive advantage in developing economies are, on the whole, intangible. However, they are not necessarily market or product specific, as might be expected. Although some qualifications are standard regardless of the level of development (for instance, first mover advantages), others are particularly important in developing economies. Global and multinational firms that are able to manage some of the imperfect conditions in developing economies benefit from being first movers; some of the benefits include economic advantages of sales volume. In general, many of the developing countries use the economics of the free market as the primary engine for growth. Hoskisson et al. (2000) investigated two groups of emerging and developing countries: (1) the developing countries in Asia, Latin America, Africa and the Middle East; and (2) the transition countries in the former Soviet Union and China. Both private and public enterprizes have had to take different paths and use different strategies in dealing with the two distinct groups of developing countries. The research has examined the different strategies and implementation paths used by private and public businesses from a number of theoretical perspectives. One of these perspectives is the RBV of the firm.

In most developing and emerging economies, the post-colonial period saw the materialization of a state-centric form of governance, especially due to the lack of private capital and the absence of sophisticated market forces. More significantly, the role of the state expanded a great deal as a result of governments' national developmental agendas in these countries. Furthermore, many economic entities were brought under the management of the state through gigantic nationalization programs in order to end foreign economic dominance (cases in point are Egypt and Algeria). These programs brought with them immediate needs for basic services such as education and health that had to be provided by government in the absence of private sector initiatives (Haque, 2002). In fact, most of these initiatives were often supported by international aid agencies prior to the 1980s. However, since the early 1980s the mode of governance has changed in developing and emerging countries. This is due to the impact of globalization demanding the substitution of state agencies market oriented-driven mechanisms supported by economic policies and institutions under a new political economy model.

In responding to the new political economy, developing and emerging governments have attempted to reduce the range of public governance through various measures such as privatization, deregulation, and downsizing, and to restructure its functions by emphasizing the state's role as a facilitator while assigning the main role to the private sector (Haque, 2002). For instance, as a result of pressure from international agencies such as the World Bank and the International Monetary Fund, gigantic privatization and deregulation initiatives have been undertaken in most Asian, African, and Latin American countries. Some of the well-known examples include Argentina, Brazil, Chile, Indonesia, Malaysia, Mexico, Nigeria, Pakistan, the Philippines, South Korea, and Thailand. In these countries different approaches to privatization have been adopted in major sectors such as telecommunications, airlines, electricity, petroleum, automobiles, television, fertilizer, tobacco, banking, insurance, etc (Haque, 1999).

This unparalleled process of privatization has significantly reduced the state's economic control in these countries. In addition, most governments have also taken initiatives to directly downsize the public sector to create greater avenues for the private sector. As a case in point, and under the influence of the World Bank and the Asian Development Bank, Malaysia has implemented measures to downsize the public sector, the Philippines has adopted the strategy of 'streamlining the bureaucracy' to reduce staff by 5–10 percent, Singapore has applied a zero manpower growth policy in order to ultimately reduce the number of public employees by 10 percent, and Thailand has put on hold new employment (Haque, 2002). Similarly, India has decided to downsize the public sector by reducing public employment by 30 percent, and Sri Lanka has introduced an early retirement policy and retrenched thousands of government employees (Haque, 2001). In Latin America, governments have elected to reduce or freeze public sector employment in cases such as Argentina, Bolivia, Brazil, and Mexico. A recent study shows that between the early 1980s and 1990s, as a percentage of total population, the number of central government employees decreased from 2.6 to 1.1 percent in Asia, 1.8 to 1.1 percent in Africa, and 2.4 to 1.5 percent in Latin America (Schiavo-Campo, 1998, p. 465).

These downsizing exercises express the growing tendency of developing and emerging economies to reorganize public governance in line with the overall agenda for its diminishing role in socioeconomic activities. In recent years, the governments in India, Malaysia, Pakistan, Singapore, Sri Lanka, and Thailand have de-emphasized the role of public bureaucracy as the primary actor in socioeconomic development, redefining its role to facilitate or enable the business sector to take more active initiatives to deliver services (Haque, 2002). According to the World Bank (1996), in Arab countries like Algeria and Jordan the recent structural adjustment programs have led to a greater role for private enterprizes and investors, while the public sector has to enable rather than constrain such enterprizes and investors. The overall objective of this restructuring of the role of public governance vis-à-vis business sector management has been to reduce the prominence of interventionist states and to expand the sphere of national and global market forces.

In line with the assumption of the new political economy, there have emerged a number of reform initiatives to restructure the organization and management of public governance based on the experiences of the private sector. The trends are toward commercializing government entities, adopting corporate practices, managing public agencies like private companies, and forming partnerships with business enterprizes (Haque, 2001). These worldwide trends in restructuring governance can be observed today in many Asian, African, and Latin American countries.

More specifically, various government ministries and departments have been converted into businesslike 'autonomous agencies' enjoying considerable operational autonomy in financial, personnel, and administrative matters. Following the examples of developed nations, many developing and emerging countries have introduced these structural changes in governance. In South Asia, Pakistan has introduced such a structure in specific sectors such as railway, telephone, and rural energy. In Southeast Asia, Singapore has introduced the most complete program to convert almost all government departments into autonomous agencies based on a comprehensive restructuring of the budget and personnel systems. In various degrees, managerial autonomy in governance has also emerged in Indonesia, Malaysia, the Philippines, and Thailand. These new structural movements in governance represent an unmatched shift from the traditional bureaucratic model practiced in developing countries.

In addition to these internal restructuring initiatives, there are external structural changes, especially in terms of increasing partnership between the public and private sectors. In embarking on new projects, initiating new policies, and delivering services, such public–private partnership or alliance has expanded in Asian countries like India, Indonesia, Malaysia, Pakistan, the Philippines, Singapore, Thailand, and Vietnam, although this deeper public-private alliance often creates potential for conflict of interest between public agencies and business firms (Haque, 2001). The number of joint ventures has also increased in various African and Latin American countries like Argentina, Mexico, and South Africa. The above businesslike restructuring of public agencies and expansion of public–private collaboration imply diminishing boundaries between the public and private sectors.

E-COMMERCE AS A SOURCE OF RADICAL TECHNOLOGY

The worldwide trends of globalization, deregulation, technical evolution, and market liberalization are restructuring markets and challenging traditional approaches to gaining competitive advantage (Chakravarthy, 1997; Hamel 2000). It is becoming harder for firms to retain a competitive advantage based on physical or financial assets, or even on a new technology, as competitors with access to the same open market conditions can easily acquire similar assets and technologies, and even leapfrog to newer technologies. Consequently, firms need to concentrate on developing distinctive capabilities that are more difficult for competitors to imitate (Barney, 1997; Wernerfelt, 1984). Such development has become the focus of attention not only among academics, but also among business consultants, journalists, government officials, and business leaders (Miyazaki, 1995).

A prevailing paradigm for understanding how and why firms gain and sustain competitive advantage is the resource-based view of the firm (Mahoney and Pandian, 1992; Schendel, 1994). From this perspective, capabilities and resources enable firms to conceive and implement strategies to generate above-normal rates of return (Barney, 1997; Dierickx and Cool, 1989). Sustainable competitive advantage is viewed as the outcome of discretionary rational managerial choices, selective capability accumulation and deployment, strategic industry factors, and factor market imperfections. Notwithstanding its important insights, the existing literature has concentrated on explaining the exploitation of existing firm-specific capabilities and on the attributes of firm resources (eg, their rarity, uniqueness, difficulty-to-copy, or non-substitutability).

The emergence of pervasive digital networks, especially the public Internet, has created business opportunities in both established and emerging sectors of the economy. Firms that have embraced these digital networks – net-enabled organizations (Straub and Watson, 2001) – can execute transactions, rapidly exchange information, and innovate through new business processes at an unprecedented pace (Weill and Vitale, 2001). Net-enabled organizations (NEOs) have new channels for accessing customers, real-time integration with supply chain partners, new efficiencies in internal operations, and offer new digital products or services. These net-enabled business innovations, which are the first step in an organization-wide process of net-enablement (NE), require timely and ongoing reconfiguration of firm resources.

Opportunities for NE are also creating a strategic and tactical quagmire for many firms. They struggle to assimilate the rapid pace of innovation in IT and the emerging business practices they make possible. It is in this context that business leaders must often make defensive and offensive strategic investments in new NE business practices before a credible measurement of prior investments can be ascertained (Sambamurthy, 2000; Sambamurthy et al, 2003).

At face value, some firms seem to be better at managing and executing NE business innovation than other firms. Some firms with outstanding brands in the physical world have net-enabled their products and services to the delight of their customers, while other great brands have suffered from tardy and dismal efforts at NE. Our research question asks, are there measurable, organizational capabilities that comprize the ongoing work of net-enablement? If so, what are these capabilities? Do these capabilities distinguish successful NEOs from less successful organizations?

The need for NE (and the development of NEOs) is most visible in hypercompetitive environments. Hypercompetitive industries are characterized by rapid changes in technology, relative ease of entry and exit by rivals, ambiguous consumer demands, and fleeting periods of competitive advantage (Bogner and Barr, 2000). Others refer to similar market dynamism as 'high velocity markets' where successful business models and industry structure are unclear (Eisenhardt and Martin, 2000). These competitive conditions fuel a demand for innovation and speed while digital networks offer both speed and an opportunity for innovating (Sambamurthy et al, 2003). Both require firms to develop reliable capabilities for continual IT innovation for competitive necessity and to exploit short-term competitive advantage.

The utility of NE is also applicable in non-hypercompetitive environments. Even mature industries, where competitive advantage may still flow from industry position or ownership of unique resources, are subject to opportunities, new efficiencies, or even competitive threats posed by digital networks. Net-enablement can provide new growth opportunities or establish defensive positions with customers and suppliers. Firms can preemptively become NEOs even though they do not currently experience the pace of competitive change in hypercompetitive environments. Alternatively, they may use a series of net-enabled innovations to erode the existing basis of long-term competitive advantage while they reap a series of imitable, short-term gains.

The dominant business configuration for NEOs is a network, web, or hub connected via IT. Suppliers, customers, complementors, and alliance partners engage in 'coopetition' as they collaborate via alliances and compete via coalitions (Brandenburger and Stuart, 1996; Moore, 1996; Mitchell and Singh, 1996; Afuah, 2003). As firms become net-enabled, their competitive advantage may rest on tacit, inimitable collaborative relationships as a network or hub with its coopetitors. These coopetitors provide a critical source of innovations (Allen, 1977; von Hippel, 1988; Ahujah, 1996), knowledge transfer (Kogut, 1988), complementary products (Grove, 1996), and critical resources (Brower, 1970) for collectively garnering competitive advantage as a network of resources or complementary competencies. We believe that participation in these network relationships provides greater potential to lead in net-enabled business innovation.

CONCLUSION

This chapter was dedicated to the coverage of the resource-based theory. The central questions addressed by the RBV deal with why firms and economies differ and how they achieve and sustain competitive advantage. It has been argued that heterogeneous competences give economic entities their unique characters and are the fundamental nature of competitive advantage.

For our purpose, resources are based in an environment, and depending on the characteristics of that environment, focusing on one resource or another could create strategic (dis)advantage which might lead to positive (negative) outcomes. Few scholars analyzed the issue of an economic entities' sustainable advantage in terms of resource-based and institutional factors and suggested that entities are able to create or develop institutional capital to enhance optimal use of resources (Oliver, 1997). Consequently, economic entities have to manage the social context of their resources and capabilities in order to be profitable.

Research using resource-based theory and examining macro strategy difference in the social context of developing economies is absent. Similar to most resources that create competitive advantage at the micro level, resources for competitive advantage at the macro level in developing economies are mainly intangible. Although some capabilities are standards across all economies (for example, first mover advantage), others are particularly significant in developing economies (Hoskisson et al, 2000). The economic literature has paid attention to the revenue-generating promises of developing economies, and as such, has focused, mainly, on big developing and emerging economies such as China, India, and Russia. Firms which are able to manage the discouraging environments in developing economies grab hold of the benefits of first-mover advantages. In developing economies, however, such advantages are very difficult to come by without good institutional infrastructure. Consequently, it is essential to understand the relationship between economic success (failure) and the changing nature of the institutional environment.

NOTE

1. Italics are the authors'.

REFERENCES

Afuah, A.N. (2003), *Innovation Management: Strategies, Implementation, and Profits*, London: Oxford University Press.

Ahujah, G. (1996), 'Collaborations and innovation: a longitudinal study of inter firm linkages and firm patenting performance in the global advanced material industry', dissertation, University of Michigan.

Allen, T.J. (1997), *Managing the Flow of Technology*, Cambridge, MA: MIT Press.

Amit, R. and P. Schoemaker (1993), 'Strategic assets and organizational rent', *Strategic Management Journal* **14**, 33–46.

Ansoff, H.I. (1965), *Corporate Strategy*, New York: McGraw-Hill.

Argyris, N. (1996), 'Evidence on the role of firm capabilities in vertical integration decisions', *Strategic Management Journal*, **17**, 129–50.

Barney, J.B. (1986), 'Strategic factor market: expectation, luck and business strategy', *Management Science* 32(10), 1231–41.

Barney, J.B. (1991), 'Firm resources and sustained competitive advantage', *Journal of Management* **17**(1), 99–120.

Barney, J.B. (1992), 'Integrating organizational behavior and strategy formulation research: a resource based analysis', in P. Shrivastiva, A. Huff and J. Dutton (eds), *Advances in Strategic Management*, **8**, Greenwich, CT: JAI Press, pp. 39–62.

Barney, J.B. (1997), *Gaining and Sustaining Competitive Advantage*, Reading, MA: Addison-Wesley.

Barney, J.B. (2001), 'Is the resource-based "view" a useful perspective for strategic management research? Yes', *Academy of Management Review* **26**(1), 41–56.

Barney, J.B. (2002), *Gaining and Sustaining Competitive Advantage*, 2nd edn, Upper Saddle River, NJ: Prentice Hall.

Barney, J.B. and E.J. Zajac (1994), 'Competitive organizational behavior: towards an organizationally-based theory of competitive advantages', *Strategic Management Journal* **15**, 5–9.

Bartlett, C.A. and S. Ghoshal (1989), *Managing Across Borders: The Transnational Solution*, Cambridge, MA: Harvard Business School Press.

Bharadwaj, A.S. (2000), 'A resource-based perspective on information technology capability and firm performance', *MIS Quarterly* **24**(1), 169–98.

Black, J.A. and K.B. Boal (1994), 'Strategic resources: traits, configurations and paths to sustainable competitive advantage', *Strategic Management Journal* **15**, 131–48.

Bogner, W.C. and P.S. Barr (2000), 'Making sense in hypercompetitive environments: a cognitive explanation of high velocity competition', *Organizational Science*, **11**(2) (March–April), 212–26.

Bogner, W.C. and H. Thomas (1994), 'Core competence and competitive advantage: a model and illustrated evidence from the pharmaceutical industry', in G. Hamel and A. Heene (eds), *Competence-based competition*, New York: Wiley, pp. 111–44.

Bowman, C. and V. Ambrosini (2000), 'Value creation versus value capture: towards a coherent definition of value in strategy', *British Journal of Management*, **11**, 1–15.

Brancheau, J.C., B.D. Janz and J.C. Wetherbe (1996), 'Key issues in information systems: 1994–1995 SIM Delphi results', *Management Information Systems Quarterly*, **20**(2), 225–42.

Brandenberger, Adam and Harborne Stuart (1996), 'Value-based business strategy', *Journal of Economics and Management Strategy*, 5(1), 5–24.

Brower, J. (1970), *Managing the Resources Allocation Process*, Boston, MA: Harvard University Press.

Brown, S.L. and K.M. Eisenhardt (1997), 'The art of continuous change: linking complexity theory and time-paced evolution in relentlessly shifting organizations', *Administration Science Quarterly*, **42** 1–34.

Brown, S.L. and K.M. Eisenhardt (1998), *Competing on the Edge: Strategy as Structured Chaos*, Boston, MA: Harvard Business School Press.

Brumagin, A.L. (1994), 'A hierarchy of corporate resources', in P. Shrivastava and A. Huff (eds), *Advances in Strategic Management*, vol 10A, Greenwich, CT: JAI Press, pp. 81–112.

Burns, T. and G. Stalker (1961), *The Management of Innovation*, London: Tavistock.

Cable, J. and M. Dirrheimer (1983), 'Hierarchies and markets: an empirical test of the multidivisional hypothesis in West Germany', *International Journal of Industrial Organization* **1** (1), 43–62.

Castanias, R.P. and C.E. Helfat (1991), 'Managerial resources and rents', *Journal of Management* **17**, 155–71.

Chandler, A. (1990), Scale and Scope: the Dynamics of Industrial Capitalism, Cambridge, MA: Harvard University Press.

Chakravarthy, Bala (1997), 'A new strategy framework for coping with turbulence', *Sloan Management Review*, **38**(2), 69.

Chatterjee, S. and B. Wernerfelt (1991), 'The link between resources and type of diversification: theory and practice, *Strategic Management Journal* **12**, 33–48.

Chepaitis, E.V. (1996), 'The problem of data quality in a developing country', in P. Palvia, S. Palvia, and E.M. Roche (eds), *Global Information Technology and Systems Management*, Nashua, NH: Ivy League Publishing, pp. 104–22.

Child, J. and Y. Lu (1996), 'Institutional constraints on economic reform: the case of investment decisions in China', *Organization Science* **7**, 60–67.

Christensen, C.M. and M. Overdorf (2000), 'Meeting the challenge of disruptive change', *Harvard Business Review*, (March–April), pp. 67–76.

Coase, R.H. (1937), 'The nature of the firm', *Economica* **4**, 386–405.

Coff, R.W. (1999), 'When competitive advantage doesn't lead to performance: the resource-based view and stakeholder bargaining power', *Organization Science* **10**(2), 119–33.

Cohen, W.M. and D.A. Levinthal (1990), 'Absorptive capacity: a new perspective on learning and innovation', *Administration Science Quarterly*, **35**, 128–52.

Collis, D.J. (1991), 'A resource-based analysis of global competition: the case of the bearings industry', *Strategic Management Journal* **12** (summer special issue), 49–68.

Collis, D.J. (1994), 'How valuable are organizational capabilities?', *Strategic Management Journal* **15** (winter special issue), 143–52.

Conner, Kathleen R. (1991), 'A historical comparison of resource-based theory and five schools of thought within industrial Organization Theory: do we have a new theory of the firm', *Journal of Management* **17**(1), 121–55.

D'Aveni, R.A. (1994), *Hypercompetition: Managing the Dynamics of Strategic Manoeuvering*, New York: The Free Press.

D'Aveni, Richard (1999), 'Strategic supremacy through disruption and dominance', *Sloan Management Review* **40**(3), 127–36.

Davison, E. and E. Jordan (1998), 'Group support systems: barriers to adoption in a cross-cultural setting', *Journal of Global Information Technology Management*, **1**(2), pp. 37–50.

Deans, P.C., Karwan, K.R., Goslar, M.D., Ricks, D.A. and Toyne, B. (1991), 'Identification of key international information systems issues in US based multinational corporations', *Journal of Management Information Systems* **7**(4), pp. 27–50.

Demsetz H. and K. Lehn (1985), ,The structure of ownership: causes and consequences', *Journal of Political Economy*, **93**, 1155–77.

Dierickx, Ingemar and Karel Cool (1989), 'Asset stock accumulation and sustainability of competitive advantage', *Management Science* **35**(12) 1504–11.

Dyer, J.H. and H. Singh (1998), 'The relational view: cooperative strategy and sources of interorganizational competitive advantage', *Academy of Management Review*, **23**, 66–79.

Eisenhardt, Kathleen M. and Jeffrey A. Martin (2000), 'Dynamic Capabilities: what are they?', *Strategic Management Journal* **21**(10/11), 110–21.

Fiol, C.M. (1991), 'Managing culture as a competitive resource', *Journal of Management* **17**, 191–211.

Foster, R. and S. Kaplan (2001), *Creative Destruction: Why Companies That Are Built to Last Under Perform the Market – and How to Successfully Transform Them*, New York: Doubleday.

Geroski, P. and T. Vlassopoulos (1991), 'The rise and fall of a market leader', *Strategic Management Journal* **12**, 467–78.

Ghemawat, P. and J. Costa (1993), 'The organizational tension between static and dynamic efficiency', *Strategic Management Journal*, (winter special issue), 59–73.

Globerman, S., T.W. Roehl and S. Standifird (2001), 'Globalization and electronic commerce: inferences from retail brokerage', *Journal of International Business Studies* **32**, 749–68.

Grant, R.M. (1991), 'The resource-based theory of competitive advantage: implications for strategy formulation', *California Management Review* **33**(3), 114–35.

Grove, A.S. (1996), *Only the Paranoid Survive*, New York: Doubleday.

Gruca, T. and D. Nath (1994), 'Regulatory change, constraints on adaptation, and organizational failure: an empirical analysis of acute care hospitals', *Strategic Management Journal* **15**, 345–63.

Hall, R. (1992), 'The strategic analysis of intangible resources', *Strategic Management Journal* **13**, 135–44.

Hall, R. (1993), 'A framework linking intangible resources and capabilities to sustainable competitive advantage', *Strategic Management Journal* **14**, 607–18.

Hambrick, D.C. and S. Finkelstein (1987), 'Managerial discretion: a bridge between polar views of organizational outcomes', in L.L. Cummings and B. Staw (eds), *Research in Organizational Behavior* **9**, Greenwich, CT: JAI Press, pp. 369–406.

Hambrick, D.C. and P.A. Mason (1984), 'Upper echelons: the organization as a reflection of its managers', *Academy of Management Review*, **9**, 193–206.

Hamel, G. (2000), *Leading the Revolution*, Boston, MA: Harvard Business School Press.

Hamel, G. and A. Heene (1994), *Competence-based Competition*, New York: Wiley.

Hamel, G. and C.K. Prahalad (1994), *Competing for the Future*, Boston: Harvard Business School Press.

Hansen, G.S. and B. Wernerfelt (1989), 'Determinants of firm performance: the relative importance of economic and organizational factors', *Strategic Management Journal* **10**, 399–411.

Haque, M.S. (1999), 'Globalization of market ideology and its impact on Third World development', in A. Kouzmin and A. Hayne (eds), *Essays in Economic Globalization, Transnational Policies and Vulnerability*, Amsterdam: IOS Press, pp. 75–100.

Haque, M. Shamsul (2001), 'Recent transition in governance in South Asia: contents, dimensions and implications', *International Journal of Public Administration*, **24**(12), 1405–36.

Haque, M.S. (2002), 'Globalization, new political economy, and governance: a Third World view', *Administrative Theory & Praxis* **24**(1), 103–24.

Harris, J., J. Hunter and C.M. Lewis (1995), *The New Institutional Economics and Third World Development*, London: Routledge.

Hartmann, R.S. and D.J. Teece (1990), 'Product emulation strategies in the presence of reputation effects and network externalities: some evidence from the minicomputer industry', *Economics of Innovation and New Technology*, **1**(2), 157–82.

Heene, A. and R. Sanchez (eds) (1997), *Competence Based Strategic Management*, Chichester, England: Wiley.

Henderson, R.M. (1994), 'The evolution of integrative capability: innovation in cardiovascular drug discovery', *Industrial and Corporate Change*, **3**, 607–30.

Henderson, J. and N. Venkatraman (1993), 'Strategic alignment: leveraging information technology for transforming organizations', *IBM Systems Journal* **32**, 4–16.

Henderson, R. and I. Cockburn (1994), 'Measuring competence: exploring firm-effects in pharmaceutical research', *Strategic Management Journal* **15**, 63–84.

von Hippel, E. (1988), *The Sources of Innovations*, London: Oxford Unoversity Press.

Hofstede, G.H. (1980), *Culture's Consequences: Comparing Values, Behaviours, Institutions, and Organizations across Nations*, Thousands Oaks, Ca: Sage.

Hoskisson, R.E., M.A. Hitt, W.P. Wan and D. Yiu (1999), 'Theory and research in strategic management: swings of a pendulum', *Journal of Management* **25**(3), 417–56.

Hoskisson, Robert R, Lorraine Eden, Chung Ming Lau and Mike Wright (2000), 'Strategy in emerging economies', *Academy of Management Journal* **43**(3), 249–68.

Iansiti, M. and K.B. Clark (1994), 'Integration and dynamic capability: evidence from product development in automobiles and mainframe computers', *Industrial and Corporate Change* **3**, 557–605.

Ijiri, Y. and H. Simon (1977), *Skew Distributions and the Size of Business Firms*, New York: North Holland.

Itami, H. and T. Numagami (1992), 'Dynamic interactions between strategy and technology', *Strategic Management Journal* **13**, 119–35.

Itami, H. (1987), *Managing Invisible Assets*, Cambridge, MA: Harvard University Press.

Itami, H. and T. Roehl (1987), *Mobilizing Invisible Assets*, Boston: Harvard University Press.

Itami, H. and T. Numagami (1992), 'Dynamic interactions between strategy and technology', *Strategic Management Journal* **13**, 119–35.

Jefferson, G.H. and T.G. Rawski (1995), 'How industrial reform worked in China: the role of innovation, competition and property rights', in *Proceedings of the World Bank Annual Conference on Development Economics*, Washington, DC: World Bank, pp. 129–56.

Johnson, N.B., R.B. Sambharya and P. Bobko (1989), 'Deregulation, business strategy, and wages in the airline industry', *Industrial Relations* **28**, 419–30.

Karake Shalhoub, Z. and L. Al Qasimi (2003), *The UAE and Information Society*, ESCWA report, Beirut, Lebanon: United Nations.

Kelly, D. and Amburgey, T.L. (1991), 'Organizational inertia and momentum: a dynamic model of strategic change', *Academy of Management Journal* **34**, 591–612.

Khosrow-Pour, M. (2004), *The Social and Cognitive Impacts of E-Commerce on Modern Organizations*, Hershey, PA: Idea Group Publishing.

Kirzner, I.M. (1979), *Perception, Opportunity, and Profit*, Chicago: University of Chicago Press.

Kogut, B. (1988), 'Joint ventures: theoretical and empirical perspectgive', *Strategic Management Journal*, **9**(4), 319–32.

Kogut, B. and U. Zander (1992), 'Knowledge of the firm, combinate capabilities, and the replication of technology', *Organization Science* **3**(3), 383–97.

Kraatz, M.S. and E.J. Zajac (1997), 'Resource heterogeneity and its effects on strategic change and performance in turbulent environments', working paper, University of Illinois at Urbana-Champaign.

Kwon, H.S. and A. Chidambaran (1998), 'A cross cultural study of communication technology acceptance: comparison of celular phone adoption in South Korea and in the United States', *Journal of Global Information Technology Management*, **1**(3), 43–58.

Lado, A.A. and M.C. Wilson (1994), 'Human resource systems and sustained competitive advantage: a competency-based perspective', *Academy of Management Review* **19**, 699–727.

Lado, A.A., N.G. Boyd and S.C. Hanlon (1997), 'Competition, cooperation, and the search for economic rents: a syncretic model', *Academy of Management Review* **22**, 110–41.

Lado, A.A., N.G. Boyd and P. Wright (1992), 'A competency model of sustained competitive advantage', *Journal of Management* **18**, 77–91.

Lau, C.M. (1998), 'Strategic orientations of chief executives in state-owned enterprises in transition', in M.A. Hitt, J.E. Ricart, I. Costa and R.D. Nixon (eds), *Managing Strategically in an Interconnected World*, Chichester: Wiley, pp. 101–17.

Lawrence, P. and J. Lorsch (1967), *Organization and Environment*, Boston: Harvard University Press.

Levinthal, D. and J. Myatt (1994), 'Co-evolution of capabilities and industry: the evolution of mutual fund processing', *Strategic Management Journal* **15**, 45–62.

Lippman, S.A. and R.P. Rumelt (1982), 'Uncertain irritability: an analysis of interfirm differences in efficiency under competition', *Bell Journal of Economics* **13**, 418–38.

Mahoney, J.T. and J. Pandian (1992), 'The resource-based view within the conversation of strategic management', *Strategic Management Journal* **13**, 363–80.

Mathews, J. (2002), *Dragon Multinational: A New Model for Global Growth*, Oxford: Oxford University Press.

McGrath, R.G., I.C. MacMillan and S. Venkatraman (1995), 'Defining and developing competence: a strategic process paradigm', *Strategic Management Journal* **16**, 251–75.

Miller, D. (1988), 'Relating Porter's business strategies to environment and structure', *Academy of Management Journal* **31**, 280–309.

Miller, D. and P.H. Friesen (1984), *Organizations: A Quantum View*, Englewood Cliffs, NJ: Prentice-Hall.

Mitchell, Will and K. Singh (1996), 'Business survival of firms using hybrid relationships in the American hospital software systems industry, 1961–1991', *Strategic Management Journal*, **17**(3), 169–95.

Miyazaki, K. (1995), *Building Competencies of the Firm*, London: Macmillan.

Montgomery, C.A. (1995), 'Of diamonds and rust: a new look at resources', in C.A. Montgomery (ed.), *Resource-based and Evolutionary Theories of the Firm: Towards a Synthesis*, Boston: Kluwer Academic, pp. 251–68.

Montgomery, C.A. and S. Hariharan (1991), 'Diversified entry by established firms', *Journal of Economic Behavior and Organization* **15**, 71–89.

Montgomery, C.A. and B. Wernerfelt (1988), 'Diversification, Ricardian rents, and Tobin's q', *Rand Journal of Economics* **19**, 623–32.

Moore, James F. (1996), *The Death of Competition: Leadership and Strategy in the Age of Business Ecosystems*, New York: HarperCollins.

Morris, R.L. (1964), *The Economic Theory of 'Managerial' Capitalism*, New York: Free Press.

Nelson, K.G. and T.D. Clark Jr (1994), 'Cross-cultural issues in information systems research: a research program', *Journal of Global Information Management*, **2**(4), 19–28.

Nelson, R.R. and S.G. Winter (1982), *An Evolutionary Theory of Economic Change*, Cambridge: Belknap Press.

Niederman, F., J.C. Brancheau and J.C. Wetherbe (1991), 'Information systems management issues for the 1990's', *MIS Quarterly* **17**(4), 475–500.

Nonaka, I. (1994), 'A dynamic theory of organizational knowledge creation', *Organization Science* **5**(1), 14–37.

Nonaka, I. and H. Takeuchi (1995), *The Knowledge-creating Company*, New York: Oxford University Press.

North, D. (1990), *Institutions, Institutional Change and Economic Performance*, New York: Cambridge University Press.

Oliver, C. (1997), 'Sustainable competitive advantage: combining institutional and resource based views', *Strategic Management Journal* **18**, 697–713.

Palmer, D.A., P.D. Jennings and X. Zhou (1993), 'Late adoption of the multidivisional form by US corporations: institutional, political, and economic accounts', *Administrative Science Quarterly* **38**, 100–31.

Palvia, P., S. Palvia and R.M. Zigli (1992), 'Global information technology environment: key MIS issues in advanced and less developed nations', in S. Palvia, P. Palvia and R.M. Zigli (eds), *The Global Issues of Information Technology Management*, Harrisburg, PA: Idea Group Publishing.

Palvia, P.C., S.C.J. Palvia and J.E. Whitworth (2002), 'Global information technology: a meta analysis of key issues', *Information and Management* **39**, 403–14.

Parsons, G.L. (1983), 'Information technology: a new competitive weapon', *Sloan Management Review*, Fall, 3–14.

Peng, M.W. and P.S. Heath (1996), 'The growth of the firm in planned economies in transition: institutions, organizations, and strategic choice', *Academy of Management Review* **21**, 492–528.

Penrose, Edith (1959), *The Theory of Growth of the Firm*, New York: Wiley.

Peteraf, Margaret (1993), 'The cornerstone of competitive advantage: a resource-based view', *Strategic Management Journal* **14**(3), (March), 179–91.

Pinsonneault, A. and K.L. Kraemer (1997), 'Middle management downsizing: an empirical investigation of the impact of information technology', *Management Science* **43**, 659–79.

Pinsonneault, A. and S. Rivard (1998), 'Information Technology and the nature of managerial work: from the productivity paradox to the icarus paradox', *MIS Quarterly* (September), 287–311.

Porter, M.E. (1980), *Competitive Strategy*, New York: Free Press.

Porter, M.E. (1985), *Competitive Advantage*, New York: Free Press.

Porter, M. (1991), 'Towards a dynamic theory of strategy', *Strategic Management Journal* **12**, 95–117.

Porter, M. (1996), 'What is strategy?' *Harvard Business Review* **74** 61–78.

Porter, M. and V. Millar (1985), 'How information gives you competitive advantage', *Harvard Business Review*, **63**, 149–60.

Powell, T.C. and A. Dent-Micallef (1997): 'Information technology as competitive advantage: the role of human, business and technology resources', *Strategic Management Journal* **5**(18), 375–405.

Prahalad, C.K. and G. Hamel (1990), 'The core competence of the corporation', *Harvard Business Review* **68**(3), 79–91.

Priem, R.L. and J.E. Butler (2001), 'Tautology in the resource-based view and the implications of externally determined resource value: further comments', *Academy of Management Review* **26**, 57–66.

Rawski, Thomas G. (1995), 'Implications of China's Reform Experience', *China Quarterly* **144**, 1150–73.

Reed, R. and R.J. DeFillippi (1990), 'Causal ambiguity, barriers to imitation, and sustainable competitive advantage', *Academy of Management Review* **15**, 88–102.

Richardson, G.B. (1972), 'The organization of industry', *Economic Journal* **82**, 883–96.

Robins, J.A. and Wiersema, M.F. (1995), 'A resource-based approach to the multi-business firm: empirical analysis of portfolio interrelationships and corporate financial performance', *Strategic Management Journal* **16**, 277–99.

Rubin, P.H. (1973), 'The expansion of firms', *Journal of Political Economy* **81**, 936–49.

Rumelt, R.P. (1987), 'Theory, strategy, and entrepreneurship', in D.J. Teece (ed.), *The Competitive Challenge: Strategies for Industrial Innovation and Renewal*, Cambridge, MA: Ballinger, pp. 137–58.

Sambamurthy, V. (2000), 'The organizing logic for an enterprise's IT activities in the digital era: a prognosis of practice and a call for research', *Information Systems Research*, **11**(2), 105–14.

Sambamurthy, V., A. Bharadwaj and V. Grover (2003), 'Shaping agility through digital options: reconceptualizing the role of IT in contemporary firms', *MIS Quarterly*, **27**(2), 237–63.

Sanchez, R., A. Heene and H. Thomas (1996), *Dynamics of Competence Based Competition*, Oxford: Elsevier Press.

Schendel, D. (1994), 'Introduction to competitive organizational behaviour: toward an organizationally based theory of competitive advantage', *Strategic Management Journal*, **13**(5), 363–80.

Schiavo-Campo, S. (1998), 'Government employment and pay: the global and regional evidence', *Public Administration and Development* **18**, 457–78.

Schmookler, J. (1966), *Invention and Economic Growth*, Cambridge MA: Harvard University Press.

Schumpeter, J.A. (1934), *The Theory of Economic Development*, Cambridge, MA: Harvard University Press.

Schumpeter, J.A. (1942), *Capitalism and Democracy*, Cambridge, MA: Harvard University Press.

Selznick, P. (1957), *Leadership in Administration: A Sociological Interpretation*, New York: Harper and Row Publishers.

Sen, A. (1999), *Development as Freedom*, Oxford: Oxford University Press.

Shen, T.Y. (1970), 'Economies of scale, Penrose-effect, growth of plants and their size distribution', *Journal of Political Economy* **78**, 702–16.

Shore, B. and A.R. Venkachalam (1995), 'The role of national culture on systems analysis and design', *Journal of Global Information Management* **3**(3), 5–14.

Slater, M. (1980), 'The managerial limitations to the growth of firms', *Economic Journal* **90**, 520–28.

Smith, K.G. and C.M. Grimm (1987), 'Environment variation, strategic change and firm performance: a study of railroad deregulation', *Strategic Management Journal* **8**, 363–76.

Soulsby, A. and E. Clark (1996), 'The emergence of post-Communist management in the Czech Republic', *Organization Studies* **17**(2), 227–47.

Stigler, G.J., S.M. Stigler and C. Frieland (1995), 'The journals of economics', *Journal of Political Economy* **103**(2), 331–59.

Straub, D.W. and R.T. Watson (2001), 'Research commentary: transformational issues in researching IS and net-abled organizations', *Information Systems Research*, **12**(4) (December), 337–45.

Suhomlinova, O. (1999), 'Constructive destruction: transformation of Russian state-owned construction enterprises during market transition', *Organization Studies* **20**(3), 451–84.

Teece, D.J. (1980), 'Economies of scope and the scope of the enterprise', *Journal of Economic Behavior and Organization* **1**, 223–47.

Teece, D.J. and G. Pisano (1994), 'The dynamic capabilities of firms: an introduction', *Industrial and Corporate Change* **3**, 537–56.

Teece, D., G. Pisano and A. Shuen (1997), 'Dynamic capabilities and strategic management', *Strategic Management Journal* **18**, 509–33.

Thompson, J.D. (1967), *Organizations in Action*, New York: McGraw-Hill.

United Nations Conference on Trade and Development (UNCTAD) (2003), *E-commerce and Development Report*, New York: United Nations.

Weill, P. and M.R. Vitale (2001), *Place to Space: Migrating to Ebusiness Models*, Boston, MA: Harvard Business School Press.

Wernerfelt, Birger (1984), 'A resource-based view of the firm', *Strategic Management Journal* **5**, 171–80.

Wernerfelt, B. and A. Karnani (1987), 'Competitive strategy under uncertainty', *Strategic Management Journal* **8**, 187–94.

Winter, S. (1987), 'Knowledge and competence as strategic assets', in D. Teece (ed.), *The Competitive Challenge*, Boston: Harvard Business School Press, pp. 159–84.

World Bank (1996), *World Bank Annual Report 1996*, Washington, DC: International Bank for Reconstruction and Development.

World Bank (2000), *Attacking Poverty: World Bank Report*, Washington, DC: World Bank.

4. Methodology and development of hypotheses

INTRODUCTION

The resource-based view (RBV) of the firm argues that the performance of an economic entity is, *inter alia*, a function of the resources and skills that are in place, and, of those economic entity-specific characteristics which are rare and difficult to imitate or substitute. This concept is in essence based on Coase's theory of the firm which maintains that the firm is a combination of alliances that have linked themselves in such a way as to reduce the cost of producing goods and services for delivery to the marketplace (Coase, 1937). An enhancement of this RBV is that an economy can create a competitive advantage by building resources that work together to generate organizational and country-based capabilities (Bharadwaj, 2000). These capabilities permit economic entities and economies as a whole to adopt and adapt processes that enable them to realize a greater level of output from a given input or, maintain their level of output from a lower quantity of input.

In this chapter we will develop a set of hypotheses with the objective of conducting a systematic cross-country analysis of electronic commerce (e-commerce) and electronic government (e-government) activities in a sample of developing and emerging economies. The overall premise, and based on resource-based theory, is that in addition to the physical infrastructure which explains much of the variation in basic Internet use and country electronic readiness, e-commerce and e-government activities also depend significantly on a supportive institutional environment such as national respect for the 'rule of law', the availability of credible payment channels such as credit cards, the support of top leadership, and the existence of cyberlaw, etc.

Despite its widely cited potential to transform global economies, e-commerce is, as yet, predominantly a North American phenomenon. Estimates vary, but it is generally accepted that more than 75 percent of online transactions are confined within the United States borders. The slow development of e-commerce in other countries is paradoxical, given the intuitive appeal of the notion that the digital age brings with it the 'death of distance' (Cairncross, 1997). In addition, some developing and emerging economies such as the United Arab Emirates, Singapore and Bahrain have done much better than others in digitizing their e-commerce. While this puzzle has been the subject of much speculation, systematic analysis is sparse. In particular, to our knowledge, there has been little empirical analysis of the conditions necessary for the development of viable online markets in developing countries.

In general, research on information technology (IT) and e-commerce impact on the economy in terms of productivity and business value can be classified into two categories: (1) the production–economics-based approach and (2) the process-oriented approach (Barua and Mukhopadhyay, 2000). The production–economics-based approach employs production functions to examine the relationship between output events and production inputs such as IT and non-IT classified capital and labor. Notwithstanding the many years of debate on the contested 'productivity paradox', several researchers were able to estimate production functions and to find a, somehow, positive relationship between investment in IT, including investment in e-commerce technology, and productivity. These findings were supported by several other studies and prompted a large stream of literature in this area (Brynjolfsson and Yang, 1996). As Hitt and Brynjolfsson (1996) point out, while the theory of production envisages that lower prices for IT will generate benefits in the form of lower production costs for a given level of output, it is unclear on the question of whether economic entities will raise its performance advantages in terms of supra-normal profitability.

The process-oriented approach aims at explaining the process through which IT investments improve intermediate operational performance, which in turn may affect higher levels of financial performance. An early study by Mukhopadhyay et al (1995) assessed the business value of electronic data interchange (EDI) in a manufacturing setting. Their findings indicate that EDI facilitated the effective use of information to systematize material movements between manufacturers and their suppliers, which resulted in considerable cost savings and inventory cutback. As an inter-organizational information system, EDI has some features in common with Internet-based initiatives, but it also shows signs of important differences as EDI is, by and large, a more expensive, proprietary technology under the control of one large manufacturer or supplier. In contrast, Internet technologies may induce large-scale variations within an organization as well as in its dealings with customers and suppliers. It is important to note that most of these studies were carried out before the extensive use of the Internet, and as such they logically did not include variables associated with Internet initiatives and e-commerce capabilities.

A promising framework for enhancing the theoretical basis of e-commerce value is the RBV of the economy, which links economic performance to economic and organizational resources and capabilities. Economic entities create performance advantages by assembling resources that work together to create added capabilities (Penrose, 1959; Peteraf, 1993; Wernerfelt, 1984). To create sustainable advantages, these resources, or resource combinations, would have to be economically valuable, relatively scarce, difficult to imitate, or imperfectly mobile across economic entities (Barney, 1991). Resources can be combined and integrated into unique clusters that enable distinctive abilities within an economic entity firm (Teece et al, 1997).

In the information systems literature, the RBV has been used to explain how firms can create competitive value from IT assets, and how sustainability resides more in the available skills to leverage IT than in the technology itself. Information technology payoffs depend heavily on how the various IT resources work together in creating synergy. Computers, databases, technical platforms, and communication networks form the core of an entity's overall IT infrastructure resources. Although the individual components that go into the IT infrastructure are commodity-like, the process of integrating the components to develop an integrative infrastructure tailored to a firm's strategic context is complex and imperfectly understood (Milgrom and Roberts, 1990; Weill and Broadbent, 1998).

The RBV has been extended with the dynamic capabilities perspective (DCP) to tackle the practicality of unstable markets and swift technological change. The DCP refers to the ability of a firm to achieve new forms of competitive advantage by renewing technological, organizational, and managerial resources to *fit* with the changing business environment (Teece et al, 1997; Eisenhardt and Martin, 2000). In this environment, capabilities that enable rapid and purposeful reconfiguration of a firm's resources are the means through which both industry position and timely unique resources can be obtained. This model implies that dynamic capabilities are essentially change-oriented capabilities that help economic entities reconfigure their resource base to meet growing customer demands and competitor strategies.

The ability to anticipate technological change and adopt the appropriate strategies may create a path of growth that would generate a performance advantage (Teece et al, 1997). Resources are dynamic because the economic entities are continually building, adapting, and reconfiguring internal and external competences to attain congruence with the changing business environment when the rate of technological change is rapid, time-to-market is critical, and the nature of future competition and markets are difficult to determine (Teece et al, 1997). Dynamic capabilities create resource configurations that generate value-creating strategies (Eisenhardt and Martin, 2000). Consistent with DCP, e-commerce can be considered to be a dynamic capability. Internet-enhanced organizations continually reconfigure their internal and external resources to employ digital networks to exploit business opportunities. Thus, Internet-enhanced organizations exemplify the characteristics of dynamic capabilities as they engage routines, prior and emergent knowledge, analytic processes, and simple rules to turn IT into customer value (Bharadwaj et al, 2000; Sambamurthy et al, 2001; Wheeler 2002).

As this book seeks to extend the IT value literature to the domain of Internet-enabled e-commerce and e-government initiatives in developing countries, it is natural to ask if Internet initiatives are different from pre-Internet technologies (eg, personal computer (PC), mainframe, legacy systems). In fact, the economic characteristics of the Internet are significantly different from those of pre-Internet computer technologies. The Internet is unique in terms of connectivity, interactivity and open-standard network integration (Kauffman and Walden, 2001; Shapiro and Varian, 1999). These characteristics have very different bearings on customer reach and richness of information. Prior to the Internet, firms often used stand-alone, proprietary technologies to communicate inadequate data. It was difficult and/or costly for a firm to relate to its customers, suppliers, and business partners. In contrast, the Internet facilitates a two-way, real-time information exchange between a firm and its customers and suppliers.

Given these unique potentials of the Internet, many countries have adopted e-commerce as a strategy for growth and development. Yet, the way that e-commerce is ingrained in business processes differ from one country to another. In fact, it is how economic entities leverage their investments to generate unique Internet-enabled resources and entity-specific competence that determine overall effectiveness of e-commerce. Economic entities, in the public or private sectors, benefit from the Internet when they embed e-commerce capability in their fabric in a way that creates sustainable resource synergy. For instance, the integration of e-commerce capability and IT infrastructure may improve connectivity, compatibility, and responsiveness of an economic unit at the micro level, which results in better efficiency and lower costs at the macro level.

The connectivity and open-standard data exchange of the Internet may help remove incompatibility of the legacy information systems. A mainframe-based legacy IT system (such as EDI) that only marginally improves performance under ordinary conditions may produce substantial advantages when combined with the Internet. The Internet's greater connectivity allows for more direct interaction with customers and tighter data sharing with suppliers. Internet-based e-commerce can be adopted to enhance traditional IT systems in many ways. For example, using Web-based, graphical interface to improve the user-friendliness of enterprize resource planning (ERP) systems, implementing Internet-based middleware to make EDI-connections more flexible and affordable for smaller businesses, connecting various legacy databases by common Internet protocol and open standard, using XML-based communication to increase the ability of exchanging invoice and payment documents online between companies, and analyzing online data to better understand customer demand.

Based on the above, it is vital to concentrate on resource synergy as a promising path to e-commerce and e-government effectiveness. The RBV provides a solid theoretical foundation for studying the contexts and conditions under which e-commerce and Internet-based economies may produce more productivity and performance improvements in emerging and developing economies. Particularly, it directs us toward a well-adjusted and stable position, one that recognizes the commodity view of the technology per se, while permitting the possibility of synergetic associations arising from combining the capabilities of e-commerce, other IT infrastructure and other resources.

Unarguably, the most significant impediment to the development of e-commerce in many developing countries is the lack of necessary physical infrastructure, particularly household access to PCs and a cost-effective telecommunications system. However, indications from New Institutional Economics (NIE) support the notion that we should look beyond these immediate indicators to examine how the institutional environment in a country contributes to (or undermines) confidence in a new market such as e-commerce/e-government and supports private investment in the new medium. Empirical evidence has revealed that the integrity of the institutional environment, particularly with respect to the 'rule of law', is important for the development of e-commerce and e-government. Only in such an environment can participants in electronic transactions have confidence in satisfactory performance, or adequate legal recourse should the transaction break down.

Research done by Oxley and Yeung (2001) discusses the issue of transactional reliability in online markets and explores the role of institutions in supporting the growth of e-commerce. The authors develop an analytical framework for cross-country comparisons of the environment for e-commerce, focusing on both the direct facilitators of growth – such as physical infrastructure – and on the underlying, intangible features of the institutional environment.

Based on the above, it is fair to assume that capabilities afforded by information communication technology (ICT) are one major component of economies' capabilities, and recent studies have identified a number of specific ICT capabilities that provide competitive advantage. Bharadwaj (2000) classifies an entity's key ICT capability as comprising (1) a physical IT infrastructure, (2) human IT resources (including technical IT skills, and managerial IT skills), and (3) IT technology-enabled resources (such as, customer orientation, knowledge assets, and synergy). We add to these other intangible factors such as those identified by Oxley and Yeung, above.

THE NATURE OF RESOURCES

As stated in Chapter 3 and according to Wernerfelt (1984, p. 172), resources can include 'anything that might be thought of as a strength or weakness of a given firm' and so 'could be defined as those [tangible and intangible assets] which are tied semi permanently to the firm'. Applying Wernerfelt ideas to the setting of a developing country, resources are said to give long-term competitive advantages to a country to the extent that they are rare or hard to imitate, have no direct substitutes, and enable economic entities to pursue opportunities or avoid threats (Barney, 1991). However, if all other economic entities have those resources, they will be unable to contribute to superior returns, and their general availability will defuse any special advantage. Thus, resources must be difficult to create, buy, substitute, or imitate. This last point is central to the arguments of the RBV (Barney, 1991; Lippman and Rumelt, 1982; Peteraf, 1993).

Evidently, there are many resources that may satisfy these criteria, though with differing effectiveness under different circumstances: important patents or copyrights, brand names, prime distribution locations, exclusive contracts for unique factors of production, subtle technical and creative talents, and skills at collaboration or co-ordination (Black and Boal, 1994).

There are a number of directions in which the RBV can be directed, when applied to developing economies. Of paramount importance is to make some fundamental distinctions among the different categories of resources that can produce unusual economic returns. In addition, to supplement its internal focus, the RBV needs to define the external environments in which various resources would be largely beneficial (Burns and Stalker, 1961; Thompson, 1967). In addition, the RBV must start to consider the circumstances within which various kinds of resources will have the best influence on performance (Amit and Schoemaker, 1993). According to Porter (1991, p. 108), 'Resources are only meaningful in the context of performing certain activities to achieve certain competitive advantage. The competitive value of resources can be enhanced or eliminated by changes in technology, competitor behavior, or buyer needs which an inward focus on resources will overlook'.

Based on the resource-based theory literature, resources can be thought of in two broad categories: property-based and knowledge-based resources. Property-based resources are tangible (land, building, equipment, machinery, etc.), while knowledge-based resources are intangible (skills, competences, experience, relationships, alliances, intra-organizational structures and systems).

A number of researchers have attempted to classify resources based on various criteria and schematic frameworks. Barney (1991) argued that resources could be classified as physical, human, and capital. Grant (1991) added to the classification list financial, technological, and reputation-based resources. Other researchers revisited some of these initial criteria to come up with new typologies.

As stated above, a pivotal criterion in resource based theory is barriers to the imitation of resources. Some resources cannot be imitated because they are protected by property rights, such as contracts, deeds of ownership, or patents. Other resources are protected by knowledge barriers preventing competitors from imitating an entity's processes or skills.

Property rights deal with the control of resources that bind a specific and well-defined asset (Barney, 1991). When an entity has exclusive ownership of a precious resource that cannot be legally imitated by competitors, it controls that resource. It can in that way acquire higher returns until conditions change to bring down the value of the resource. Any competitor desiring to have a hold of the resource will have to pay the discounted future value of its expected economic returns (Barney, 1991). Enforceable long-term contracts that monopolize scarce factors of production embody exclusive rights to a valuable technology, or tie up channels of distribution are examples of property-based resources. Such resources shield an organization from competition by creating and protecting assets that are not available to competitors or would-be competitors (Black and Boal, 1994).

Most rivals will be conscious of the value of a competitors's property-based resources, and they may even have the knowledge to replicate these resources, but they do not have the legal right to imitate them successfully. In fact, one might make the case that in order for property-based resources to generate unusual economic return, they require protection from exclusionary legal contracts, trade restrictions, or first-mover preemption (Conner, 1991; Grant, 1991).

Property rights resources are protected from imitation by property rights and knowledge-based resources are protected from imitation by knowledge barriers. These resources cannot be duplicated because they are, to a large degree, unique and hard to understand since they require talents that are elusive and whose connection with results is difficult to determine (Lippman and Rumelt, 1982). Knowledge-based resources often take the form of specific skills, including technical, creative, and collaborative. They allow organizations to flourish not by preventing competition, but by providing entities with the skills to adapt their products to market needs and to deal with competitive challenges. It is important to point out here that the protection of knowledge barriers is not absolute; it may be possible for others to develop similar knowledge and talent, but this usually takes time, and by then, a firm may have gone on to develop its skills further and to learn to use them in distinct ways (Lado and Wilson, 1994).

In addition to property-based and knowledge-based resources, insights from the NIE suggest that we should look beyond these direct indicators to look into how the institutional environment in a country contributes to (or damages) confidence in a new market and supports private investment in the new means. Not only institutional physical resources, but knowledge resources are important determinants of how successful e-commerce and e-government can be applied in a developing economy.

The New Institutional Economics is an attempt to integrate a theory of institutions into economics. However in contrast to the many earlier attempts to overturn or replace neo-classical theory, the new institutional economics builds on, transforms, and extends neo- classical theory to allow it to deal with a host of issues beyond its knowledge. What it maintains and builds on is the basic assumption of scarcity. What it discards is instrumental rationality. New Institutional Economics views economics as a theory of choice subject to constraints; it makes use of price theory as a crucial part of the analysis of institutions.

INSTITUTIONAL ENVIRONMENT

It is likely that e-commerce will be among the most powerful transmission mechanisms through which technology-induced change will spread across many developing and emerging countries. The application of ICT to, for instance, health or education can certainly contribute to the achievement of basic development objectives and can, in the long term, lead to productivity increases. However, the upward movement of economic growth that e-commerce can bring about would probably result in a more immediate and sustainable contribution to the reduction of poverty and economic progress, one of the Millennium Goals specified by the United Nations (UN).

Addressing the comparatively low levels of productivity in a large number of developing countries, the adoption of e-commerce in these countries can yield particularly to large relative improvements in productivity. In most cases, these gains are not derived directly from the technology itself but through incremental improvements resulting from organizational changes in the production process that are made possible (or indispensable) by the technology. An encouraging factor is that e-commerce seems to be spreading in a number of developing countries faster than was the case in previous technological revolutions. To grease the wheels of e-commerce and e-government and facilitate their spread, the institutional environment in developing and emerging economies has to be favorable.

According to Davis and North (1971, pp. 6–7), the institutional environment is '[that] set of fundamental political, social and legal ground rules that establishes the basis for production, exchange and distribution. Rules governing elections, property rights and the right of contract are examples'. There is now an established tradition of research within NIE connecting characteristics of the institutional environment to the extent and nature of private investment. Some of this work has examined the impact of general characteristics of the nation-state (eg Levy and Spiller, 1996; Henisz and Zelner Bennet, 2001), while others have focused on specific aspects of the legal or regulatory environment (eg Oxley, 1999).

An important question that needs to be addressed is what aspects of the institutional environment are most important for promoting transactional integrity in e-commerce, and hence in supporting investment in these new markets? From an institutional perspective, and based on past research, this question can be analyzed from the following key features:

(1) the overall integrity of the nation's legal system, related to the degree to which the economy is governed by the rule of law;
(2) the credibility of payment channels available to e-commerce participants, which in turn is a function of the country's financial institutions and regulations, and the existence of a law that governs e-commerce transactions; ie cyberlaw.

Developing and emerging countries can profit from the opportunities provided by e-commerce for exploiting competitive advantages not achievable in the 'old economy'. E-commerce gives small- and medium-size enterprises (SMEs) the ability to access international markets that used to be difficult to enter due to high transaction costs and other market access barriers. Labor intensive services can now be delivered online, providing new opportunities for developing countries with relatively cheap labor. The emergence of successful industries such as software development or tele-servicing in several countries is an example of this. Thanks to e-commerce, entrepreneurs in developing countries can also access cheaper, better-quality trade-related services (for instance, finance or business information), thus escaping local de facto monopolies. Finally, e-commerce can stimulate growth in developing countries by helping to improve the transparency of the operation of markets and public institutions. For instance, by simplifying business procedures, e-commerce not only reduces the cost for businesses of complying with domestic and international trade-related regulations, but also reduces the cost of corruption, a burden that often most severely affects the SMEs and other weaker players in the economy.

For all these promising benefits to happen, a number of institutional measures and mechanisms are required in order to create an enabling environment for e-commerce, and address areas such as infrastructure, applications, payments systems, human resources, the legal framework, taxation, etc.

The following analysis of e-commerce and e-government success in a cross-section of developing countries should prove that not only physical infrastructure measures are most important in explaining variations in basic e-commerce adoption and Internet use, but also intangible institutional measures that are critical to the success of e-commerce. This chapter will examine the degree of dependence of e-commerce and e-government success on the strengths of a number of institutional, knowledge-based, and physical resources.

In the following sections, we will cover four indicators developed by different agencies to measure a country's IT and e-commerce readiness. These are the information society index (ISI), the e-government index, the economic freedom index, and the networked readiness index. We then move to the development of hypotheses and summarize the chapter with a concluding section. Operational measurements, data collection, statistical methods, and data analysis will be covered in Chapter 5, in addition to empirical findings.

Information Society Index

The Information Society Index is the world's first measure of 55 nations' abilities to participate in the information revolution. It provides government planners, global IT and telecommunications corporations, and global asset management firms with the data and analysis required for measuring progress toward a digital society, assessing market opportunities, and developing policies.

The 2003 World Times/IDC Information Society Index (ISI) measures the global impact of IT and Internet adoption rate in 55 countries around the world. These 55 countries navigating the Information Superhighway account for 98 percent of all IT investment around the world. The ISI establishes a standard by which all nations are measured according to their ability to access and absorb information and information technology. While gross domestic product (GDP) measures economic wealth, ISI measures information capacity and wealth. The ISI is designed to help countries assess their position relative to other countries and to guide companies to future market opportunities. To develop the ISI index, countries are evaluated on 23 variables in four different categories: computer infrastructure, information infrastructure, Internet infrastructure, and social infrastructure (IDC, 2004).

In the seventh annual ISI, Sweden kept its lead for 4 years in a row and surpassed countries such as the US in its information-society sophistication. Prepared by World Times and the International Data Corporation, ISI 2003 reveals that, in digital terms, the rich countries are getting richer while the poor are too, but that digital divides between groups of societies will eventually grow larger and larger. While all societies are benefiting from the information revolution's rising tide, they are advancing at rates as far apart as the oceans are wide. The ISI divides the 55 countries into four groups: Skaters, Striders, Sprinters and Strollers.

Skaters
Although telecommunications, computer, Internet and social infrastructures are well established and distributed among business, government and individual users in 'skater' countries, emphasis on further development must not slacken without risk of even the most advanced country falling back. Sweden's surge past the US in the ISI 2003 shows that there is always room for improvement even in the most sophisticated information society. Sweden skated ahead of the US and other developed countries because of a government and corporate partnership designed to dramatically increase the number of PCs through a subsidy for home PC purchases. Also skating ahead are other Nordic countries. Only two economies in our sample are among the skaters group, and they are Singapore and Hong Kong.

Striders
Among the striders in our group which are moving purposefully into the information age, with much of the necessary infrastructure in place, are Taiwan, Korea, Israel, the UAE, and the Czech Republic.

Sprinters
One third of the 55 countries tracked by the ISI each year are sprinters; these are countries that are moving forward in spurts before having to catch up and shift priorities due to economic, social and political pressures. This group includes most of the countries of Latin America, Russia, the Philippines and Thailand. Like short-distance runners, they each have the capacity to speed up for a period of time before needing to catch their breath and shift priorities because of economic, social and political pressures.

Many of these countries are either in the early stages of privatization or have yet to move in that direction. Among this group of sprinters in our sample are Poland, Romania, Chile, Argentina, Malaysia, Bulgaria, South Africa, Russia, Saudi Arabia, Brazil, Ecuador, Mexico, Turkey, Colombia, the Philippines, and Thailand.

Strollers

Strollers are those countries that are moving ahead, but inconsistently, often because of limited financial resources in relation to their vast populations. Sampled countries in this category are Jordan, Egypt, China, Indonesia, Peru, India and Pakistan.

Electronic Government Index

National e-government program development among the UN member states has advanced dramatically in the 2001–2005 period. Countries whose web presence in previous years consisted of one or two static government Web pages began offering content rich, well-designed, citizen-centric sites. However, despite creative initiatives, national e-government program development in many of the countries remains overwhelmingly at the information provision stage. The level of sophistication in which countries are using the Internet to deliver quality information does, however, vary considerably.

Full-fledged commitment to e-government implies that a country's leadership recognizes the fact that information has become a social and economic asset, and just as important and valuable as traditional commodities and natural resources. Information benefits most the individuals and industries which have easy access to its acquisition, and the self-determination to convert essential data into knowledge. Several in our sample such as Mexico, Brazil, the UAE, and Chile were able to overcome unrelenting infrastructure limitations, like inadequate hardware availability or scarce internal access, and rigorous human capital challenges, to develop complete e-government programs. In Mexico, the UAE, Egypt and Brazil, the commitment on the part of the political leadership has been solid and unremitting.

Naturally, a country's social, political and economic composition correlates closely with its e-government program; there are exceptions, however. Key factors such as the state of a country's telecommunications infrastructure, the strength of its human capital, the political will and commitment of the national leadership and changing policy and administrative priorities play important roles. Each of these factors affects how decision makers, policy planners and public sector managers elect to approach, develop and implement e-government programs.

In 2001, of the 190 UN Member States, 88.9 percent of their governments used the Internet in some role to provide information and services. For 16.8 percent of these governments, their presence on the Internet was just beginning to emerge. The official information offered in these countries was often static in content and limited to only a few independent websites. Countries with an enhanced Internet presence – where users have access to an increasing number of official websites that provide advanced features and dynamic information – represented 34.2 percent, the highest number among the UN Member States. Thirty percent of the countries surveyed offer interactive online services where users have access to regularly updated content, and can, among other things, download documents and email government officials. The capacity to conduct transactions online, where citizens can actually use the Internet to pay for a national government service, fee or tax obligation, was available in 17 countries or only 9 percent of the UN Member States.

The e-government index (EGI) developed by the UN attempts to (1) objectively quantify critical enabling environmental factors, and (2) establish a 'reference point' for which a country can measure future progress. The index incorporates a country's official online presence, evaluates its telecommunications infrastructure and assesses its human development capacity. As stated earlier, the results of the e-government index tend to reflect a country's economic, social and democratic level of development.

The UN report classified a country's online presence in one of five categories based on (1) presence of an official website, (2) type of services delivered, (3) provision of services in education, health, labor, welfare and financial services, (4) use of a single entry portal, and (5) fidelity to strategic plans and use of e-government teams. The five categorical stages are: emerging, enhanced, interactive, transactional, and fully integrated or seamless. The following section will discuss each of the five categorical stages and classify the sample countries accordingly.

Emerging stage

A country classified as having emerging presence is one that commits to becoming an e-government player. In such a country, a formal but limited Web presence is established thorough a few government websites providing uses with static organizational and political information. Qatar is the only country in our sample that fits this category.

Enhanced presence stage

A country where online presence begins to expand with increasing official websites is classified as a country with enhanced presence. Here content will consist more of dynamic and specialized information that is frequently updated with government publications and legislation. Sites also have search features and email addresses for communication purposes. Eight countries in our sample satisfied these conditions: Algeria, Ecuador, Indonesia, Iran, Kazakhstan, Nigeria, Oman, and Vietnam.

Interactive presence stage
A country is classified under the interactive presence classification when its presence on the Internet is spread out considerably, providing access to a wide range of government institutions and services, and exhibiting a more sophisticated level of formal interactions between citizens and service providers such as email and post comments areas. The capacity to search specialized databases and download forms and applications or submit them is also available and the content of information is regularly updated. The majority of countries in our sample (28), were classified under this category: Argentina, Bolivia, Bulgaria, Chile, China, Colombia, Czech Republic, Egypt, Hungary, India, Israel, Jordan, Lebanon, Malaysia, Pakistan, Peru, Philippines, Poland, Romania, Russia, Saudi Arabia, Slovakia, South Africa, Sri Lanka, Thailand, Turkey, Ukraine, and Uruguay.

Transactional presence stage
Only five in our sample were classified under the category 'transactional presence' according to the EGI: Brazil, Mexico, Korea, the UAE, and Singapore. Countries in this classification have electronic systems where complete and secure transactions like obtaining visas, passports, birth and death certificates, and licenses can be performed. The user can actually pay online for a service performed. Digital signatures may be recognized in an effort to facilitate procurement and doing business with the government.

Fully integrated/seamless presence stage
Twelve countries in our sample (or 27 percent), were classified as countries with high e-government capacity or as global leaders (see Table 4.1). In terms of geographic spread, we have two countries in the Asia-Pacific region (Singapore and Korea); four countries in the Middle East (Israel, the UAE, Kuwait, and Lebanon); five countries in Latin America (Argentina, Brazil, Chile, Mexico and Uruguay); and only one in Eastern Europe (Czech Republic). None of the countries in Africa were among the e-government leaders, as classified by the UN.

Economic Freedom Index

The year 2004 marks the tenth anniversary of the Heritage Foundation/Wall Street Journal Index of Economic Freedom. The Economic Freedom Index (EFI) covers 10 different country attributes or factors. In the earlier years,

Table 4.1   E-government leaders

Country	Rank on e-government index
Singapore	4th
Korea	15th
Israel	17th
Brazil	18th
UAE	21st
Mexico	22nd
Kuwait	26th
Czech Republic	30th
Argentina	31st
Uruguay	34th
Chile	35th
Lebanon	36th

Source: Benchmarking E-governments (United Nations, 2001).

some countries were missing certain ratings or were missing entirely, so the number of available countries ranged from 98 to 161 over the 9 calendar years. The idea of producing a user-friendly 'index of economic freedom' as a tool for policymakers and investors was first discussed at The Heritage Foundation in the late 1980s. The goal then, as it is today, was to develop a systematic, empirical measurement of economic freedom in countries throughout the world. To this end, the decision was made to establish a set of objective economic criteria that, since 1994, have been used to study and grade various countries for the annual publication of the Index of Economic Freedom.

The EFI, however, is more than just a dataset based on empirical study; it is a careful theoretical analysis of the factors that most influence the institutional setting of economic growth. Moreover, although there are many theories about the origins and causes of economic development, the findings of the Heritage Foundation/Wall Street study are straightforward: the countries with the most economic freedom also have higher rates of long-term economic growth and are more prosperous than are those with less economic freedom.

The 2004 Index of Economic Freedom measures how well 161 countries score on a list of 50 independent variables divided into 10 broad factors of economic freedom. Low scores are more desirable. The higher the score on a factor, the greater the level of government interference in the economy and the less economic freedom a country enjoys. These 50 variables are grouped into the following categories:

- Trade policy,
- Fiscal burden of government,
- Government intervention in the economy,
- Monetary policy,
- Capital flows and foreign investment,
- Banking and finance,
- Wages and prices,
- Property rights,
- Regulation, and
- Informal market activity.

Based on the 2004 report, that year economic freedom had advanced throughout the world: the scores of 75 countries are better, the scores of 69 are worse, and the scores of 11 are unchanged. The countries of Latin America and the Caribbean continue to suffer from their own counterproductive policies. Economic freedom in the region has not increased: it has decreased. Of the 26 countries that had been graded in 2004, 11 improved in their overall level of economic freedom and 13 were worse. In fact, of the 10 countries with the world's largest declines in economic freedom, two were Latin American: Venezuela and Argentina.

The lack of economic vitality in these two countries reflects the evaporation of economic rights. Argentina's economic plight worsens as it marches toward a closed economy. The downward spiral of its economy has been accompanied by price controls, financial restrictions, high inflation, and a history of violating property rights. Argentina's new President, Nestor Kirchner, aims to jump-start the economy by financing public works. Inevitably, he will discover that such methods kill economic growth, not create it. The economic history of the former Soviet Union is a telling example.

Venezuela's situation is even darker. President Hugo Chávez has introduced exchange controls that have made it difficult for business, both foreign and domestic, to operate. As a result, 80 percent of Venezuelans live below the poverty level. Venezuela is now ranked as a 'repressed' economy and possesses the least amount of economic freedom in the region. With an improved monetary policy score, Chile has shifted from a 'mostly free' to a 'free' country this year and is by far the most free economy in the region. Chile has completed free trade agreements (FTAs) with the European Union (EU) and the US and will be phasing out complex non-tariff barriers as a result of the FTA with the US.

In 2004 North Africa and the Middle East had the same net amount of economic freedom as in the previous year. The scores of eight countries in this region have improved, while those of eight are worse. The region has no countries that are ranked as 'free'. Of the 10 factors measured in the EFI, the fiscal burden factor both improved in the most countries (seven) and worsened in the most (nine), resulting in an overall net loss of two. The trade policy factor experienced the largest net gain, with three countries improving and not a single country declining in openness to trade. The largest net loss was in the wages and prices factor, where no countries improved and three countries declined. The journal and the foundation reported in the *2003 Index of Economic Freedom Index* that the problems of bureaucracy, corruption and uncertainty make it difficult to build a business bigger than a market stall in much of the region. The EFI used figures in the *Arab Human Development Report*, (UNDP, 2003) issued for the first time in 2003 by the UN Development Program, to describe the economic difficulties that engulf most of the region. In Chapter Two of the index, dealing with the Middle East, it was stated that strengthening the rule of law is the key element to expanding economic freedom in Arab countries. Without rule of law, people cannot benefit from property rights, or have the ability to settle disputes peacefully and fairly. The report goes further to indicate that the rule of law is more important than privatization. Good governance and market-oriented reforms are central elements of the Free Trade Agreements that the US has negotiated or is negotiating with Arab countries.

The *2003 Index* identified Bahrain as the most economically free country in the region, and as tied for the sixteenth place for the freest economy in the world. Saudi Arabia, the UAE, Kuwait, Qatar, Oman, Jordan, Morocco and Tunisia were categorized in the index as 'mostly free' economies. While the UAE is the third freest economy in the region, its overall score worsened by the third largest margin in the world. The UAE's fiscal burden of government, banking and finance, wages and prices, and informal market scores were worse in 2003. The UAE has a bloated public employment sector, subsidized services, and government handouts. There is, however, a glimmer of hope: Abu Dhabi is spearheading the privatization of utilities and seeking to attract foreign investment in the power and water sectors.

Commenting on Qatar's economy, the *Index* noted that its ruler has undertaken a bold program of political and economic reform since coming to power in 1995. Programs were initiated to liberalize the political system, give women the right to vote, and to create a democratically elected Municipal Council.

The 2003 *Index* grouped together Lebanon, Algeria, Egypt, Yemen and Syria in the 'mostly unfree' category; Iran and Libya were put in the group of 'repressed' economies and Iraq was not given a ranking because of lack of information.

On net, economic freedom continues to improve in Sub-Saharan Africa, with 21 countries' economic freedom scores improving and 15 countries' scores declining. The majority of countries (30 out of 42) remain 'mostly unfree'. Of the 10 factors used to grade countries in the *Index*, government intervention showed the greatest net improvement, with 18 countries improving and only four declining. The largest net loss was in the fiscal burden factor, with 14 countries improving and 21 declining. Five countries in this region (Rwanda, Ethiopia, Cape Verde, Senegal, and Mauritania) are among the world's 10 most improved. At the same time, four others (Namibia, Madagascar, Lesotho, and Gabon) are among the 10 whose scores worsened by the world's widest margins.

In addition, of all the countries in the 2003 edition of the *Index*, Rwanda experienced the single greatest degree of improvement overall: an amazing feat when one considers that the previous year it was one of the countries showing the greatest decline in economic freedom. Rwanda has improved its trade policy, government intervention, monetary policy, and regulation scores. Zimbabwe continued to be the least-free country in the region. Despite improving its fiscal burden of government and government intervention scores, it remained 'repressed'. As a result, unemployment was at 80 percent, inflation was over 200 percent, and millions of Zimbabweans were facing starvation.

At the other end of the spectrum, Botswana remained the freest country in the region despite a worse score in 2003. Both its trade policy and fiscal burden of government scores were worse. The second freest was Uganda, which had privatized 74 businesses over the past decade and was targeting 85 more.

Sub-Saharan Africa needs trade liberalization. The trade policy factor improved in only five countries, and 10 countries closed their markets further in 2003. South Africa had a free trade agreement with the EU. Additionally, South Africa, Lesotho, Swaziland, and Namibia form the Southern African Customs Union, which, with an average common external tariff rate of 11.4 percent, was negotiating a free trade agreement with the US.

The scores of the Asia–Pacific region were worse for five countries, with scores for 11 countries improved and scores for 16 countries worse in 2003. This was drastically different from the previous year when, on net, the scores of six countries improved. Of the 10 factors, fiscal burden and monetary policy exhibited the greatest improvement overall, and the greatest number of countries declining in economic freedom occurred in the government intervention factor.

Although most countries in the region were ranked 'mostly unfree', the Asia–Pacific region also contained the world's three freest economies: Hong Kong, Singapore, and New Zealand. Additionally, Fiji and Laos were among the world's 10 most improved countries. Not surprisingly, Indonesia was among the 10 countries whose scores worsened by the widest margin worldwide. Indonesia's fiscal burden of government, government intervention, capital flows and foreign investment, and wages and prices scores were all worse that year. Indonesia's economy began growing, albeit slowly, and the list of changes needed for faster growth included lower taxes, less government intervention in the economy, lower barriers to investment, lower level of restrictions on banking and finance, stronger protection of property rights, less regulation, and a significant reduction in the informal market. Indonesia continued to suffer from many of the problems that made it so vulnerable to the Asian financial crisis.

North Korea remained the least free country in the region. In addition to earning more revenue from illegal drugs than from legitimate business, North Korea scored poorly on every factor and has nowhere to go but up – if it should ever choose to do so. Once again, Hong Kong was the poster country for economic freedom, both in the region and around the world. With a duty-free port, Hong Kong is a model for free trade. It was also at the time the world's tenth largest trading entity. Likewise, as the world's second freest country, Singapore has a weighted average tariff rate of approximately zero percent. Singapore has a high level of government intervention in the economy and a moderate cost of government; Hong Kong has a low level of government intervention in the economy and a low cost of government. In fact, Hong Kong's government intervention score improved in 2003.

Most of the world's economically repressed countries lie in Asia, which experienced a net loss of economic freedom in five countries. (At the same time, however, the top three countries in the 2004 rankings were also located in Asia.) Latin America and the Caribbean experienced a net loss of two countries. North Africa and the Middle East had no change.

By factor, the results were more evenly split. Four factors of the *Index* had a greater net number of countries with expanded freedom, four had less freedom, and two had no net change. The fiscal burden factor marked the greatest number of improvements (57) and the greatest number of losses (71), for an overall net loss of 14. This was the largest net loss. The biggest net gain was in the monetary policy factor, with 30 countries improving and nine worsening for a net gain of 21. The government intervention factor experienced a net gain of 11, with 41 countries improving and 30 countries declining.

Openness to foreign investment had a net setback of 11, with two countries improving and 13 declining. The level of protection that countries maintain in their trade policy was worse, with 15 countries improving and 20 countries declining for a net loss of five. Banking and finance remained the same overall, as 10 countries had freer financial markets but 10 found their freedom slipping. Regulation also remained the same overall with a gain of one and a loss of one. Wages and prices experienced a net loss of eight, with three countries improving and 11 declining. The informal market experienced a net gain of one country, with 15 countries improving and 14 declining.

Between 2001 and 2003, the report noted a worldwide trend toward a decline in the protection of property rights. Regrettably, 2004 was no different. Many countries continue to disregard the important relationship between maintaining strong property rights and attracting investment. The protection of property rights experienced a net loss of seven countries, with seven countries declining in their protection and none demonstrating improvement.

In order to grow, countries must implement policies that attract investors and encourage entrepreneurs. Without strong property rights, investors cannot be sure of their ability to lay claim to their business; as a result, the level of risk involved in a business venture increases, and investors and entrepreneurs are left reluctant, skeptical, and likely to put their money elsewhere. Hong Kong and Singapore have good investment climates characterized by strong property rights. Both countries have also been magnets for investment and have prospered, each one having a GDP per capita over US$24,000.

By contrast, countries that fail to implement strong property rights suffer the consequences of that failure. Governments that refuse to embrace property rights and other economic freedoms sentence their citizens to an impoverished life. Table 4.2 lists the countries, along with their EFI and ranking.

The Networked Readiness Index

The Networked Readiness Index (NRI) was developed by the Center for International Development at Harvard University. The main objective is to understand technology's pivotal role in economic development in countries around the world. The NRI, published in 2004, is a summary measure that helps to focus attention on overall levels of ICT development in 102 countries, representing more than 85 percent of the world's populations and 90 percent of its economic output. The NRI is defined as 'the degree of preparation of a nation or a community to participate in and benefit from ICT developments' (Dutta and Jain, 2004). The index, which was introduced in 2002 and was further refined in 2003, is based upon the

Table 4.2   Economic Freedom Index

Country	Score	EFI Rank
Algeria	4.6	118
Argentina	5.8	86
Bolivia	6.5	58
Brazil	6.2	74
Bulgaria	6.0	78
Chile	7.3	22
China	5.7	90
Colombia	5.3	107
Czech Republic	6.9	41
Ecuador	5.6	94
Egypt	6.2	74
Hong Kong	8.7	1
Hungary	7.3	22
India	6.3	68
Indonesia	5.8	86
Iran	6.0	78
Israel	6.6	51
Jordan	7.0	36
Kazakhstan[a]		
Korea	7.1	31
Lebanon[a]		
Malaysia	6.5	58
Mexico	6.5	58
Nigeria	5.7	90
Oman	7.4	18
Pakistan	5.7	90
Peru	6.8	44
Philippines	6.1	51
Poland	6.4	61
Qatar[a]		
Romania	5.4	103
Russia	5.0	114
Saudi Arabia[a]		
Singapore	8.6	2
Slovakia	6.6	51
South Africa	6.8	44
Sri Lanka	6.0	78
Taiwan	7.3	22
Thailand	6.7	50
Turkey	5.5	100
UAE	7.5	16
Ukraine	5.3	107
Uruguay	6.4	44
Vietnam[a]		

Note: a. Country not included in the study.

following: (1) consideration of the various stakeholders who are involved in the development and use of ICT; namely individuals, businesses, and governments; (2) significance of the macroeconomic and regulatory environment for ICT; and, (3) examination of the degree of usage of ICT by the various stakeholders. Based on these three considerations, the index is an amalgam of three indices. The first is an environment index, comprising market environment, information and regulatory environment. In other words, it looks at the environment for ICT offered by a given country or community. The second is a readiness index which weighs the readiness of a community's key stakeholders (individuals, businesses, and governments) to use ICT. Finally, there is the usage index which measures the usage of ICT amongst these stakeholders. All these sub-indices are weighted equally. The component index and subindex rankings served to identify key areas where a nation is under- or over-performing.

Environment index
The environment component index is designed to measure the degree of conduciveness of the environment that a country provides for the development and use of ICT. This is measured by evaluating (1) the market or availability of skilled human resources; (2) the political and regulatory environment; and, (3) the ICT infrastructure in terms of the availability and quality. In our sample, Singapore (2), Taiwan (8), Hong Kong (11), Israel (13) and Korea (20) rank among the top 20 on the environmental component index.

Readiness index
Readiness of a nation is a measure of the capability and willingness of the three principal agents of a country (individuals, business, and governments) to influence the potential of ICT. Capability and willingness are influenced, in turn, by the existence of ICT skills, access and affordability of use, and government use rate of ICT. Only three countries in our sample rank among the top 20 on the readiness component index: Singapore (4), Taiwan (17), and Korea (19).

Usage index
The usage component aims to measure the degree of usage of ICT by the principal stakeholders; namely, individuals, businesses, and governments. This component provides an indication of the changes in behaviors, lifestyles, and other economic and non-economic benefits brought about by the adoption of ICT. Singapore in our sample is the top performer on this component (ranked second among the 102 countries studied, only

after Norway). Three other countries in our sample rank among the top 20 worldwide: Hong Kong (15), Israel (16) and Korea (17).

Examining Table 4.3, which shows the overall ratings of countries in our sample on the NRI index, one can see that, in our sample, Singapore is the top ranked Asian and Oceanic country (2), followed by Taiwan (17) and Korea (20). Among the Middle Eastern and North African countries, Israel ranks among the top 25 countries in the world (16), followed by Jordan (46), and Egypt (65). Furthermore, one can observe that the top ranked Latin American countries are Chile (32), Brazil (39) and Mexico (44). Slovenia (30) takes the lead among the Central and Eastern European countries, followed by the Czech Republic (33), and Hungary (36).

DEVELOPMENT OF HYPOTHESES

The set of hypotheses in the current research addresses the determinants of success of e-commerce and e-governments in developing and emerging economies. The following section will identify economic resources and constraints that might support (undermine) the success of e-commerce in developing and emerging countries. Chapter 5 will cover the choice of the sample of countries, methodology, and operational variables which will be included in the analysis.

Human Resources

The first type of constraints faced by a developing country is the quantity and quality of its human resources available to society. Since financial resources are only a means to acquire productive assets, resources critical to e-commerce and e-governments are primarily embedded in technical infrastructure and human skill sets. Most policy makers agree that unless businesses and consumers in a country are educated about the opportunities and benefits offered by information/communication technologies and unless they are trained to use the Internet, e-commerce and e-government will not be successful. Some go further to argue that training and education are the main challenges for most developing and emerging countries seeking to participate in the digital economy (ILO, 2001). Training and education are fundamental to the effective use of the Internet and e-commerce. In a networked society, many of the benefits relate directly to the capability to use data and information to create new knowledge. Therefore, IT skills of human resource are considered to be a core component of a successful information society (IS) strategy.

Table 4.3   NRI Score for Countries in the Sample (2004)

Country	Score	NRI Rank
Algeria	2.75	87
Argentina	3.45	50
Bolivia	2.66	90
Brazil	3.67	39
Bulgaria	3.15	67
Chile	3.94	32
China	3.38	51
Colombia	3.28	60
Czech Republic	3.80	33
Ecuador	2.68	89
Egypt	3.19	65
Hong Kong	4.61	18
Hungary	3.74	36
India	3.54	45
Indonesia	3.06	73
Iran[a]		
Israel	4.64	16
Jordan	3.53	46
Kazakhstan[a]		
Korea	4.60	20
Lebanon[a]		
Malaysia	4.19	26
Mexico	3.57	44
Nigeria	2.92	79
Oman[a]		
Pakistan	3.03	76
Peru	3.09	70
Philippines	3.10	69
Poland	3.51	46
Qatar[a]		
Romania	3.26	61
Russia	3.19	63
Saudi Arabia[a]		
Singapore	5.4	2
Slovakia	3.66	41
South Africa	3.72	37
Sri Lanka	3.15	66
Taiwan	4.62	17
Thailand	3.72	38
Turkey	3.32	56
UAE[a]		
Ukraine	2.96	78
Uruguay	3.35	54
Vietnam	3.13	68

Note: a. No data available.

In many developing countries, the literacy rate is low and the level of education is insufficient for the full implementation of the changes required to move into an information society. In addition, given the fast technological change related to ICTs, continuous learning is required, which means that employees and citizens of any country need to improve skills or acquire new ones on a continuous basis. Governments can play an important role in enhancing information and technological literacy through the country's education system. Training teachers in the use of the Internet and communications technologies in the classroom will lead to a new generation of IT-literate children. The UAE is a representative example of government support of education in this respect. In 2003, one of the authors was appointed by the Minister of Education and Youth to head a committee which was charged with revamping the K-12 education system in order to incorporate ICT and Internet technologies into the curriculum of schools. The work of the Committee was completed in June 2004, with a report and a list of recommendations to the Ministry. This document was adopted by the Ministry in October 2004, and work on implementing the Committee recommendations has not started yet, but is expected to start in the 2006–07 academic year.

The quantity and quality of a country's existing skilled personnel limit expansion of its economic base; what is referred to as the 'Penrose effect' (Marris, 1963). Edith Penrose has been credited by several authors espousing a resource-based perspective as having been instrumental to the development of this perspective. Edith Penrose's much cited work on the theory of the growth of the firm provides arguably the most detailed exposition of a RBV in the economics literature. She notes that a firm is more than an administrative unit; it is also a collection of productive resources the disposal of which between different users and over time is determined by administrative decisions. When we regard the function of the private business firm from this point of view, the size of the firm is best gauged by some measure of the productive resources it employs (Penrose, 1959).

The 'Penrose effect' is more pronounced in a developing economy than it is in a developed one. In the former, the new staff, either nationals or expatriates, have to go through a time-consuming integration process before they become productive team players. The constraint is a result of the intimate relationship between human (especially managerial at the executive level) and organizational resources. The two types of resources have to be well balanced in order that successful measures by local and federal governments can be taken. Hence the first hypothesis:

Hypothesis 1: a country's success in e-commerce is positively related to the level of skills of its human resource component

Financial Resources

Another common resource constraint is the country's existing financial base. The RBV of the firm regards the firm (in our case, the unit of analysis is the economy) as a collection of resources and capabilities that are derived internally by factors such as its assets, skills, knowledge, or culture. The RBV has been used by several authors in their research as a mechanism for understanding the manner in which firms operate. From the RBV perspective, resources are often copied by competitors, although cost may be a barrier to imitation. This research will use the economy as a unit of analysis from a resource-based perspective instead of a firm. In addition, the country's capabilities, which may be defined as complex interactions and co-ordination of people and other resources, are the means by which an economy reaches a competitive advantage. However, in order to achieve a competitive advantage, economic actors must enable it to perform value-creating activities, which are determined by market forces, better than its competitors. For e-business to be effective, there needs to be an appropriate infrastructure in place. Electronic Data Interchange (EDI) and extranets are among the basic infrastructure components for Business-to-Business (B2B) e-commerce. Each has its own unique characteristics with respect to access, security, and ease of use.

Even though the domestic financial sector and the capital account in developing countries were heavily regulated for a long time; Kaminsky and Schmukler (2002) show how restrictions have been lifted over time. These authors developed an index of financial liberalization that takes into account restrictions on the domestic financial system, the stock market, and the capital account. They illustrate the gradual lifting of restrictions in both developed and emerging countries during the last 30 years. They also show that developed countries have tended to use more liberal policies than developing countries. Although there has been a gradual lifting of restrictions over time, there were periods of reversals in which restrictions were reimposed. The most substantial reversals took place in the aftermath of the 1982 debt crisis, in the mid-1990s, and after the Argentine crisis in Latin America.

The literature identifies six main reasons to explain the new wave of liberalization and deregulation of the financial sector by governments of different countries. First, governments found capital controls increasingly costly and difficult to maintain effectively. Second, as Errunza (2001) and the World Bank (2001) argue, policymakers have become increasingly aware that government-led financial systems and non-market approaches have failed. Thirdly, recent crises have heightened the importance of foreign capital to finance government budgets and smooth public consumption and investment. Also, foreign capital has helped governments capitalize banks with problems, conduct corporate restructuring, and manage crises. Fourthly, opening up the privatization of public companies to foreign investors has helped increase their receipts. Fifthly, although governments can also tax revenue from foreign capital, they might find this harder to do than with other factors of production because of its footloose nature. Finally, governments have become increasingly convinced of the benefits of a more efficient and robust domestic financial system for growth and stability of the economy and for the diversification of the public and private sectors' investor base.

Financial institutions, through the internationalization and globalization of financial services, are also a major driving force of financial liberalization. As discussed by the International Monetary Fund (IMF) (2000), changes at the global level and changes in both developed and developing countries explain the role of financial institutions as a force of globalization and liberalization.

At a global level, the gains in IT have diminished the importance of geography, allowing international corporations to service several markets from one location. As discussed in Crockett (2000), the gains in IT have had three main effects on the financial services industry:

(1) they promoted a more intensive use of international financial institutions;
(2) they led to a major consolidation and restructuring of the world financial services industry; and
(3) they gave rise to global banks and international conglomerates that provide a mix of financial products and services in a broad range of markets and countries, blurring the distinctions between financial institutions and the activities and markets in which they engage.

Demographic changes and the increased sophistication of small investors around the world have intensified competition for savings among banks, mutual funds, insurance companies, and pension funds. Households have bypassed bank deposits and securities firms to hold their funds with institutions better able to diversify risks, reduce tax burdens, and take advantage of economies of scale.

In developing countries, the liberalization of the regulatory systems has opened the door for international firms to participate in local markets. The privatization of public financial institutions has provided foreign banks with an opportunity to enter local financial markets. Macroeconomic stabilization, a better business environment, and stronger fundamentals in emerging markets have ensured a more attractive climate for foreign investment.

In recent years, then, there has been a revival of interest in the role played by financial development in long-term economic growth. A host of studies carried out over the past decade, beginning with King and Levine (1993), have found evidence in favor of the Schumpeterian view that a well-developed financial system promotes growth by channeling credit to its most productive uses. This has now become the conventional wisdom. Also, in the Information Age, the most productive use of finances is investments in e-commerce and Internet-based technologies:

Hypothesis 2: a country's success in e-commerce is positively related to the strengths of its financial base

Access and Technical Capabilities

Another related factor is the indigenous technical capability of the developing country, which is indicated by a number of variables such as national research and development (R&D) expenditure, the rate of capital formation, national investment in education and the number of technical personnel per capita. Technology and technical skills are driving growth at every level of any economy. For example, most economists now agree that three ingredients are essential to economic growth: capital, labor, and technology. Of these three components, technology and technical skills are the most important. Eminent economists estimate that technical growth and technological maturity have accounted for the bulk of economic growth in the most developed countries over the past 50 years. Of course, technology improves the productivity of labor. However, leading economists who have analyzed the role of technical progress in the postwar period found a greater influence on the productivity of capital.

The fact that more and more people are using the Internet, which is a must for the growth of e-commerce, is not necessarily a sign of the survival of such expansion or of its speed. Some estimates of the numbers of Internet users count anyone (including, for instance, children) who has had access to the Internet in the previous 30 days. A much higher frequency of access is necessary in order to acquire the familiarity and generate the confidence that is needed in order to become an e-commerce practitioner particularly in the case of those engaged in B2B e-commerce, whose use of the Internet cannot be of some hours per month, but of hours per day. Indeed, when asked about the use they make of the Internet, people in developing and emerging countries rarely mention e-commerce as a frequent online activity.

Email is the most popular use of the Internet in developing countries. It is safe to assume that in developing countries the proportion of Internet users who are also e-commerce practitioners is lower than average, owing of course to lower per capita incomes, but also to other well-known factors such as low credit card usage, lack of relevant products or services or poor logistics and fulfillment services.

Without an appropriate technological infrastructure, there will be little use of e-commerce and electronic means by the business community. The network infrastructure needs to be accessible, affordable and of good quality. The telecommunications sector in many of the developing countries is run by the public sector, where the scope and modalities of privatization and liberalization pose difficult problems. It is worth noting here that countries that have carried out telecommunications sector reforms have experienced significant improvements in their drive to become information societies. For example, since adopting a new national ICT plan in 1999, Egypt has successfully increased telephone capacity and teledensity, the numbers of mobile phone subscribers and international circuits, and the capacity of international links to the Internet, while reducing access costs (OECD, 2002).

Developing and emerging countries need to take into consideration the fact that establishing telecommunications infrastructure is costly, and that they might need inflows of foreign direct investment. In general, technological development and technical growth in a developing economy can take place through the transfer of technology and expertize from more advanced and developed countries. A study of 33 countries using American technology showed that there was a positive relationship between rate of development (ie as measured by the indigenous technical capability) and the proportion of licensing arrangements which were used as the means of absorbing technology (Contractor, 1980). Furthermore, in transitional economies such as China, the successful transfer of hard technology often has to be accompanied by the transfer of soft technologies like management know-how (Hendryx, 1986).

All in all, we see the growth-inducing power of technology at the industry level in developed countries. In the US, for instance, research-intensive industries (aerospace, chemicals, communications, computers, pharmaceuticals, scientific instruments, semiconductors, and software) have been growing at about twice the rate of the economy as a whole in the past two decades. In developed countries, we also see technology's growth-inducing power at the level of the individual firm. Recent studies show that firms with access to advanced technologies are more productive and profitable, pay higher wages, and increase employment more rapidly than firms that do not. The evidence is mounting. At the macroeconomic level, the industry level, and the firm level, access to technical resources constitute the engine of economic growth.

In the realm of technology, the so-called enabling technologies are the most important factors in this economic growth equation. Throughout the twentieth century, enabling technologies (such as mass production, machine numerical control, and the transistor) have been powerful engines of growth. The integrated circuit is, perhaps, the defining enabling technology of the twentieth century. Since its invention more than 40 years ago, it has enabled a whole range of new products and industries (from the computer to satellite communications) and it has had a profound impact on existing products and processes from automobiles, consumer electronics, and home appliances, to a broad range of advanced industrial systems. The integrated circuit sowed seeds for the knowledge-based economy and the Information Age that are rapidly unfolding.

Without access to PCs and Internet connections at a reasonable cost, consumers in developing economies are unable to migrate from traditional markets to electronic markets. However, even with access to the necessary equipment, people will not become active e-participants unless they have reasonable confidence in the truthfulness of transactions undertaken online. Thus, the presence of an adequate Internet infrastructure is a necessary but not sufficient condition for the development of e-economies:

Hypothesis 3: a country's success in electronic commerce is positively related to its indigenous technical capability

Rule of law

Social theorists, legal scholars, and historians concur that law has played a central role in the transformation and industrialization of the West over the past 200 years. The mounting complexity of formal legal systems and the development of constitutionalism and the rule of law during this period are thought to have been key determinants of economic growth and prosperity. Max Weber went as far as affirming that a well developed legal system was a prerequisite for the development of capitalism (Weber, 1981). Kinship relations, reputation bonds enforced by relatively closely united communities and a multitude of self-enforcing mechanisms form the most important governance and enforcement mechanisms. Several historical and comparative studies (Ellickson, 1991; Greif, 1989; Redding, 1990) have revealed that these mechanisms can be extremely successful.

For developing and emerging countries, providing an enabling legal framework is a determining factor to e-commerce and e-government success, as it affects the ability to conduct transactions online. The main legal challenge of e-commerce is the dematerialization problem; ie, the lack of tangible information. Due to this and other unique characteristics of e-commerce, national legal frameworks need to be adapted to enable the development and success of e-commerce. It is important to remember, though, that adjusting the legislative framework to e-commerce will not solve fundamental problems inherent in the existing legal system of a country. Although it is known that commerce and technology often advance ahead of the law needed to regulate them, it is equally true that technology needs to take into account relevant legal requirements. Furthermore, efficient regulation of e-commerce issues such as spam and digital rights management requires that legislative solutions go hand in hand with technical solutions (UNPD, 2003).

It has been argued that institutional and legal perspectives would offer researchers a vantage point for conceptualizing the digital economy as an emergent, evolving, embedded, fragmented, and provisional social production that is shaped as much by cultural and structural forces as by technical and economic ones. Faced with new forms of electronic exchange, distribution, and interaction, information/communication technology researchers cannot reasonably confine their interests to the problems of developing and implementing technologies or even to studying a technology's impact on local contexts. A world of global networking (both technological and organizational) raises issues of institutional interdependence whose understanding requires an appreciation for how prior assumptions, norms, values, choices, and interactions create conditions for action and how subsequent action produces unintended and wide-reaching consequences (Orlikowsk and Barley, 2001). Recognition of the institutional implications of e-commerce would focus attention on such complex issues as the blurring of corporate boundaries, national sovereignty, organizational control, intellectual property, individual privacy, and internetworking protocols. Without an institutional structure, e-commerce and e-government research might focus more narrowly on technological designs, economic imperatives, or psychological impacts, thus missing important social, cultural, and political aspects of technology diffusion.

A number of reasons have been put forward in the resource-based literature to explain why valuable resources, both tangible and intangible, are imperfectly imitable by competitors (Dierickx and Cool, 1989; Grant, 1991; Lippman and Rumelt, 1992). The most well-known reason is casual ambiguity, which is said to exist 'when the link between the resources controlled by a firm's sustained competitive advantage is not understood or understood only very imperfectly' (Barney, 1991, pp. 108–09). Discussions of casual ambiguity are usually focused on the core competencies of a firm that account for its competitive advantage (Reed and DeFillippi, 1990). These competencies are a complex combination of productive services offered by the firm's physical, human and organizational resources. In view of the intricacies of the relationships and processes involved, even senior management of the firm may not fully understand the exact nature of the casual connections between actions and results.

However, the situation for a stand-alone technology would be very different. Casual ambiguity is less a problem here. Imitation by competitors can be a real danger, especially when the technology has been substantially codified. It is in the firm's interest to guard against the leakage of its crucial technical know-how. How far intellectual property rights are protected in the host country is a critical factor economic agents should consider. Studies have found that the risk of patent infringement may provide an internalization motive for foreign direct investment (Caves, 1971; Dunning, 1979; Horstmann and Markusen, 1987). In developing countries where the record of patent protection is poor, the firm would prefer transfer modes like joint ventures or even wholly owned subsidiaries so that it has more control over the use of the technology and minimize the leakage. Of course, as mentioned earlier, public policy of the host country is an important factor as well. For instance, China has preference for joint ventures as a means of importing foreign technology (Tsang, 1995). Firms using other transfer modes will lose the economic incentives offered to joint ventures.

A country with a strong rule of law is defined as one having a strong court system, a well-defined political institution, and citizens who are willing to accept the established institutions and to make and implement laws and arbitrate disagreements. North (1986) argues that the key to economic growth is 'efficient economic organization', involving, among other things, a well-specified legal system, an impartial judiciary and a 'set of attitudes towards contracting and trading that encourage people to engage in [markets] at low cost' (North, 1986, p. 236).

The strength of the rule of law affects transactional integrity in e-commerce, and thus investment in such markets, in three ways. First, a strong rule of law generates greater transparency and stability regarding the boundaries of acceptable behavior. This reduces transactor's uncertainty about what legal protection they can expect, and enhances their ability to successfully litigate at least the more serious cases of fraudulent online dealings. Wherever the rule of law is weak, that ability is undermined. Secondly, effective punishment of transgressors lowers the cost of reputation-building for honest businesses, as signals are more credible when defectors face high sanctions. Thirdly, a strong rule of law influences people's general attitudes, increasing the level of trust in markets and contracting. This trust is particularly important in e-commerce, given our earlier discussion of information asymmetries in online markets.

To illustrate the importance of these features of a strong rule of law, consider countries where citizens grant little legitimacy to legal contracts, relying on more informal approaches when conducting business. Here, personal relationships are important, and people will likely be apprehensive of any business dealings with faceless strangers (and, conversely, may not hesitate to cheat a stranger with whom they *do* trade).

What is meant by Rule of Law, then, is the presence of a clear governance arrangement that respects individual and commercial rights and which is enforced consistently and fairly as an important prerequisite for promoting effective use of technology and knowledge. If commercial contracts are not respected, and if businesses can be arbitrarily seized and/or if bureaucratic red tape stifles creative energy, any incubation project will be doomed to failure.

The pervasive growth in e-commerce in recent years has raised concerns that existing legal and regulatory regimes are too inconsistent or inadequate in dealing with the issues that e-commerce raises. Most commentators have, however, noted that ironically it is the lack of substantial legal or regulatory infrastructure that has made the unbridled growth of e-commerce possible, and this has caused some to worry that the application of too much traditional regulation will stifle growth. Many development economists and technologists have taken the point further and argue that modern information markets should largely be defined by agreements and other manifestations of market choice rather than by regulation. At various stages during the development of the Internet, several observers have also expressed disappointment with the inadequacy of domestic legal systems in dealing with issues in cyberspace. This is hardly surprising as the principles developed to deal with legal issues in the physical world are sometimes inadequate in dealing with the emerging legal challenge thrown up by the Internet.

The fast growth of the Internet, and consequently e-commerce transactions, greatly increases the ease of accessing, reproducing, and transmitting information. This ease raises a host of legal issues including the risk of copyright infringement, the protection of patent rights, and the preservation of trade secrets. The Internet also raises privacy concerns and issues pertaining to the validity and enforcement of agreements entered into via the medium of the Internet. Conflict of law issues take on an added dimension of complexity and confusion due to the inherent fluid nature of the Internet. Users habitually trigger the application of the laws of multiple jurisdictions in a matter of seconds. It is becoming increasingly evident that the process of mapping existing legal concepts and tools into this new domain is not straightforward, and that a number of familiar legal concepts will need to be rethought and perhaps re-engineered before they can be efficiently applied in the new environment. Most governments act reactively and amend or create regulations after industry acceptance of these technologies has taken place. This gives rise to the maddening and steadily widening gap between new technologies and adequate government regulation. The existing body of law is, however, not entirely helpless and oftentimes the law is able to adapt and tackle some of the emerging legal issues thrown up by e-commerce. This is done through the process of drawing from precedents and on reasoning by analogy. There is, unfortunately and perhaps understandably, a limit to the ability of the law to adapt itself to emerging technologies: timely legislative intervention to supplant the existing law and to fill in the existing lacunae is often needed to ensure that the law remains current and relevant.

Many governments and regulatory bodies in developing and emerging countries are starting to recognize the economic potential of e-commerce and e-government and are considering a number of policy initiatives designed to encourage further development and application of this technology. These initiatives include attempts to overhaul or effect amendments to existing laws to deal with the emerging legal issues that e-commerce raises. In Singapore, for instance, various amendments to existing legislation and subsidiary legislation have been put in place rationalizing the existing law to cope with moves in various industries towards the electronic framework. The amendments have collectively dealt with computer and electronic evidence, copyright, income tax concessions for cyber-trading, electronic dealings in securities and futures, electronic prospectuses and deregulation of the telecommunications industry.

In Malaysia, the Multimedia Development Corporation has been working on a National Electronic Commerce Master Plan, which is designed to facilitate the creation of a favorable environment for the development of e-commerce in Malaysia. The four key elements in this Master Plan are to boost confidence in on-line trading, prepare a regulatory framework, build a critical mass of Internet users and introduce an electronic payment system.

In the Philippines, the passage of the Electronic Commerce Act of 2002 underpins the Philippine government's resolve to create an environment of trust, predictability and certainty in the Philippine system – so as to enable e-commerce to flourish. In India, there have been feverish attempts to update the Indian legal and regulatory framework to make them more relevant in the face of rapid developments in IT and communications. The internet service provider (ISP) and gateway markets have been liberalized and the national long-distance sector has been opened up. In addition, discussions are ongoing for the liberalization of the international long-distance sector and India's up linking policies are slated to become more liberal.

A closer examination of the legislative activity in this area, however, leaves an uncomfortable feeling that what is taking place across a large part of the developing world is probably a reaction to perceived legal problems presented by e-commerce, rather than a careful and considered response to the actual issues that this new method of doing business raises.

Most countries have sought to respond to the novel legal problems that crop up in cyberspace by enacting new legislation, while others have sought to extend the ambit of their current laws to cover the novel scenarios occurring in cyberspace. In this flurry of activity, it is not surprising that most countries have not addressed the fundamental issue of whether it would be wise or desirable to apply existing national laws, which have evolved mainly to deal with 'territorial-based' concepts and rights, to the realm of cyberspace. Accordingly, there have been calls to treat cyberspace as a separate jurisdiction for the purposes of legal analysis. Some analysts have suggested that a separate law of cyberspace, similar to the law of the high seas, should be formulated. Others have proposed that the norms and practices of the users of the Internet could be relied upon in determining the applicable and appropriate legal principles that should apply to transactions conducted via the medium of the Internet. This would include 'Netiquette', which has the potential to constitute the foundation pillars of a workable uniform cyberspace law.

Based on the above discussion, on a ceteris paribus basis, we expect the following proposition to hold:

Hypothesis 4: a country's success in electronic commerce is positively related to level of protection in terms of law, regulation and payment

Cyberlaw

Frenetic activity in the past few years has ensured that lawyers and policy makers specializing in IT law are kept busy monitoring developments that are taking place in many parts of Asia as well as in other parts of the world. Examples of legislation passed or sought to be passed in Asia include Australia's Electronic Transactions Act 1999, Broadcasting Services Amendment (On-Line Services) Act 1999, Privacy (Private Sector) Bill and the Copyright Amendment (Digital Agenda) Bill 1999; South Korea's Electronic Transaction Basic Act 1998; Singapore's Electronic Transaction Act 1998; Hong Kong Electronic Transactions Ordinance 2000; Japan's Draft Bill Concerning Electronic Signatures and Certification Authorities and the Law Partially Amending the Trade Mark Law; Malaysia's Malaysian Communications and Multimedia Commission Act 1998, Communications and Multimedia Act 1998, Digital Signature Act 1997, Computer Crimes Act 1997 and Telemedicine Act 1997; the Philippines' Electronic Commerce

Act; India's Information Technology Act 2000, and the Cyberlaw of Dubai, UAE (2002).

Broadly speaking, cyberspace symbolizes a conceptual distinction between activities that take place in the physical or real world and those that occur online or in virtual reality. Beyond conceptual distinctions, we might say that the infrastructure of cyberspace is basically digital code, and that this aspect of cyberspace makes the virtual landscape unique. As a practical matter, both the increasing importance and the expanding utility of the Internet are making distinctions between real-space and cyberspace less noticeable. Even so, cyberspace still presents a remarkable number of novel legal questions involving how computer users carry out various transactions involving e-commerce through the interconnection of computing and communications technologies. Although the lack of reliable or relevant precedent renders legal practice in this area difficult and, quite often, annoying, the challenges are also exciting. In cyberlaw, one cannot easily escape the feeling that despite the apparent absence of physical matter, cyberspace is a bleeding edge of the law.

Not surprisingly, because of the unique nature of the Internet, its use creates unique legal questions and issues, particularly with respect to intellectual property rights and cybercrime. In addition, e-government requires a regulatory and public policy environment conducive to e-commerce, protection of rights, and an enabling legal framework for the digital transformation of government operations. Policy agendas include issues such as privacy, security, digital signatures, consumer protection, international trade, telecommunications, taxation and the digital divide. Industrial age laws, their interpretation and intent are many times not applicable or, worse, detrimental to a growing digital economy and society. Investment in the education of legislators around technology issues is a prerequisite to successful e-government. Without digital signatures, for instance, companies are hard pressed to engage in e-commerce. Businesses require assurance that an electronically signed document can be enforced against the sender. At present, there is no definitive court decision ruling that an electronic document can be 'signed' electronically in legal systems and in circumstances where the signature remains as a formal requirement of law. This 'signature' issue is intimately related to a technical, legal issue of proof. In a court case, a party seeking to enforce a contract has the burden of proving that (1) the document was signed by the person who it purports to have come from, and (2) that the document presented is, in fact, the one that was signed.

Many developing and emerging countries have realized the importance and necessity of law to regulate cyberspace. In October 2004, the government of Singapore announced that it would the next year introduce jail terms and stiff fines for people who break software and Internet copyright laws (http://www.channelnewsasia.com). People found to be illegally using software or downloading off the Internet will face a maximum six months in jail and a fine of 20,000 Singapore dollars (US$11,900) for their first offence, according to amendments to the Copyright Act introduced into parliament. Repeat offenders face 3 years in jail and a fine of 50,000 Singapore dollars. The laws specifically refer to people who break the law 'to obtain a commercial advantage' or infringe significantly; meaning that individuals who download a limited number of songs or movies off the Internet for personal use may be exempt. This implies that the courts would be left to interpret the definition of 'significant'. The tougher laws are part of Singapore's commitments to its FTA signed with the US that came into effect in 2003. Previously, people who breached software and Internet copyright laws in Singapore were only subject to civil action.

Development of cyberlaw is still evolving in developing and emerging countries. The proposed Digital Signature and E-Commerce proposed regime in Thailand, for instance, has been strongly criticized. The two separate laws – one on electronic transactions and the other on electronic signatures – have been merged into one following a review by the Office of the Juridical Council. This new draft, which was approved by the Cabinet, is opposed by the IT industry, because the Cabinet's regulatory authority lies with digital signatures rather than the much broader issue of e-commerce. Industry feels strongly that these two areas are fundamentally different and should be clearly distinguished. Moreover, IT experts find the new draft overly broad and too vague. Notwithstanding the criticism, the Bill passed its first reading in parliament on 23 August 2000. On 27 September 2000, a revised version of the Electronic Commerce law was scheduled for its second reading in parliament. The draft law was rewritten to remove concerns about too much government control over e-commerce and some unclear sections of the law. Basically, it seemed that the responsibility of the e-commerce committee would be confined to regulating electronic signatures (e-signatures) instead of the broader issue of electronic commerce again. In October 2000, it became clear, however, that the bills would be stalled and delayed at least five months or until the next government takes office.

Other developing and emerging countries, however, have been very slow (or reluctant) to develop an e-commerce law. In 2003, Egypt, for instance, drafted an e-signature law, which has been approved by the Cabinet (it is awaiting discussion by the Parliament); however Egypt is deferring a broader e-commerce law that will address such issues as domain names, customs and duties, and the creation of a certificate authority to verify e-signatures. The development of e-commerce in Egypt has been impeded by concern about the lack of security on computer networks, the relatively high prices charged by ISPs, and the limited number of Internet users in the country.

The country of Lebanon is a perfect example of disinclination and reluctance. Lebanon has not yet adopted an e-signature law, which would allow companies to conduct business and keep records electronically, although a draft of the law has circulated in Parliament since 2000! In addition, a telecom liberalization and privatization law passed in 2002 remains unimplemented.

Based on the above, it is reasonable to assume cyberlaws contribute to better diffusion of electronic commerce and electronic governments; hence:

Hypothesis 5: a country's success in e-commerce is positively related to the existence of cyberlaw

Credible Payment Channels

Developing a borderless or seamless international environment that supports the growth of e-commerce, especially its more sophisticated offerings, will require multilateral, regional and bilateral action on a number of fronts, including financial payment systems, data protection and privacy, protection of intellectual property, electronic transaction law, technical standards, consumer protection, content regulation, taxation, and cross-border trade issues. Payment systems are central to developing e-commerce and to the success of e-governments in developing countries because transactions in goods and services are matched by the transfer of some form of money.

Accordingly, payments technology is being developed in parallel with technology connecting consumers and businesses around the world. The most important developments are in relation to electronic substitutes for cash, which may be stored in intermediate forms such as stored value cards before entering an e-commerce communications network. The willingness of consumers to use stored value cards for e-commerce will depend critically upon consumer confidence and trust. The main public policy issues associated with electronic cash are soundness of the issuer and systems, security of the payment instrument and the transaction, the need for legal recognition of digital signatures, privacy issues, international compatibility of standards and international interoperability of systems and law enforcement.

Consumers in developing economies typically prefer to transact in cash or debit cards, and the rate of use of credit cards is low. To understand the importance of credible payment channels to e-commerce, consider the role of traditional financial intermediaries, such as credit card companies, in combating potential online fraud. Credit card companies play an important monitoring and certification role in commercial transactions, providing assurance to both buyers and sellers. If a buyer pays with a credit card, rather than with a check, the seller's payment is assured. On the other side of the transaction, the buyer also has some protection. In the US, for example, in the case of a disputed charge, the buyer has the right under the Fair Credit Billing Act of 1993 to withhold payment while the credit card company investigates the claim. In the event that the card number is stolen and used for illegitimate charges, the card holder's liability is limited to US$50, provided it is reported in a timely fashion. The major credit card companies extend similar rights in other countries, although there is significant variation in local laws (Consumers International, 1999).

Customer trust, the main asset of banks and credit card companies, is getting harder to protect with the increasing volume of Internet financial transactions and storage of customer data online. According to Gartner Group, the credit card industry is predicting a triple-digit growth in security compromises, given the determination of criminals to penetrate systems and the ability of viruses and Trojan horses to collect passwords and other data (ePayment.com, 2004). For this reason, Visa and MasterCard are working to align security at physical world stores and data processors with the standards set for e-commerce. Initially, only Visa's large Internet merchants had to comply with its security policy, as online transactions were believed most vulnerable to hackers, *Bank Systems Online* reports. Visa has since extended its Cardholder Information Security Program to all e-tailers which take its cards, and from September 2004, all Visa card-accepting merchants have had to comply with the program. MasterCard's approach differs slightly with its website data-protection program and SecureCode program for online transactions, while third parties are advized on protecting merchants' customer data. Encrypting credit card data, as practiced by 10 percent of US firms, is not an answer, as data-intensive processes slow the retrieval and management of information, for which businesses could lose customer support. Similarly, encryption keys have to be available for easy end-user access without a risk of compromising the system. Ultimately, no bullet-proof solution exists for ID and customer-data theft, so businesses will require multiple solutions and security layers to best defend themselves against an unquantified risk.

Thus, credible electronic payment channels, such as those that credit card companies provide, can at least partially assure satisfactory performance, which may otherwise be lacking in online markets. As a consequence, credit cards or other credible electronic payment (e-payment) channels are important facilitators of e-commerce.

The low level of credit card ownership in a large number of developing countries is a major impediment to the spread of e-commerce, especially business-to-consumer (B2C). Governments, however, have been moving to adopt flexible regulations and create a supportive environment to encourage the introduction of e-payments, Internet banking, and other electronic finance (e-finance) facilities. Thailand's e-payment strategy for 2002–04, under the leadership of the Bank of Thailand, has created an industry payment body to involve other stakeholders including commercial banks in order to take leading responsibility for the development of e-payment systems and technologies. Online security is a key factor restraining the development of e-commerce in many developing countries. Citizens of these countries consider credit card security their number one concern about conducting electronic transactions.

In some countries, like China, holders of credit or debit cards are legally responsible for the amount they charge on their cards, even in cases where the card is stolen. In some developing and emerging countries there are very few secure servers, leading to an increase of credit card misuse. Recently, though, we see that governments in a growing number of developing countries and in cooperation with the private sector are creating e-payment and e-finance friendly regulatory environments and developing secure methods of electronic storage and transmission of commercial messages, e-signatures, and electronic contracts (UNDP, 2003). Hence, the following hypothesis is formulated:

Hypothesis 6: a country's success in e-commerce is positively related to the degree of credibility of existing payment channels

CONCLUSION

This chapter has covered the nature of resources and the foundation of institutional environment theory. In addition, it has covered the four indicators developed by different agencies to measure a country's IT and e-commerce readiness. These are the information society index (ISI), the electronic government index (EGI), the economic freedom index (EFI), and the networked readiness index. In addition to covering the methodology of these indices, the chapter also analyzed the state of countries in our sample, based on each index.

A number of hypotheses, dealing with what is believed to determine the success of e-commerce and e-governments in developing economies, were then developed. The first had to do with the quantity and quality of human resources available to society. It is believed that training and education are fundamental to the effective use of the Internet and thus to the success of e-commerce. Since the quantity and quality of the country's existing skilled personnel limit the expansion of its economic base (the Penrose effect), it is hypothesized that a country's success in e-commerce is positively related to the level of skills of its human resources.

The second hypothesis has to do with the financial resources available to the country. In recent years, a host of studies have found evidence of a positive relationship between the strength of the financial base of a country and its economic growth. It is hypothesized that, in the information age, financial investment in Internet-based technologies is positively correlated with economic growth.

Access to Internet-based resources and technical capabilities constitute the basis of the third hypothesis. Without access to computers and Internet connections at a reasonable cost, citizens in developing economies will be unable to migrate from traditional markets to electronic markets. The fourth hypothesis deals with the role the rule of law plays in facilitating the use of Internet-based technologies in a developing country. Scholars, from all professional backgrounds, agree that law plays a vital role in the transformation and development of societies. It is believed that, in the developed world, the development of constitutionalism and the rule of law have been the major drivers of economic growth and progress. A number of reasons have been advanced in the resource-based literature to highlight the role a strong rule of law plays in economic growth and development. The argument goes that a strong rule of law affects transactional integrity in an Internet-based society, and thus investment in such markets.

Cyberlaw is hailed to be one of the major drivers of e-commerce and Internet-based business. Due to the unique nature of the Internet, its use creates legal issues and questions, especially in areas related to intellectual property rights and cybercrime. Few countries in the developing world have drafted cyberlaw; and those who have, are still struggling to perfect its implementation. In this chapter, the authors argued that the existence of cyberlaw leads to a better diffusion of e-commerce, and subsequently to economic growth and development. Hence the fifth hypothesis was formulated to state that success in e-commerce is positively related to the existence of cyberlaw. The sixth and last hypothesis set forth in this chapter has to do with the existence of credible payment channels. It is argued that payment systems are fundamental to developing Internet-based activities and to the success of e-governments, in particular. Hence, success of any e-commerce project is positively related to the existence of a credible payment system in a country.

Chapter 5 will now cover the formulation of methodology, collection of data, and the testing of the six hypotheses formulated in this chapter.

REFERENCES

Amit, R. and P. Schoemaker (1993), 'Strategic assets and organizational rent', *Strategic Management Journal* **14**, 33–46.

Baker and McKenzie E-Law Alert (2004), 'Singapore to introduce jail terms, fines, for software and internet piracy', accessed at www.channelnewsasia.com.

Barney, J. (1991), 'Firm resources and sustained competitive advantage', *Journal of Management* **17**(1) 99–120.

Barua, A. and T. Mukhopadhyay (2000), 'Information technology and business performance: past, present and future', in R. Zmud (ed.), *Framing the Domains of IT Management: Projecting the Future Through the Past* Cincinnati, OH: Pinnaflex Educational Resources.

Bharadwaj, A. (2000), 'A resource-based perspective on IT capability and firm performance: an empirical investigation', *MIS Quarterly* **24**(1) 169–96.

Black, J.A. and K.B. Boal (1994), 'Strategic resources: traits, configurations and paths to sustainable competitive advantage', *Strategic Management Journal* **15**, 131–48.

Brynjolfsson, E. and S. Yang (1996), 'Information technology and productivity: a review of the literature', *Advances in Computing* **43**, 179–214.

Burns, T. and G. Stalker (1961), *The Management of Innovation*, London: Tavistock.

Cairncross, F. (1997), *The Death of Distance*, Boston, Massachusetts: Harvard Business School Press.

Caves, R.N. (1971), 'International corporations: the industrial economics of foreign investment', *Economica* **38**, 1–27.

Coase, R.H. (1937), 'The nature of the firm', *Economica*, **4**, 386–405.

Conner, K.R. (1991), 'A historical comparison of resource-based theory and five schools of thought within industrial economics', *Journal of Management* **17**, 121–54.

Consumers International (1999), 'Consumers@shopping: an international comparative study of electronic commerce, accessed at www.consumersinternational.org.

Contractor, F.J. (1980), 'The composition of licensing fees and arrangements as a function of economic development of technology recipient nations', *Journal of International Business Studies*, Winter 47–62.

Crockett, Andrew (2000), 'Commentary: how should financial market regulators respond to the new challenges of global economic integration?', in *Global Economic Integration: Opportunities and Challenges*, proceedings of a symposium sponsored by the Federal Reserve Bank of Kansas City, Jackson Hole, WY, August 24–26, pp. 121–28.

Davis, L. E. and D.C. North (1971), *Institutional Change and American Economic Growth*, Cambridge: Cambridge University Press.

Dierickx, I. and K. Cool (1989), 'Asset stock accumulation and sustainability of competitive advantage', *Management Science* **35**, (12) 1504–11.

Dunning, J.H. (1979), 'Explaining changing patterns of international production: in defense of the eclectic theory', *Oxford Bulletin of Economics and Statistics* **41**(4), 269–95.

Dutta, Soumitra and Amit Jain (2004), 'The networked readiness index 2003–2004: overview and analysis framework', accessed 12 April at www.weforum.org/pdf/Ger/GITR 20 03 2004/Framework Chapter.pdf.

Eisenhardt, K. and J. Martin (2000), 'Dynamic capabilities: what are they?', *Strategic Management Journal* **21**, 1105–122.

Ellickson, Robert C. (1991), *Order Without Law: How Neighbors Settle Disputes*, Cambridge, Mass: Harvard University Press.

ePayment.com (2004), 'Credit card firms trying to retain customer trust', accessed 29 May at www.ePayment.com.

Errunza, Vihang R. (2001), 'Foreign portfolio equity investments, financial liberalization, and economic development', *Review of International Economics* **9** (November) 703–26.

Grant, R.M. (1991), 'The resource-based theory of competitive advantage: Implications for strategy formulation', *California Management Review* **33**(3), 114–35.

Greif, Avner (1989), 'Reputation and coalitions in medieval trade: evidence on the Maghribi traders', *Journal of Economic History* **49**(3), 857–82.

Hendryx, S.R. (1986), 'Implementation of a technology transfer joint venture in the People's Republic of China: a management perspective', *Columbia Journal of World Business*, (Spring) 57–66.

Henisz, Witold J. and A. Zelner Bennet (2001), 'The institutional environment for telecommunications investment', *Journal of Economics & Management Strategy* **10**(1), 123–47

Hitt, L. and E. Brynjolfsson (1996), 'Productivity, business profitability, and consumer surplus: three different measures of information technology value', *MIS Quarterly* **20**(2), 121–42.

Horstmann, I. and J.R. Markusen (1987), 'Licensing versus direct investment: a model of internalization by the multinational enterprise', *Canadian Journal of Economics* **20**(3), 464–81.

IDC (2004), *Information Society Index: 2003*, Washington, DC: IDC.

International Labour Organization (ILO) (2001). *World Employment Report*, Geneva: ILO.

International Monetary Fund (IMF), (2000), *International Capital Markets*, Washington, DC: IMF.

Kaminsky, Graciela and Sergio L. Schmukler (2002), 'Short-run pain, long-run gain: the effects of financial liberalization', *World Bank Policy Research* working paper no. 2912.

Kauffman, R. and E. Walden (2001), 'Economics and electronic commerce: survey and directions for research', *International Journal of Electronic Commerce* **5**(4), 5–116.

King, R. and R. Levine (1993), 'Finance and growth: Schumpeter might be right', *Quarterly Journal of Economics* **108**(3), 681–737.

Lado, A.A. and M.C. Wilson (1994), 'Human resource systems and sustained competitive advantage: a competency-based perspective', *Academy of Management Review* **19**, 699–727.

Levy, Brian and Pablo T. Spiller (1996), *Regulations, Institutions and Commitment*, Cambridge: Cambridge University Press.

Lippman, S.A. and R. Rumelt (1982), 'Uncertain imitability: an analysis of interfirm differences in efficiency under competition', *Bell Journal of Economics* **13**, 418–38.

Marris, R.L. (1963), 'A Model of the "Managerial" Enterprise', *Quarterly Journal of Economics* **77**, 185–209.

Milgrom, P. and J. Roberts (1990), 'The economics of modern manufacturing: technology, strategy, and organization', *American Economic Review* **80**(3), 511–28.

Mukhopadhyay, T., S. Kekre and S. Kalathur (1995), 'Business value of information technology: a study of electronic data interchange', *MIS Quarterly* **19**(2), 137–56.

North, D.C. (1986), 'The new institutional economics', *Journal of Institutional and Theoretical Economics* **1**.

OECD (2002), *Communications Outlook*, Paris: OECD.

Orlikowski, W.J. and Barley, S.R. (2001), 'Technology and institutions: what can research on Information Technology and research on organizations learn from each other?', *MIS Quarterly* **25**:2, 145–65.

Oxley, J. and B. Yeung (2001), 'E-commerce readiness: institutions and international competitiveness', *Journal of International Business Studies* **32**(4).

Oxley, Joanne Elizabeth (1999), 'Institutional environment and the mechanisms of governance: the impact of intellectual property protection on the structure of inter-firm alliances', *Journal of Economic Behavior and Organization* **38**(3), 283–310.

Penrose, E.T. (1959), *The Theory of the Growth of the Firm*, New York: Wiley.

Peteraf, M.A. (1993), 'The cornerstones of competitive advantage: a resource-based view', *Strategic Management J.* **14**(3), 179–91.

Porter, M. (1991), 'Towards a dynamic theory of strategy', *Strategic Management Journal*, **12**, 95–117.

Redding, S.G. (1990), 'The Spirit of Chinese Capitalism', *Studies in Organization* **22**, New York: W. de Gruyter.

Reed, R. and R.J. DeFillippi (1990), 'Causal ambiguity, barriers to imitation, and sustainable competitive advantage', *Academy of Management Review* **15**(1), 88–102.

Shapiro, C. and H. Varian (1999), *Information Rules: A Strategic Guide to the Networking Economy*, Boston, MA: Harvard Business Press.

Teece, D.J., G.A. Pisano and A. Shuen (1997), 'Dynamic capabilities and strategic management', *Strategic Management Journal* **18**, 509–33.

Thompson, J.D. (1967), *Organizations in Action*, New York: McGraw-Hill.

Tsang, E.W.K. (1995), 'The implementation of technology transfer in Sino-foreign joint ventures', *International Journal of Technology Management* **10**(7/8), 757–66.

United Nations Development Programme (UNDP) (2003), *The Arab Human Development Report*, New York: United Nations.

Weber, Max (1981), *General Economic History*, New Brunswick, NJ: Transaction Books.

Weill, P. and M. Broadbent (1998), *Leveraging the New Infrastructure How Market Leaders Capitalize on Information Technology*, cambridge, MA: Harvard Business School Press.

Wernerfelt, B. (1984), 'A resource-based view of the firm', *Strategic Management Journal* **5**, 171–80.

Wheeler, B.C. (2002), 'NEBIC: a dynamic capabilities theory for assessing net-enablement', *Information Systems Research* **13**(2), 125–46.

World Bank (2001), *Finance for Growth: Policy Choices in a Volatile World*, a World Bank policy research report, Oxford: Oxford University Press and World Bank.

5. Data collection and empirical results

INTRODUCTION

The literature on electronic commerce (e-commerce) diffusion is novel but has already established a foundation for discussions. The rapid expansion of the Internet holds substantial promise for developing countries, which can benefit to a great extent from the Internet's communication and information capacity to help meet their economic, social and political needs. The increasing speed of inserting information into electronic media is making information resources based anywhere in the world available to all citizens of the globe through the Internet. Developing countries are the number one beneficiaries of the recent revolution in communication and information technology. The revolution serves, and can serve, all sectors of society. The areas of education, health, social policy, commerce and trade, government, agriculture, communications, and research and development (R&D) all are prime winners.

The correlation between information, communication, and economic growth is well known, making the usefulness of networks nearly self-evident. Electronic networking is a strong, speedy, and economical way to communicate and to exchange information. When networks are available, collaboration among various entities and individuals seems to come into being almost spontaneously.

Forrester estimates that the growth of e-commerce has been overwhelming and reached US$6.8 trillion in 2004 (Forrester Research, 2003). In many countries, government and business entities have used the Internet to decrease transaction costs, reach a wider audience and improve profitability. Customers are the prime beneficiaries: they use the Internet as a way to gather information and increase their search efficiency and effectiveness. Furthermore, the growth of e-commerce has created new sources of products and superior choices for consumers similar to benefits achieved by business. Unfortunately, not many developing countries have jumped on the bandwagon of the Internet and e-commerce, which has led to a widening digital divide.

The digital divide is a very serious matter for those who are currently behind in Internet access, for they are not able to enjoy many benefits of being wired and are handicapped in participating fully in society's economic, political and social life. These benefits include finding lower prices for goods and services, working from home, acquiring new skills using distance learning, making better-informed decisions about healthcare needs, and getting more involved in the education of their children. These are only some of the myriad benefits conferred by Internet access. Thus, for citizens of developing countries, lagging behind in Internet access entails further lagging behind in economic progress in the quality of life. Developing countries lagging behind in the European Community (EC) find themselves in an increasingly difficult position as they attempt to promote their exports, attract capital investment and jobs, and transform their economies. A variety of reasons have been suggested for the digital divide, from the lack of telecommunications infrastructure, dearth of computer skills on the part of business and consumers, failure of regulatory reform and standards, as well as the poor state of physical infrastructure, such as roads, rail, etc.

Developing countries now play an increasingly important role in international trade and investment. Since 1980, their share of world manufactured exports has doubled from 10 to 20 percent. According to World Bank (1997) projections, their share of world trade and output could roughly double to 50 percent and 30 percent, respectively, by 2020. The greatest obstacle to the growth of global trade, including global e-commerce, is the continued imposition of trade barriers (White, 2000) that block a potentially vast range of new goods and production processes. It has been calculated that a cumulative negative effect of 20 percent on investment and profits results from a 10 percent duty on imports (Richman, 1993).

The fastest growing developing countries are those with the highest degree of openness to imports and exports (Sachs and Warner, 1995; Edwards, 1998). A similarity exists with trade liberalization and Internet adoption. The majority of the countries cited as failing to liberalize trade are found to have very low Internet penetration rates, mainly as a result of poor investment in their telecommunications infrastructure and availability of computers. Stephenson and Ivascanu (2001) illustrate that within the Western hemisphere, Internet use is highest in those countries where density of telephone use is greater, where the provision of telecommunication services is more competitive, and where the combined costs required to access and use the Internet are lower.

The literature on e-commerce adoption in developing countries is extremely limited, although some evidence exists describing the impediments (Travica, 2002). Petrazzini and Kibati (1999) report on e-commerce impediments characterizing Argentina, Armenia, India, and Kenya. These include limited

Internet accessibility, a lack of competition in international telephone traffic that makes access to the international network expensive, a lack of intra-regional infrastructure, and a disproportionate penetration of the telephone in the urban as opposed to rural, more populated areas. South Korea shares the problems of customers' distrust in online merchants (Lee, 1999). Plant (1999) identifies obstacles to e-commerce in Latin America, such as the lack of customer protection laws, tradition of remote shopping, methods of non-cash payment and Internet culture. Montealegre (1999) draws on King et al (1994) and suggests that both society and culture must be considered for successful adoption in developing countries. He illustrates examples of Latin American countries that have successfully adopted technology using varying combinations of government, non-governmental, and business organizations. Other cases (Peha, 1999; Clark, 1999) cite examples from Haiti and China, respectively, where the successful adoption of telecommunications technology had been achieved as a result of competition between government agencies (that formerly controlled the telecommunications networks) and private entities. Davis (1999) indicates that accessibility to technology is the limiting factor, while in reality it is a combination of infrastructure and organizational culture.

In recent years, economists have analyzed the impact of a technology developed in an industrialized country which is copied by a developing country. They have shown that the rate of growth of the developing country depends on its initial stock of knowledge and the costs of imitation (Barro and Sala-I-Martin, 1995). They have further argued that if the costs of imitation are lower than the costs of innovation, the poorer country can grow faster than the richer one by leapfrogging technologies development through participating and competing in global trade and sharing information globally (Srikantaiah and Xiaoying, 1998). For instance, countries with an underdeveloped telecommunications infrastructure can implement a digital telecom network and avoid the costs many developed countries incurred in first laying out an analogue system.

Yet, even when developing countries adopt e-commerce, the technologies are not always optimized. A survey by the International Trade Center (ITC) discovered that businesses in developing countries view their Internet connectivity as a valuable communications tool, but failed to incorporate the technology as an aspect of their competitive strategy (Barclay and Domeisen, 2001). Business perception contributes to the fact that less than one third of the surveyed countries included electronic trade as a component of their national export development strategies, an excellent indicator of the need for close cooperation between government and business during this technology adoption.

To facilitate the introduction of the Internet and eventually electronic commerce/services, the necessary and sufficient condition is the creation of the communication's infrastructure. For developing countries, financial resources needed to invest in communication infrastructure are one of the major barriers since most countries rely on foreign aids. A number of initiatives undertaken by developed countries are helping to narrow the digital divide, albeit limited in terns of scope and weight; the Leland Initiative, for instance, is a 5-year US$15 million project sponsored by the United States (US) government to provide Internet connectivity in more than 20 African countries. In addition to developing infrastructure, the objective of the program is to create a sustainable supply of Internet services including training, marketing, and extension into rural areas, as well as support and training for small to medium-sized businesses (USAID, 2003). The user-based initiative relies on the partnerships of local banks, companies, and governmental entities. Expanding on the development of the communications infrastructure projects, for example, the Leland initiative, is the creation of community learning centers (CLCs), which have their roots in former post and telegraph offices that served as central points for public information and communication. These centers, widely popular in some countries in Africa and Latin America, provide inexpensive Internet access plus a variety of business services such as faxing, photocopying, word processing, and printing that reduce the cost of equipment and connection fees. In addition to these services, the CLCs provide training and education in both technology and business management issues (Fountaine, 2003).

A number of infrastructure development challenges include: (1) the development of physical telecommunications infrastructure; (2) the provision of universal access at a reasonable cost; (3) the achievement of interconnection and interoperability of telecommunications; and, (4) the establishment of networks and services.

The reminder of this chapter deals with data collection on the various variables identified in Chapter 4, the proposed operational measurements of the independent variables and the dependent variable, discussion of methodology, and analysis of the empirical results.

DATA COLLECTION

In order to assess the significance of the various economic resources in explaining the development of e-commerce in developing countries, the authors assembled cross-sectional data for 44 emerging and developing economies which have implemented e-commerce initiatives. Data on Internet usage and other indicators of e-commerce activities were collected. Table 5.1 shows our sample countries organized according to the World Bank classification. According to this classification, economies are divided according to their 2003 gross national income (GNI) per capita, calculated using the World Bank Atlas method. The groups are: low income, with GNI of US$765 or less; lower middle income, with GNI of US$766 – US$3,035; upper middle income, with GNI of US$3,036 – US$9,385; and high income, with GNI of US$9,386 or more.

In calculating GNI (formerly referred to as Gross National Product (GNP)) and GNI per capita in US dollars for certain operational purposes, the World Bank uses the Atlas conversion factor. The purpose of the Atlas conversion factor is to reduce the impact of exchange rate fluctuations in the cross-country comparison of national incomes.

The Atlas conversion factor for any year is the average of a country's exchange rate (or alternative conversion factor) for that year and its exchange rates for the two preceding years, adjusted for the difference between the rate of inflation in the country, and through the year 2000, that in the G5 countries (France, Germany, Japan, the United Kingdom, and the US). For 2001 onwards, these countries include the Euro Zone, Japan, the United Kingdom, and the US. A country's inflation rate is measured by the change in its gross domestic product (GDP) deflator.

The inflation rate for G5 countries (through 2000, and the Euro Zone, Japan, the UK, and the US for 2001 onwards), representing international inflation, is measured by the change in the special drawing rights (SDR) deflator (SDRs are the International Monetary Fund's (IMF's) unit of account.) The SDR deflator is calculated as a weighted average of the G5 countries' GDP deflators in SDR terms, the weights being the amount of each country's currency in one SDR unit. Weights vary over time because both the composition of the SDR and the relative exchange rates for each currency change. The SDR deflator is calculated in SDR terms first and then converted to US dollars using the SDR to dollar Atlas conversion factor. The Atlas conversion factor is then applied to a country's GNI. The resulting GNI in US dollars is divided by the mid-year population to derive GNI per capita.

OPERATIONAL MEASUREMENTS

In the current research, the level of e-commerce activities is the dependent variable. The proposed measurements of the dependent and independent variables are presented below.

E-commerce Activities (Dependent Variable)

Developing practical measures of actual e-commerce activity is a considerable challenge. At present only a few developed countries, such as

Table 5.1   World Bank Classification

Country	GNI group	Country	GNI group
Algeria	Lower Middle	Mexico	Upper Middle
Argentina	Upper Middle	Nigeria	Low
Bolivia	Lower Middle	Oman	Upper Middle
Brazil	Upper Middle	Pakistan	Low
Bulgaria	Lower Middle	Peru	Lower Middle
Chile	Upper Middle	Philippines	Lower Middle
China	Lower Middle	Poland	Upper Middle
Colombia	Lower Middle	Qatar	High
Czech Republic	Upper Middle	Romania	Lower Middle
Ecuador	Lower Middle	Russia	Lower Middle
Egypt	Lower Middle	Saudi Arabia	Upper Middle
Hong Kong	High	Singapore	High
Hungary	Upper Middle	Slovakia	Upper Middle
India	Low	South Africa	Lower Middle
Indonesia	Lower Middle	Sri Lanka	Lower Middle
Iran	Lower Middle	Taiwan	Middle
Israel	High	Thailand	Lower Middle
Jordan	Lower Middle	Turkey	Lower Middle
Kazakhstan	Lower Middle	UAE	High
Korea	High	Ukraine	Low
Lebanon	Upper Middle	Uruguay	Upper Middle
Malaysia	Upper Middle	Vietnam	Low

Source: GNI World Bank classification, World Bank, Washington, DC.

the US, the UK and Australia, have initiated national data collection on the value of goods purchased online. Estimates of e-commerce activities in different parts of the world are available from consulting firms focusing on e-commerce, but this category of data is not suitable for cross-country comparisons. Most companies provide data only for some, not all, regions. Those with more complete global coverage use different methodologies for estimates in different regions and cannot provide reliable data at the country level (Oxley and Yeung, 2001). As a result, there is wide variation in detailed assessments of e-commerce activity at the country level, although there is general agreement that activity is concentrated in the US and, secondarily, in Europe.

Since reliable data on e-commerce activities is not readily available, the authors elected to use the number of 'Internet users per capita' (PCINTU) as a proxy measure for e-commerce activities. Notwithstanding the number of shortcomings associated with the number of Internet users as a proxy for the diffusion of e-commerce and electronic government (e-government) in an economy, it is still the best indicator available.

Data on the number of Internet users in a country are available from the International Labor Union (ILO) 2004 *Statistical Yearbook.*

Human Resources

The Human Development Index (HDI) is a widely discussed relatively new measure of the effect of economic development on the well being of the people. The United Nations Development Program (UNDP) developed the HDI during the early 1990s when, in the economic literature, 'per capita income' was considered as an inadequate measure of development (especially, for emerging and developing countries). It was argued, 'real' gross domestic product (GDP) per person growth was not necessarily a good guide to growth of living standards in the twentieth century; it was probably a considerable underestimate (Crafts, 1999). The HDI shifted the focus of economic development from (per capita) income to a much broader achievement in human life.

The HDI measures the overall achievement of a country in three basic dimensions of human development; longevity, knowledge, and decent standard of living, all of which we consider as indigenous resources. Longevity is measured by life expectancy at birth, knowledge (or educational attainment) is measured by a combination of adult literacy (two-thirds weights) and the combined primary, secondary and tertiary enrolment (one-third weight), and standard of living is measured by real GDP per capita (US$PPP). To calculate the HDI score, at first, for each indicator of human development, a range (a maximum and a minimum) is established. Then, the difference of score of a country on each indicator (actual score minus minimum of the range) is divided by the range itself. The HDI is a simple average of the three indicators so obtained.

Despite its popularity as an index, it is not far from criticism. The concept of human development has a broad meaning and cannot be captured by an index or a set of indicators (Streeten, 1994). The index was also criticized on various grounds. These include the construction of the scale and measurement (Dasgupta and Weale, 1992; Desai, 1991; Luchters, 1996; Srinivisan, 1994), methodology (Srinivisan, 1994), and data quality/ limitations issues (McGillivray and White, 1993). Despite its limitations, the HDI is a useful measure to gauge the status of human development in a country. Economists agree that while there is a strong relationship between development and income, human outcomes do not depend on economic growth and levels of national income alone. They also depend on how these resources are used. For instance, democratic participation in decision making and equal rights for men and women are two of the most important human development indicators but they do not depend on income or GDP.

The HDI is derived from the *2004 Human Development Index Report* published by the United Nations (UN). This report presents an extensive set of indicators, including 33 tables and 200 variables, on important human outcomes realized in countries around the world.

The HDI focuses on three measurable dimensions of human development: living a long and healthy life, being well-educated, and having a decent standard of living. Table 5.2 shows the values of the three dimensions of the HDI index along with the HDI index for each country in our sample. These figures are compiled from the *2004 Human Development Index Report*, published by the UN.

A close examination of Table 5.2 reveals that Israel is ranked number one in our sample with an HDI value of 0.908, closely followed by Hong Kong (0.903) and Singapore (0.902). The country that ranked at the bottom of the list in our sample is Nigeria with an HDI of 0.466, followed by Pakistan (0.497) and India (0.595). The average HDI value for all countries in our sample is 0.766, with a standard deviation of 0.094. This small standard deviation indicates a narrow distribution where all values cluster around the mean.

In our statistical analysis the HDI index will be utilized to measure human development in a country.

Financial Resources

As discussed in Chapter 4, information technology (IT) has led to the promotion of a more intensive use of international financial institutions and gave rise to global international conglomerates. In addition, previous studies have found evidence that a well-developed, sound financial system promotes growth in the economy by channeling credit to its most productive uses.

A robust, well-functioning financial sector is vital for economic growth and successful electronic activities, especially for developing economies. It is critical for vigorous sustained growth. As an economy grows and matures, its financial sector must grow with it. It must be able to fit with the increasingly sophisticated demands that are placed on it. To help in the process of development and changes in the structural underpinning of the economy, financial institutions must adapt as economies mature. However, as economies grow and become more digitized, their agricultural and manufacturing sectors expand; their services sectors then develop and grow, and their banking sectors need to keep up. Decisions as to which activities

Table 5.2   HDI values of sample countries

Country	Life Expectancy Index	Education Index	GDP Index	HDI Value
Algeria	0.74	0.69	0.68	0.704
Argentina	0.82	0.96	0.78	0.853
Bolivia	0.64	0.86	0.53	0.681
Brazil	0.72	0.88	0.73	0.775
Bulgaria	0.77	0.91	0.71	0.796
Chile	0.85	0.90	0.77	0.839
China	0.76	0.83	0.64	0.745
Colombia	0.78	0.84	0.69	0.773
Czech Republic	0.84	0.92	0.84	0.868
Ecuador	0.76	0.85	0.60	0.735
Egypt	0.73	0.62	0.61	0.653
Hong Kong	0.91	0.86	0.93	0.903
Hungary	0.78	0.95	0.82	0.848
India	0.64	0.59	0.55	0.595
Indonesia	0.69	0.80	0.58	0.692
Iran	0.75	0.74	0.70	0.732
Israel	0.90	0.94	0.88	0.908
Jordan	0.76	0.86	0.62	0.750
Kazakhstan	0.69	0.93	0.68	0.766
Korea	0.84	0.97	0.86	0.888
Lebanon	0.81	0.84	0.63	0.758
Malaysia	0.80	0.83	0.75	0.793
Mexico	0.81	0.85	0.75	0.802
Nigeria	0.44	0.59	0.36	0.466
Oman	0.79	0.71	0.82	0.770
Pakistan	0.60	0.40	0.49	0.497
Peru	0.74	0.86	0.65	0.752
Philippines	0.75	0.89	0.62	0.753
Poland	0.81	0.96	0.78	0.850
Qatar	0.78	0.83	0.88	0.833
Romania	0.76	0.88	0.70	0.778
Russia	0.69	0.95	0.74	0.795
Saudi Arabia	0.79	0.71	0.81	0.768
Singapore	0.88	0.91	0.92	0.902
Slovakia	0.81	0.91	0.81	0.842
South Africa	0.40	0.83	0.77	0.666
Sri Lanka	0.79	0.83	0.60	0.740
Taiwan	0.78	0.79	0.77	0.780
Thailand	0.74	0.86	0.71	0.768
Turkey	0.76	0.80	0.69	0.751
UAE	0.83	0.74	0.90	0.824
Ukraine	0.74	0.94	0.65	0.777
Uruguay	0.84	0.94	0.73	0.833
Vietnam	0.73	0.82	0.52	0.691

to finance are crucial for rapid growth. Growing economic complexity is, of course, an inevitable consequence of growth. It means that the benefits of efficient credit allocation rise; that efficient credit allocation is financing investments where the payoff is highest. However, it also means that the challenges for those assessing alternative loan applicants mount. They must develop the means of allocating credit among competing needs. They must learn to assess business plans and identify and manage risk.

For our purpose, we will use the following two variables to assess the financial strength of an economy: (1) access to sound money, as related to monetary policy; and (2) banking and finance as they relate to credit market regulations. The ranking of the countries based on these four components is taken from the *2005 Heritage Foundation Index of Economic Freedom.*

A country's monetary policy affects the stability of its financial base. With a stable monetary policy, people can rely on market prices for the foreseeable future. Hence, investment, savings, and other longer-term plans are easier to make, and individuals enjoy greater economic freedom. Inflation not only confiscates wealth, but also distorts pricing, misallocates resources, raises the cost of doing business, and undermines the movement of capital and investment into the society.

In the majority of countries, banks provide the essential financial services that facilitate economic growth; they lend money to start businesses, purchase homes, and secure credit that is used to buy durable consumer goods, in addition to furnishing a safe place in which individuals can store their earnings. The more banks are controlled by the government, the less free they are to engage in these activities. Hence, heavy bank regulation reduces opportunities and restricts economic growth and therefore, the more a government restricts its banking sector, the lower its level of economic growth and the higher its score.

Table 5.3 shows the sample countries rated on the four components measuring the financial strengths of the economies. The two variables used to measure the soundness of the financial base in a country are (1) access to sound money (ACSMNY) and (2) credit market regulations (CRDREG).

Access and Technical Capabilities

Countries are usually at very different starting positions in the task of building their digital infrastructure to facilitate the development and diffusion of e-commerce applications. E-commerce infrastructure determines the level of access and technical capabilities of an economy, and is defined as the share of total economic infrastructure used to support electronic business processes and conduct e-commerce transactions. The

Table 5.3   Financial strengths of countries in the sample

Country	Size of Government Expenditures, Taxes and Enterprises	Access to Sound Money	Credit Market Regulations
Algeria	4.1	6.7	4.5
Argentina	7.7	7.0	6.7
Bolivia	7.3	9.7	7.9
Brazil	6.5	7.7	5.6
Bulgaria	4.6	8.3	7.9
Chile	6.1	9.2	8.3
China	3.1	8.5	4.7
Colombia	4.7	7.4	7.2
Czech Republic	4.9	8.9	8.1
Ecuador	9.0	4.4	6.5
Egypt	6.9	9.6	5.3
Hong Kong	9.1	9.3	8.9
Hungary	5.7	9.1	7.9
India	7.1	6.9	5.9
Indonesia	6.8	6.4	5.2
Iran	6.5	8.2	4.8
Israel	2.6	9.2	7.2
Jordan	4.8	9.7	6.4
Kazakhstan[a]	4.3	–	–
Korea	7.4	9.2	7.4
Lebanon[a]	–	–	–
Malaysia	5.4	6.6	5.8
Mexico	8.1	7.4	7.2
Nigeria	6.3	6.6	7.5
Oman	5.8	9.9	9.6
Pakistan	7.2	6.9	7.1
Peru	7.4	9.7	8.5
Philippines	6.9	9.4	7.6
Poland	5.6	7.9	8.1
Qatar[a]	–	–	–
Romania	4.5	6.2	7.2
Russia	5.3	3.8	6.0
Saudi Arabia[a]	–	–	–
Singapore	8.0	9.7	7.9
Slovakia	4.5	8.2	7.9
South Africa	5.6	7.8	8.8
Sri Lanka	7.4	6.5	6.7
Taiwan	6.2	9.7	6.3
Thailand	6.6	6.7	7.0
Turkey	7.0	4.0	6.1
UAE	7.6	9.1	6.8
Ukraine	3.3	6.0	6.9
Uruguay	7.4	8.7	6.3
Vietnam[a]	–	–	–

Note: Data not available or incomplete.

Source: compiled from *Economic Freedom of the World: 2004 Annual Report*, The PRS Group.

innovation of Internet technology, coupled with different environment and policy externalities, leads to distinctive arrangements determining specific diffusion path among individual countries and regions. Identifying the unique resources of countries is essential for understanding e-commerce diffusion in these countries. Some large developing countries, like Brazil, are faced with obstacles and opportunities to diffuse the Internet across it economy and society. Telecommunication infrastructure is often a stumbling block for developing countries. Based on this statement, countries lagging behind a certain level of telephone density would be severely handicapped for e-commerce diffusion.

Our access and technical capabilities measures focus on a number of indicators describing the availability of reasonably priced access to the Internet. For most current applications, Internet access requires a personal computer (PC), plus a phone connection to the Internet, although access via a mobile phone is becoming a viable alternative in some applications and in a number of countries in our sample, such as the UAE. For the purpose of our study, we used the following infrastructure indicators: (1) total number of telephone subscribers; (2) number of Internet hosts; and (3) number of PCs. Data for 2003 on the total number of PCs, phone lines, number of Internet users, and mobile phones in each country are taken from the International Telecommunication Union yearbook (ITU, 2004). We scale each of these totals by population to produce per-capita measures: 'TLLINE', 'PCHOSTS', and 'PC#'.

Rule of Law

A major concern for scholars of development and growth is the 'rule of law' and the related concepts from other legal systems. Economic growth, political adjustment, the protection of human rights, and other admirable objectives are all thought to revolve around the 'rule of law'. Policymakers in developing and emerging economies are thus seeking ways to establish or strengthen the rule of law in their countries. Despite the assortment of definitions of the term, 'rule of law', most can be classified according to whether they emphasize formal characteristics, substantive outcomes, or functional considerations. The differences between these three conceptions and the implications of each for efforts to establish, measure, or foster the rule of law can be found in Stephenson (2001).

Levy and Spiller (1996) developed a framework to analyze the interaction of the institutional endowment of a country, the nature of its regulatory institutions, and the performance of the various sectors. They emphasize that the integrity and value of a regulatory framework differ with a country's political and social institutions. They also observe that performance can be adequate, with a wide range of regulatory measures, as soon as three complementary means limiting arbitrary administrative action are all in place: (1) substantive restraints on the discretion of the regulator; (2) formal or informal constraints on changing the regulatory structure; and (3) institutions that implement and enforce the above formal constraints.

The basic political institutions of a country refer to the nature of its judiciary and its legislative and executive institutions. Specifically, a self-governing and professional judiciary is a natural candidate for fulfilling the condition of enforcing formal constraints. A dishonest, politically motivated, judiciary will be unlikely to side against the government on sensitive matters. Thus, judicial independence and professionalism imply a more confident framework for enforcing contracts; hence increasing the confidence of customers in the economy. Levy and Spiller further emphasize the role of the contending social interests within a society and the balance between them. In actuality, the more controversial these social interests are, the higher the potential for a reversing of government policies. The higher the political instability of a country, the higher the potential for opportunistic behavior by governments, and hence the more inefficient will the performance of the sector be. Finally, Levy and Spiller stress the importance of administrative capabilities. Practically, the higher the administrative potential of the country, the higher the potential superiority of the regulatory system, and, hence, the higher the performance of the sector.

For the sake of our study, we employed the most widely accepted measure of the rule of law, which was developed by the **PRS Group**, a country risk rating agency, in its *International Country Risk Guide (ICRG)*. This measure (LAW) takes on a value between one and ten; higher values indicate a stronger rule of law in a country.

The ICRG Risk Rating System assigns a numerical value (risk points) to a predetermined range of risk components, according to a predefined scale, for each country covered in the analysis. Each scale is designed to award the highest value to the lowest risk and the lowest value to the highest risk. To allow for comparability, all countries are assessed on the same basis scale. The risk components are grouped into three risk categories: economic, financial, and political. Each risk category is made up of a number of risk components. The sum of the risk points assigned to each risk component within each risk category determines the overall risk rating for that risk category. The objective of the political risk rating is to provide a means of assessing the political stability of the countries covered on a comparable basis. To produce the political risk ratings, the following risk components are used: government stability, socio-economic conditions, investment profile, internal conflict, external conflict, corruption, military in politics, and religion in politics. Each of these components is assessed, evaluated, weighted and then they are all combined to produce the political risk factor.

The prime objective of the economic risk rating is to present a way of measuring a country's economic strengths and weaknesses. In general, if a country's strengths outweigh its weaknesses it will be classified as a low economic risk and if its weaknesses outweigh its strengths it will be classified as a high economic risk. Country's strengths and weaknesses are evaluated and measured by assigning risk points to a number of economic risk components. The minimum number of points that can be assigned to any component is zero and the maximum number is assessed based on the weight that component is given in the overall economic risk assessment (PRS, 2003). In all cases, the lower the number of points, the higher the risk. In addition, and to ensure comparability between countries, the components are based on accepted ratios between measured data within the financial and economic structures of the country. To produce the economic risk ratings, the following risk components are used: GDP per head, real GDP growth, annual inflation rate, budget balance as a percentage of GDP, and current account as a percentage of GDP.[1]

The financial risk rating provides a means of evaluating a country's ability to pay its way. Consequently, this entails a system of measuring a country's ability to finance its official, commercial and trade debt obligations. The financial risk components identified and weighted by the ICRG are: foreign debt as a percentage of GDP, foreign debt service as a percentage of exports of goods and services, current account as a percentage of exports of goods and services, net international liquidity as months of import cover, and exchange rate stability. The method of calculating the composite index is based on a formula that assigns 50 percent to political risk and 25 percent each to financial and economic ratings. Table 5.4 represents the country risk ranked by composite risk rating for 2003.

Our sample contains six countries in the very low risk category, or 13.6 percent. The bulk of our countries (20 countries in the sample) fall in the low risk category; this constitutes 45.5 percent of the countries in the sample. The moderate risk category contains 16 countries or 36.4 percent of our sample. Only two countries, or 0.05 percent, fall in the high risk category, and these are Nigeria and Lebanon. We use the composite risk factor as defined by the ICRG to assess the rule of the law in a given country. In our sample, this measure (LAW) takes on a value between 88.3 and 55.5; higher values indicate a stronger rule of law in a country.

Cyberlaw

(As discussed in Chapter 4) Table 5.5 lists the countries in our sample, whether or not the country has an e-commerce law or cyberlaw.

In Latin America, Colombia is among the leaders in terms of regulators when considering e-commerce regulation, access law and prices to the end

Table 5.4   Country risk and ranking for our sample (September 2003)

Country	Composite Risk	Rank in 2003	Risk Category
Singapore	88.3	4	Very low
Kuwait	86.3	11	Very low
UAE	84.5	16	Very low
Taiwan	83.0	19	Very low
Hong Kong	81.5	21	Very low
Korea	80.8	24	Very low
Oman	79.8	28	Low
Qatar	78.5	35	Low
Czech Republic	78.3	37	Low
China	77.3	39	Low
Chile	76.8	40	Low
Hungary	76.8	40	Low
Saudi Arabia	76.8	40	Low
Malaysia	75.8	48	Low
Poland	75.5	49	Low
Slovakia	75.5	49	Low
Thailand	75.5	49	Low
Russia	75.0	53	Low
Israel	72.5	57	Low
Kazakhstan	72.3	58	Low
Mexico	72.0	61	Low
Bulgaria	71.8	62	Low
Jordan	71.0	64	Low
Iran	70.5	65	Low
Romania	70.5	65	Low
Philippines	70.0	68	Low
Vietnam	69.8	69	Moderate
India	69.0	72	Moderate
Ukraine	68.8	73	Moderate
South Africa	68.5	75	Moderate
Peru	68.3	76	Moderate
Algeria	66.3	82	Moderate
Brazil	66.3	82	Moderate
Egypt	65.8	85	Moderate
Argentina	65.0	89	Moderate
Uruguay	64.5	91	Moderate
Colombia	63.5	94	Moderate
Pakistan	63.5	94	Moderate
Sri Lanka	63.5	94	Moderate
Ecuador	63.3	97	Moderate
Turkey	61.8	107	Moderate
Indonesia	61.3	108	Moderate
Nigeria	57.0	122	High
Lebanon	55.5	123	High

Source: PRS Group (2003).

users. Chile has also made a lot of progress having mandated a certain procedure called unbundling of the local loop, which means that the incumbent, which is Telefonica, has to provide lower charge access fees for Internet usage. Brazil also has been proactive in that sense. The laggards are countries like Venezuela, Ecuador, and Bolivia, which are less developed and in some cases still have monopoly long-distance or local service providers, and that really haven't embraced liberalization on any front.

As developing and emerging countries join the World Trade Organization (WTO) they have been adapting their legal and regulatory systems to accommodate trademark, patent and intellectual property rights (IPR) protection. Some countries have been part of the early stages of such IPR protection; others have retroactively signed the agreements and sought membership in the World Intellectual Property Organization (WIPO). Only five countries in our sample are not members of the WTO.

Developing and emerging countries' participation in interim treaties is uneven. These include the WIPO Copyright Treaty (WCT), the Trademark Law Treaty (TLT), and the Patent Law Treaty (PLT). As of September 2004, for instance, only 48 states worldwide were members of the WCT. Copyright protection extends to expressions and not to ideas, procedures, methods of operation, or mathematical concepts as such (WIPO, 2004). Only 18 countries in our sample are members of the WCT, or 41 percent. The UAE was the latest cosignatory, having become a member on July 14, 2004.

As of October 2004, only 33 countries worldwide have signed the TLT. As Table 5.5 indicates, only 11 countries in our sample are cosignatories to this treaty, or only 25 percent (Turkey became bound by the Treaty on January 1, 2005). Only 54 countries worldwide were cosignatories to the PLT. Table 5.6 shows that only 10 countries in our sample are among those, or 23 percent.

In its 2003–06 action plan, Singapore adopted three outcomes for e-government: delighted customers, connected citizens, and networked government. Singapore is in the process of reviewing its current suite of online services against the needs of the public to identify opportunities for service innovation that will yield greater value. In some cases, these action plans are not supported by an all-encompassing approach to measuring value or progress; however, in many cases such a measurement framework is planned. Mexico, for example, is developing a new project management system for e-government that will include metrics, key performance indicators and a scorecard to facilitate evaluating its e-Mexico initiative.

Given the lack of information on the soundness of cyberlaws in the various countries, the author will use the length of time the law was enacted as a proxy. It is believed that countries that have developed and implemented cyberlaws early have a better and strong commitment to moving their

Table 5.5   Cyber Law in sample countries

Country	Cyber Law (Y/N)	Year Enacted
Algeria	No	–
Argentina	Yes	2001
Bolivia	No	–
Brazil	Yes	2001
Bulgaria	Yes	1999
Chile	Yes	2002
China	No	–
Colombia	Yes	1999
Czech Republic	Yes	2000
Ecuador	Yes	2002
Egypt	No	–
Hong Kong	Yes	2000
Hungary	Yes	2001
India	Yes	1998
Indonesia	No	–
Iran	No	–
Israel	Yes	2001
Jordan	No	–
Kazakhstan	No	–
Korea	Yes	2001
Lebanon	No	–
Malaysia	Yes	1997
Mexico	Yes	2000
Nigeria	No	–
Oman	No	–
Pakistan	No	–
Peru	Yes	2000
Philippines	Yes	2000
Poland	Yes	2001
Qatar	No	–
Romania	Yes	2001
Russia	Yes	2001
Saudi Arabia	No	–
Singapore	Yes	1998
Slovakia	Yes	2002
South Africa	Yes	2002
Sri Lanka	No	–
Taiwan	Yes	2001
Thailand	Yes	2000
Turkey	No	–
UAE	No	–
Ukraine	No	
Uruguay	Yes	2000
Vietnam	Yes	2002

Source: compiled by the authors from various resources.

Table 5.6   Status of countries on intellectual property rights

Country	WTO Member	WCT	TLT	PLT member
Algeria	–	–	–	Yes
Argentina	1995	2002	–	–
Bolivia	1995	–	–	–
Brazil	1995	–	–	Yes
Bulgaria	1996	2002		
Chile	1995	2002	–	–
China	2001	–	–	–
Colombia	1995	2002	–	–
Czech Republic	1995	2002	1996	Yes
Ecuador	1996	2002	–	–
Egypt	1995	–	1999	–
Hong Kong	1995	–	–	–
Hungary	1995	2002	1998	Yes
India	1995	–	–	–
Indonesia	1995	2002	1997	–
Iran[a]				
Israel	1995	–	–	Yes
Jordan	2000	2004	–	–
Kazakhstan	2000	2004	2002	–
Korea	1995	2004	2003	–
Lebanon	–	–	–	Yes
Malaysia	1995	–	–	–
Mexico	1995	2002	–	–
Nigeria	1995	–	–	Yes
Oman	2000	–	–	–
Pakistan	1995	–	–	–
Peru	1995	2002	–	–
Philippines	1995	2002	–	–
Poland	1995	2004	–	Yes
Qatar	1996	–	–	–
Romania	1995	2002	1998	Yes
Russia[a]				
Saudi Arabia[a]				
Singapore	1995	–	–	–
Slovakia	1995	2002	1997	–
South Africa	1995	–	–	–
Sri Lanka	1995	–	1996	–
Taiwan	2002	–	–	–
Thailand	1995	–	–	–
Turkey	1995	–	–	Yes
UAE	1996	2004	–	–
Ukraine	–	–	2005	–
Uruguay	1995	–	1996	–
Vietnam[a]				

Note: a. not signatory nations.

Source: collected by the authors from various resources.

economies into the information/digital ages for the mere development of these laws is a signal and an indication to motivated businesses to move to cyberspace.

The cyberlaw index (CI) variable is constructed from information provided by the above two tables (Tables 5.5 and 5.6) and based on: (1) existence of a cyberlaw (if a country does not have a cyberlaw then a weight of zero is give to this component); (2) membership of the WTO; (3) membership of the WCT; (4) membership of the TLT; and (5) membership of the PLT. These five components are not equally weighted. The authors' judge component (1), existence of a cyberlaw, to be the most important; consequently, it is given a 40 percent weight. Next in terms of importance is membership in the WTO, with a weight of 30 percent. The remaining three components (WCT, TLT, and PLT) are weighted at 10 percent each. Table 5.7 shows the CI for the sample countries.

Table 5.7   Cyberlaw Index

Country	Cyberlaw Index (CI)	Country	Cyberlaw Index (CI)
Algeria	0.10	Mexico	0.80
Argentina	0.80	Nigeria	0.40
Bolivia	0.30	Oman	0.30
Brazil	0.80	Pakistan	0.30
Bulgaria	0.80	Peru	0.80
Chile	0.80	Philippines	0.80
China	0.00	Poland	0.90
Colombia	0.80	Qatar	0.30
Czech Republic	1.00	Romania	1.00
Ecuador	0.80	Russia	0.40
Egypt	0.40	Saudi Arabia	0.00
Hong Kong	0.70	Singapore	0.70
Hungary	1.00	Slovakia	0.90
India	0.70	South Africa	0.70
Indonesia	0.50	Sri Lanka	0.40
Iran	0.00	Taiwan	0.70
Israel	0.80	Thailand	0.70
Jordan	0.40	Turkey	0.40
Kazakhstan	0.50	UAE	0.40
Korea	0.90	Ukraine	0.10
Lebanon	0.10	Uruguay	0.80
Malaysia	0.70	Vietnam	0.40

Source: developed by the authors

Credible Payment Channels

As suggested in our earlier discussion, credit cards are important facilitators of e-commerce as they provide a credible payment channel for online transactions. Credit cards in their present form emerged in the US in the 1960s. Debit cards have been introduced more recently and together they represent the most rapidly growing method of payments in the US as well as several other countries. Credit cards are rapidly growing as the preferred method of settling small value payments associated with the purchase of specific goods and services. To facilitate the process of exchange, separate electronic clearing and settlement systems have been established by the major credit card companies. MasterCard and Visa have established their own networks which are used for verifying transactions world-wide. Electronic point of sale (POS) terminals permit card details to be verified in less than 15 seconds with networks linking the merchant, the credit card processor and the card issuer worldwide. The number of credit cards in use is growing rapidly worldwide. This confirms the basic demand which exists for more efficient electronically based payment systems. A number of constraints, however, are likely to prevent credit cards from becoming the comprehensive worldwide solution for electronic low value payments systems.

In most developing countries, low credit card penetration, low access penetration, and high access costs, as well as poor infrastructure and parcel delivery systems are all contributing to a low diffusion rate of e-commerce. One of the most lamented obstacles for developing countries' business-to-consumer (B2C) segment is the low credit card penetration rates in these countries. The total transaction volume of the 'plastic money' is increasing fast, but is starting from low levels.

The card companies, American Express Co., MasterCard International and Visa International, have recently been working tirelessly to make credit cards a global currency. Since the 1970s, they have aggressively issued cards and pushed merchant acceptance of their brands into every major economy in the world. Included in that push are developing economies such as the countries in our sample. Those efforts have paid off in a big way. Global AmEx, MasterCard and Visa credit and debit card volume totaled US$4.5 trillion in 2003, up from US$3.9 trillion a year earlier, a 15 percent increase. Visa was the biggest gainer, increasing charge volume 16.9 percent to US$2.8 trillion. AmEx posted the new biggest percentage gain, increasing its global volume by 13 percent to US$352 billion. MasterCard volume grew 10.4 percent to US$1.2 trillion (MasterCard, 2004).

We therefore include in our empirical model estimates of credit card penetration rate. This number is derived by dividing the number of credit cards in use in a certain economy by population. Data on credit cards in use in a certain economy was collected from various sources including the *CIA Factbook* (published by the US Central Intelligence Agency); *Country Commercial Guides* (published by the US Department of Commerce), reports published by various credit card companies such as Visa and MasterCard, country reports published by the countries (from Faulkner and Gray's *2000 Global Card Directory*), and, in the case of the UAE, Qatar and Bahrain, from officials in the central banks of the respective countries. The name of the variable is CCPR (credit card penetration rate). Table 5.8 shows credit card penetration rate (CCPRTE) as defined above.

Table 5.8   Credit card penetration rate

Country	CCPR (percentage)	Country	CCPR (percentage)
Algeria	1	Mexico	15
Argentina	46	Nigeria	4
Bolivia	3	Oman	18
Brazil	50	Pakistan	2
Bulgaria	1.5	Peru	13
Chile	24	Philippines	14
China	22	Poland	10
Colombia	24	Qatar	27
Czech Republic	18	Romania	15.5
Ecuador	3.8	Russia	2
Egypt	2	Saudi Arabia	15
Hong Kong	129	Singapore	237
Hungary	29	Slovakia	5
India	10	South Africa	54
Indonesia	3	Sri Lanka	4
Iran	1	Taiwan	16
Israel	48	Thailand	29
Jordan	30	Turkey	23.2
Kazakhstan	1.2	UAE	43
Korea	140	Ukraine	2
Lebanon	9	Uruguay	3
Malaysia	7	Vietnam	2

Source: Collected by the authors from various resources.

Economic Development

Since e-commerce activity, as well as several of our explanatory variables (eg, rule of law, infrastructure measures), are likely to correlate significantly with the level of economic development in a country, it is important that we control for this aspect of country difference. We therefore include in our empirical model a control variable, the natural log of per capita in each country, LPCI. These data are for 2002 (the latest available) and are drawn from the *World Development Report 2004* (World Bank, 2004).

CHOICE OF STATISTICAL METHODS

Multiple regression is used to account for (predict) the variance in an interval dependent, based on linear combinations of interval, dichotomous, or dummy independent variables. The multiple regression equation takes the form:

$$y = b1x1 + b2x2 + \ldots + bnxn + c$$

The b's are the regression coefficients, representing the amount that the dependent variable y changes when the independent changes 1 unit. The c is the constant, where the regression line intercepts the y-axis, representing the amount that the dependent y will be when all the independent variables are 0. The standardized versions of the b coefficients are the beta weights, and the ratio of the beta coefficients is the ratio of the relative predictive power of the independent variables. Associated with multiple regression is R^2, multiple correlation, which is the percent of variance in the dependent variable explained collectively by all of the independent variables.

Multiple regressions has a number of assumptions, including linearity of relationships, the same level of relationship throughout the range of the independent variable (homoscedasticity), interval or near-interval data, and data whose range is not truncated. In addition, it is important that the model being tested be correctly specified. The exclusion of important causal variables or the inclusion of extraneous variables can change markedly the beta weights, and hence the interpretation of the importance of the independent variables.

The regression coefficient, b, is the average amount that the dependent increases when the independent increases one unit and other independents are held constant. Put another way, the b coefficient is the slope of the regression line; the larger the b, the steeper the slope, and the more that the dependent changes for each unit change in the independent. The b coefficient is the unstandardized simple regression coefficient for the case of one independent. When there are two or more independents, the b coefficient is a partial regression coefficient, though it is common simply to call it a 'regression coefficient' also.

Correlation is a bivariate measure of association (strength) of the relationship between two variables. It varies from 0 (random relationship) to 1 (perfect linear relationship) or –1 (perfect negative linear relationship). It is usually reported in terms of its square (r2), interpreted as percent of variance explained. For instance, if r2 is .25, then the independent variable is said to explain 25 percent of the variance in the dependent variable.

There are several common pitfalls in using correlation. Correlation is symmetrical, not providing evidence of which way causation flows. If other variables also cause the dependent variable, then any covariance that they share with the given independent variable in a correlation will be falsely attributed to that independent. Also, to the extent that there is a non-linear relationship between the two variables being correlated, correlation will understate the relationship. Correlation will also be attenuated to the extent that there is measurement error, including use of subinterval data or artificial truncation of the range of the data. Correlation can also be a misleading average if the relationship varies depending on the value of the independent variable ('lack of homoscedasticity').

Beside Pearsonian correlation (r), the most common type, there are other special types of correlation to handle the special characteristics of such types of variables as dichotomies, and there are other measures of association for nominal and ordinal variables. There is also 'multiple correlation', which is the correlation of multiple independent variables with a single dependent. Also, there is 'partial correlation', which is the correlation of one variable with another, controlling for a third or additional variables. The statistical method that will be used to estimate the model is ordinary least squares (OLS) multiple regression. Consider the general linear model:

$$Y = XB + u$$

where y is a $(n \times 1)$ vector of observations on the dependent variable, X is a $(n \times p)$ matrix of observations on the p explanatory variables, B is a $(p \times 1)$ unknown fixed coefficient vector, and u is the $(n \times 1)$ vector of unknown random disturbances. The OLS results in an estimate of the coefficient vector B that is unbiased and has minimal variance when the following standard assumptions hold:

$$E(u) = O \; E(ut \; us) = O$$

ut is independent of all explanatory variables and normally distributed. Then, by the Gauss-Markoff theorem, OLS estimators are best linear unbiased estimates.

Interpretation of multiple regression results depends implicitly on the assumption that the explanatory variables are not strongly correlated. If there are no linear relationships among regressors, they are said to be orthogonal. Under such circumstances, it is usual to interpret a regression coefficient as measuring the change in the response variable when the corresponding explanatory variable is increased by one unit and all other explanatory variables are held constant. This interpretation may not be valid if there are strong relationships among the explanatory variables. When this ideal assumption of independent explanatory variables is violated, the variables are said to be collinear, and the data are said to be multicollinear.

The problem of multicollinearity is often cited as a serious problem in many econometric studies and is highly pronounced in the time-series production function approach because of high correlations among inputs. In our case, the basic aggregates such as outputs, capital stock, and labor force exhibit relatively regular growth: capital and labor tend to move together and are both highly correlated with time and hence with each other .

Multicollinearity is a critical statistical issue in any econometric time series study, and it should be given special and careful attention for a variety of reasons. First, the presence of multicollinearity hinders the precise estimation of economic relationships because the impact of each independent variable on the dependent variable cannot be separated, and the regression results may be ambiguous. Secondly, when the explanatory variables are collinear, the estimated values of the coefficients will have large sampling errors that affect both inferences and forecasts that are based on the regression model. Thirdly, in the presence of multicollinearity, the estimated values of the coefficients become very sensitive to slight changes in the data and to the addition or deletion of variables in the equation.

Clearly, the diagnosis of collinearity should be approached carefully. Such diagnosis consists of two related but separate elements: detecting the presence of collinear relationships among the data series and assessing the extent to which these relationships have degraded estimated parameters. Diagnostic information of this sort is an aid in determining whether and where corrective action is necessary and worthwhile.

Solutions to the Multicollinearity Problem

The approaches that are commonly suggested to deal with the multicollinearity problem can be classified into two broad categories: augmenting the current data and sample information, reducing or simplifying the specified model using improved estimation techniques based on the original data set, such as Bayes-like methods employing prior information.

Advantages and disadvantages of each measure are covered extensively in the literature on regression analysis and multicollinearity. The approach used in this study as a corrective measure for collinearity or as a remedy to the multicollinearity problem is a simplification of the specified model. Since multicollinearity is often caused by the choice of the model, such as when two highly correlated regressors are used in the regression equation, some respecification of the regression equation may lessen the impact of multicollinearity. One approach to model respecification is to redefine the regressors in a way that preserves the information content in the original regressors but reduces the ill-conditioning of the data. Malinvaud points out that the model becomes clearer for an equivalent formulation that involves fewer, but mutually independent, exogenous variables (Malinvaud, 1966, p. 187). Such a formulation will be sufficient in applications.

Autocorrelation

The fundamental assumptions in linear regression are that the error terms have zero mean and constant variance, are uncorrelated, and are normally distributed. This assumption of uncorrelated or independent errors is often not appropriate for time-series data, since the errors in time-series data frequently exhibit serial correlation, that is, $E(ut, us)$ is not zero for t different from s. Such error terms are said to be autocorrelated.

The presence of autocorrelation in the errors has several effects on the OLS regression procedure. These are summarized as:

1. The OLS estimates are still unbiased, but they are no longer minimum variance estimates. We say that these estimates are inefficient.
2. The confidence intervals and tests of hypotheses based on the t and F distributions are, strictly speaking, no longer appropriate.
3. When errors are positively autocorrelated, the residual mean squared errors (MSE) may seriously underestimate the error variance. Consequently, the standard errors of the regression coefficients may be computed as being much smaller than their true values.

Various statistical tests can be used to detect the presence of autocorrelation. The test developed by Durbin and Watson (1971) is widely used. This test is based on the assumption that the errors in the regression model are generated by a first-order autoregressive process at equally spaced time periods. As most regression problems involving time-series data exhibit positive autocorrelation, the hypotheses usually considered by the Durbin-Watson test are:

$$HO: rho = O \quad H1: rho > O$$

where rho is the autocorrelation parameter. A significant value of the Durbin-Watson statistic indicates a model specification error.

In this study the Durbin-Watson statistic is used to check for autocorrelation. In the case of the presence of autocorrelation, the problem would have been eliminated by using the method of Cochrane and Orcutt (1949) to estimate the parameters of the model, including rho.

Stability of the Estimates

Besides multicollinearity and autocorrelation, there is the issue of structural stability of estimated relations in a multiple regression analysis. When a linear regression is used to represent an economic relationship, the question often arises as to whether the relationship remains stable in two periods of time or whether the same relationship holds for two different groups of economic units.

The Chow (1960) test will be used to examine possible structural instability and parameter sensitivity. The Chow test results in conclusive evidence against instability and is based on the analysis of covariance. The method involved can be described very simply in the following way. Suppose that n observations are used to estimate a regression with p parameters. Suppose also that there are m additional observations, and one is interested in deciding whether they are generated by the same regression model as the first n observations. To perform the analysis of variance, we need the following sums of squares:

A =   sum of squares of (n + m) deviations of the dependent variable from the regression estimated by the (n + m) observations, with (n + m -p) degrees of freedom

B =   sum of squares of n deviations of the dependent variable from the regression estimates by the first n observations, with (n -p) degrees of freedom

C =   sum of squares of m deviations of the dependent variable from the regression estimated by the second m observations, with (m -p) degrees of freedom

Then the ratio $(A - B - C)/p$ to $(B + C)/(n + m - 2p)$ will be distributed as $F(p, n + m -2p)$ under the null hypothesis that both groups of observations are generated by the same regression model.

EMPIRICAL RESULTS

Table 5.9 presents the definitions of the operational variables used in the regression analysis.

Table 5.9   Definition of all operational variables

PCHOSTS:	Hosts per capita (number of hosts divided by population)
TELLINE:	Telephone subscriber per capita (# of subscribers divided by population)
PCINTU:	Internet user per capita (# of users divided by population)
PC#:	Personal computers per capita
LAW:	Composite risk factor of a country
CI:	Cyberlaw Index developed by the authors
CCPRTE:	Credit card penetration rate
PCINCOME:	Log per capita income
ACSMNY:	Country rating of access to sound money
CRDREG:	Country rating of credit market regulations
HDI:	Country rating on the human development index

Table 5.10 presents the descriptive statistics of operational variables used in the statistical analysis.

Table 5.10   Descriptive statistics

Variable	Number of observations	Mean	Standard deviation	Minimum	Maximum
PCHOSTS	44	0.01351	0.00432	0.0000042	0.122663
TELLINE	44	0.54138	0.06554	0.032459	1.698087
PCINTU	44	14.6281	2.18959	0.608228	60.34696
PC#	44	0.34282	0.23151	0.000165	0.616667
LAW	44	6.15750	0.02324	3.794416	9.46323
CI	44	0.57045	0.04452	0.0	1.0
CCPRTE	44	0.26277	0.06567	0.01	2.37
PCINCOME	44	3.46893	0.07511	2.600967	4.43685
ACSMNY	44	7.7	0.25518	3.8	9.9
CRDREG	44	6.904545	0.17683	4.5	9.6
HDI	44	0.758	0.01386	0.463	0.905

The correlation matrix in Table 5.11 reveals that the simple pairwise correlations among the variables are in most cases consistent with the formulated hypotheses in Chapter 4. For instance, Internet users and number of hosts are positively correlated with the number of PCs in a given economy on the one hand, and the number of telephones, on the other hand. As expected, there is a strong positive relationship between CCPR and the number of Internet users, on the one hand, and the number of hosts in a country, on the other. Also there is a strong relationship between CCPR and Internet users, on the one hand, and the number of PCs, on the other. In addition, per our hypothesis, there is a strong relationship between the CI and the number of Internet hosts, on the one hand and the number of PCs on the other. We do also notice a strong relationship between per capita income and the e-commerce penetration rate as measured by number of hosts per capita, and other variables in the model.

An examination of Table 5.11 reveals that almost all of the bivariate correlations are significant, which indicate the possibility of existence of multicollinearity among our independent variables. However, it is well-known that parameter estimates remain unbiased and consistent in Ordinary Least Squares Regression despite the presence of mulicollinearity. In addition, the F-statistics for the regression analysis (presented later) is found to be highly significant.

The empirical results of the regression analysis are presented in Table 5.12. These OLS estimations were conducted to explore the relationships among the different variables defined in Table 5.9 and to test the six hypotheses formulated in Chapter 4. The main objective of our analysis is to identify those resources contributing to the success of electronic commerce initiatives in lesser developed and emerging economies. As stated in Chapter 4, the authors hypothesized that in addition to physical infrastructure resources, the success of e-commerce initiatives depends on the existence of soft resources such as a well-established rule of law, cyberlaw, and credible payment systems. Results presented in Table 5.12 are quite supportive of the authors' argument. The results of the stepwise regression analysis are presented in Table 5.13.

As can be seen from the results above, there are three variables significant at the 99 percent confidence level; these are the CCPR, the CI, and the per capita income (PCINCOME). A fourth variable is significant at the 90 percent confidence level, and that is per capita number of hosts (PCHOST). The coefficient of determination for this model (R^2) is 76.1 percent, and the value of the F statistic for the entire model is 30.966 with four degrees of freedom. The model is significant at the 99 percent level.

Based on the results in Table 5.12, all variables are consistently signed; as hypothesized, the model shows a positive relationship between the degree

Table 5.11 Correlation matrix

	CCPRTE	CI	CRDREG	HDI	PCINTU	PCHOSTS	PCINCOME	LAW	PC#	ACSMNY	TELLINE
CCPR	1.000	0.246	0.306*	0.459**	0.709**	0.606**	0.531**	0.217	0.014	0.532**	0.549**
		0.108	0.043	0.002	0.000	0.000	0.000	0.158	0.926	0.000	0.000
CI	0.246	1.000	0.443**	0.415**	0.470**	0.278	0.215	0.112	0.008	0.428**	0.411**
	0.108		0.003	0.005	0.001	0.068	0.162	0.470	0.958	0.004	0.006
CRDREG	0.306*	0.443**	1.000	0.271	0.359*	0.216	0.328*	0.031	0.095	0.390**	0.345*
	0.043	0.003		0.075	0.017	0.158	0.030	0.841	0.538	0.009	0.022
HDI	0.459**	0.415**	0.271	1.000	0.677**	0.431**	0.785**	0.136	0.054	0.663**	0.709**
	0.002	0.005	0.075		0.000	0.003	0.000	0.380	0.727	0.000	0.000
PCINTU	0.709**	0.470**	0.359*	0.677**	1.000	0.669**	0.725**	0.291	0.055	0.852**	0.876**
	0.000	0.001	0.017	0.000		0.000	0.000	0.055	0.725	0.000	0.000
PCHOSTS	0.606**	0.278	0.216	0.431**	0.669**	1.000	0.548**	0.296	0.008	0.743**	0.763**
	0.000	0.068	0.158	0.003	0.000		0.000	0.051	0.957	0.000	0.000
PCINCOME	0.531**	0.215	0.328*	0.785**	0.725**	0.548**	1.000	0.199	0.027	0.767**	0.786**
	0.000	0.162	0.030	0.000	0.000	0.000		0.196	0.863	0.000	0.000
LAW	0.217	0.112	0.031	0.136	0.291	0.296	0.199	1.000	0.051	0.328*	0.358*
	0.158	0.470	0.841	0.380	0.055	0.051	0.196		0.743	0.030	0.017
PC#	0.014	0.008	0.095	0.054	0.055	0.008	0.027	0.051	1.000	0.066	0.047
	0.926	0.958	0.538	0.727	0.725	0.957	0.863	0.743		0.672	0.763
ACSMNY	0.532**	0.428**	0.390**	0.663**	0.852**	0.743**	0.767**	0.328*	0.066	1.000	0.984**
	0.000	0.004	0.009	0.000	0.000	0.000	0.000	0.030	0.672		0.000
TELLINE	0.549**	0.411**	0.345*	0.709**	0.876**	0.763**	0.786**	0.358*	0.047	0.984**	1.000
	0.000	0.006	0.022	0.000	0.000	0.000	0.000	0.017	0.763	0.000	

Notes:

1. * Correlation is significant at the 0.05 level (2-tailed); ** Correlation is significant at the 0.01 level (2-tailed).
2. See Table 5.9 for full definition of all operational variables.

246

Table 5.12   Regression analysis model summary

Model	R	R Square	Adjusted R Square
1	.872[a]	.761	.736

Notes: [a] Predictors: (Constant), PCHOST, CI, PCINCOME, CCPR

ANOVA[b]

Model		Sum of Squares	df	Mean Square	F	Sig.
1	Regression	.690	4	.172	30.966	.000[a]
	Residual	.217	39	.006		
	Total	.907	43			

Notes:
[a]   Predictors: (Constant), PCHOST, CI, PCINCOME, CCPR
[b]   Dependent Variable: PCINTU

Coefficients[a]

Model		Unstandardized Coefficients		Standardized Coefficients		
		B	Std. Error	Beta	t	Sig.
1	(Constant)	−.368	.096		−3.817	.000
	CCPRTE	.001	.000	.324	3.129	.003
	CI	.125	.040	.254	3.088	.004
	PCINCOME	.116	.029	.398	4.049	.000
	PCHOST	.932	.536	.184	1.741	.090

Note: [a] dependent variable: PCINTU

of diffusion of e-commerce in an economy and CCPR. This supports our hypothesis that a country's success in e-commerce is positively related to the degree of credibility of existing payment channels, as measured by the level of CCPR. The results also support hypothesis 5, which states that a country's success in e-commerce is positively related to the existence of cyberlaw. From Table 5.14, the CI is positively related to levels of e-commerce diffusion as measured by the per capita number of Internet users. Also, as expected, e-commerce diffusion is found to be positively related to PCINCOME.

Together these results provide support for our main argument that, in general, the diffusion of e-commerce in developing and emerging economies is dependent on the resources available in a particular economy, and in particular, physical resources in terms of telecommunications infrastructure are not sufficient alone to ensure the success of e-commerce in an economy or e-commerce diffusion. As demonstrated from our analysis above, the strength of some institutional components such as the development of cyberlaw is an additional factor to the growth and diffusion of e-commerce.

The results of the stepwise regression analysis do not necessarily indicate that the other variables that were excluded from the model do not have an impact on the diffusion of e-commerce in developing and emerging economies. As explained earlier, the problem of multicollinearity among the independent variables may be a main reason why some of the variables were shown to be statistically insignificant from the multivariate analysis. As can be seen from the correlation matrix in Table 5.11, a number of variables are highly correlated, as expected. Another problem that presents itself in this case is the size of the sample. Results from multivariate statistical analysis based on a small sample may be questionable.

In order to ensure the completeness of the analysis, especially the small sample of countries included, a check of outliers' influences was conducted using a SPSS statistical package. As can be seen from Figure 5.1 and Figure 5.2, only one significant outlier was found (case number 44); that is South Korea. This was expected, given that South Korea has a very high level of

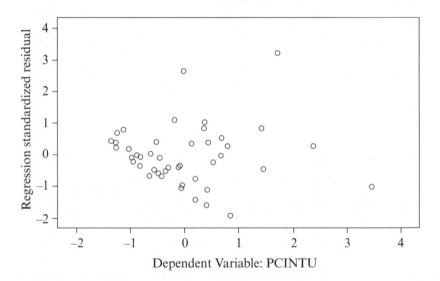

Figure 5.1   Scatter plot of the dependent variable

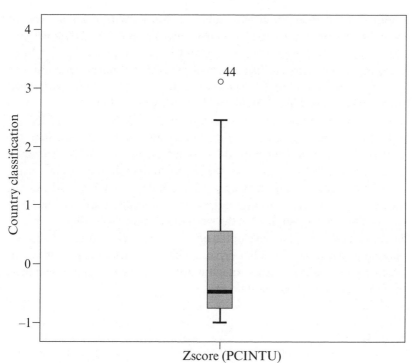

Figure 5.2   Box plot of the data in the sample

Internet penetration rate per capita. To test the influence of South Korea on our results, the country was removed from the sample and the regression analysis was run again. Removing South Korea from the analysis did not affect our original results neither their interpretations.

CONCLUSION

The literature on e-commerce adoption in developing countries is extremely limited, although some evidence exists describing the impediments, which include limited Internet accessibility, a lack of competition in international telephone traffic that makes access to the international network expensive, a lack of intra-regional infrastructure, and a disproportionate penetration of the telephone in the urban, as opposed to rural, more populated areas. To facilitate the introduction of the Internet and eventually electronic commerce/services, the necessary condition is the creation of the communication's infrastructure. For developing countries, financial resources needed to invest in communication infrastructure are one of the major barriers, since most countries rely on foreign aids. As we have demonstrated in this chapter, physical infrastructural resources might be necessary for e-commerce diffusion in developing and emerging economies, but they are not sufficient. Our statistical analysis shows that the institutional environment is as important as the physical infrastructure for the success of e-commerce initiatives. These institutional environments, it is argued, facilitate the building of transactional integrity in online transactions.

This chapter has dealt with data collection on the various variables identified in Chapter 4, discussed the proposed operational measurements of the independent variables and the dependent variable, laid out the methodology for the analysis, and presented and discussed the empirical results. Our analysis supported the main argument that the success rate of e-commerce diffusion in developing and emerging economies depends not only on physical resources but on a number of institutional mechanisms which we refer to as soft resources; this is of central concern to researchers of New Institutional Economics.

NOTE

1. For a definition of these variables and their measurement proxies, please refer to the *International Country Risk Guide* (2003).

REFERENCES

Barclay, B. and N. Domeisen (2001). 'Trade opportunities: are developing countries ready?', *International Trade* **2** Forum(1), 16–19.

Barro, R.J. and X. Sala-I-Martin (1995), 'The Diffusion of Technology', New York: McGraw Hill.

Chow, G. (1960), 'Tests of equality between sets of coefficients in two linear regressions', *Econometrica* **28**(3): 591–605.

Clark, T. (1999), 'Electronic Commerce in China', in Fay Sudweeks and Celia T. Rom (eds), *Doing Business on the Internet: Opportunities on the Internet*, London: Springer.

Cochrane, D, and G.H. Orcutt (1949), 'Application of least squares regressions to relationships containing auto correlated error terms', *Journal of the American Statistical Association* **44**, 32–61.

Crafts, Nicholas (1999), 'Economic growth in the twentieth century', *Oxford Review of Economic Policy* **15**(4): 18–36.

Dasgupta, Partha and Martin Weale (1992), 'On measuring the quality of life', *World Development*, **20**(1), 119–31.

Davis, C.H. (1999), 'The rapid emergence of electronic commerce in a developing region: the case of Spanish-speaking Latin America', *Journal of Global Information Technology Management* **5**(1): 25–40.

Desai, Meghnad (1991), 'Human development, concepts and measurement', *European Economic Review* **35** (2–3), 350–57

Durbin, J. and G.S. Watson (1971), 'Testing for serial correlation in least squares regression III', *Biometrika* **58**, 1–19.

Edwards, S. (1998), 'Openness, productivity, and growth: what do we really know?', *Economic Journal* **108**(44), 383–98.

Faulkner and Gray (2000), 'Global Card Directory', see http://www.faulknergray.com/.

Fontaine, M. (2003), 'Power to the people: entering the information age', in *Digital Opportunities for Development*, Academy for Educational Development, 42–55.

Forrester Research, Inc. (2003), 'Projections for global e-commerce', accessed at www.forrester.com.

Heritage Foundation/*Wall Street Journal* (2005), 'Index of economic freedom', accessed at www.heritage.org.

International Telecommunication Union (ITU), (2004), *Yearbook*, Geneva: ITU.

King, J.L., V. Gurbaxani, K.L Kraemer, F.W. McFarlan, K.S. Raman and C.S. Yap (1994), 'Institutional factors in information technology innovation', *Information Systems Research* **5**(2): 139–69.

Lee, O. (1999), 'An action research report of an e-commerce firm in South Korea', in Fay Sudweeks and Celia T. Rom (eds), *Doing Business on the Internet: Opportunities on the Internet*, London: Springer, pp. 246–58.

Levy, B. and P. Spiller (eds) (1996), *Regulations, Institutions, and Commitment*, New York, NY: Cambridge University Press.

Luchters, Guido (1996), 'Human development as statistical artifact', *World Development* **24**(8), 1385–92.

Malinvaud, Edmond (1966), *Statistical Methods of Econometrics*, New York: North-Holland.

MasterCard (2004), Credit Card and the Global Economy, New York: MasterCard.

McGillivray, M. and H. White (1993), 'Measuring development? The UNDP's human development index', *Journal of International Development* **5**, 183–92.

Montealegre, R. (1999), 'A temporal model of institutional interventions for information technology adoption in less-developed countries', *Journal of Management Information Systems* **16**(1), 207–32.

Oxley, Joanne E. and Bernard Yeung (2001), 'E-commerce readiness: institutional environment and international competitiveness', *Journal of International Business Studies* **32**(4), 705–24.

Peha, J.M. (1999), 'Lessons from Haiti's Internet development', *Communications of the ACM* **42**(6), 67–72.

Petrazzini, B. and M. Kibati (1999), 'The Internet in developing countries', *Communications of the ACM* **42**(6), 31–36.

Plant, R. (1999), *eCommerce: Formulation of Strategy*, Upper Saddle River, NJ: Prentice-Hall.

PRS Group (2003), *International Country Risk Guide*, online edition accessed at www.prsgroup.com/icrg/icrghtml.

Richman, L.S. (1993), 'The real toll of tariffs', *Fortune* **128**(15), 1–4.

Sachs, J. and A. Warner (1995), 'Economic reform and the process of global integration', in W. Brainard and G. Perry. (eds), *Brookings Papers on Economic Activity*, Washington, DC: Brookings Institution, pp. 1–118.

Srinivisan, T.N. (1994), 'Human development: a new paradigm or reinvention of the wheel?', *American Economic Review* **84**(2), 238–43.

Srikantaiah, T.K. and D. Xiaoying (1998), 'The Internet and its impact on developing countries: examples from China and India', *Asian Libraries* **7**(9), 199–209.

Stephenson, M. (2001), 'The rule of law as a goal of development policy', accessed at www1.worldbank.org/publicsector/legal/ruleoflaw2.htm.

Stephenson, S. and D. Ivascanu (2001), 'Electronic commerce in the Western Hemisphere', Organization of American States Trade Unit working paper, Washington, DC: OAS.

Streeten, Paul (1994), 'Human development: means and ends', *American Economic Review* **84**(2), 232–7.

Travica, B. (2002), 'Diffusion of electronic commerce in developing countries: the case of Costa Rica', *Journal of Global Information Technology Management* **5**(1), pp. 4–24.

United Nations Development Programme (UNDP) (2004), *Human Development Report 2004: Cultural Liberty in Today's Diverse World*, New York: New York University Press.

USAID (2003), *Leland Initiative*, accessed at http://www.usaid.gov/regions/afr/leland/project.htm.

US Central Intelligence Agency (2005), *CIA World Factbook*, online edition accessed at www.cia.gov/ciz/publications/factbook.

US Department of Commerce (various), *Country Commercial Guides*, Washington, DC: US Government Printing Office.

White, L.J. (2000), 'Reducing the barriers to international trade in accounting services: why it matters, and the road ahead', World Trade Organization working paper, Geneva.

World Bank (1997), *World Development Indicators*, Washington, DC: World Bank.

World Bank (2004), *World Development Report 2004: Making Services Work for Poor People*, Washington, DC: World Bank.

World Intellectual Property Organization (WIPO) (2004), http://www.wipo.org, Geneva.

6. Where do we go from here?

INTRODUCTION

In this book, we have provided a guiding framework for understanding electronic commerce (e-commerce) diffusion in developing economies from a resource-based theory perspective. The work performed here and the conclusions reached are unique in nature and have several characteristics, none of which has received attention in the information technology (IT) or economic literature. The analysis of e-commerce and electronic government (e-government) experiences in a cross-section of developing countries conducted in this study proved that not only physical infrastructure measures are most important in explaining variations in basic e-commerce adoption and Internet use, but also intangible institutional measures are critical to the success of e-commerce. This book has examined the degree of dependence of e-commerce and e-government success on the strengths of a number of institutional, knowledge base, and physical resources.

This concluding chapter outlines the flow of research that was undertaken during the study that formed the basis for this book. The purpose of the chapter is, first, to review and restate the research objectives of the study; secondly, to discuss briefly the methods employed in the research; and, thirdly, to summarize the empirical findings and sum up the answers to the research questions outlined in Chapter 1. These are to be followed by the major conclusions and implications drawn from the analysis. Finally, a number of recommendations are set forth along with suggestions for future research.

Presently, e-commerce accounts for less than 1 percent of the entire business-to-business (B2B) and business-to-customer (B2C) retail markets, worldwide. However, it is clear that many businesses and consumers are taking their first trials by purchasing inventory and buying goods on the Internet. To help developing and emerging countries solve critical economic problems and provide new services by the means of collecting data, turning data into information, and turning information into knowledge quickly enough to reflect its value as a service, governments are investing more and more in e-commerce technology.

Although the role and success of e-commerce is perceived differently by different scholars, the fact that it constitutes an integral component of global business is no longer disputable. Practically, many countries have adopted various approaches and business models to e-commerce. These business models are based on using e-commerce strategically, creating competitive opportunities, increasing the use of technology more effectively, and enhancing a more enduring connection between IT investments and strategic goals. Many governments have accepted the notion that e-commerce can play (and in fact is playing) a strategic role by creating competitive advantage rather than simply displacing cost. The adoption and diffusion of e-commerce has been of varying degrees of success among countries, depending on their level of economic development, which lead to what we call the digital divide.

The digital divide is characterized by highly unequal access and use of information and communication technologies (ICT), and exhibits itself both at the international, regional and national levels – and therefore needs to be addressed by national policy makers at the highest governmental levels as well as the international community. The adoption of ICT by the public and the private sectors requires an environment encouraging open competition, trust and security, interoperability and standardization, and the availability of the financial resources needed for the development of ICT. This requires the implementation of sustainable measures to improve access to the Internet and telecommunications and increase IT literacy at large, as well as the development of local Internet content.

The asymmetrical diffusion of technology and the disparity in access to technologies in developing and emerging economies are apparent in different ways, with considerable consequences for social, economic and political maturity. These end results are mirrored in the reality that anxiety over the digital divide now concentrates on what is referred to as 'digital exclusion'. Digital exclusion broadens the idea of digital divides based on connectivity and access to highlight ideas of exclusion or lack of participation and representation in more advanced ICTs.

The positive impact and significance of technology to economic development have long been acknowledged. This is more pronounced for ICTs, which cut across all economic operations and have a wide set of applications. ICTs offer the potential for increased availability of information, new means of communication, the reorganization of productive processes and improved efficiency in many different economic activities.

Despite the potential benefits that can be offered by ICT, developing and emerging countries face significant obstacles to ICT connectivity and access. The underlying causes of low levels of penetration of ICT and low level of adoption and diffusion of e-commerce in these countries include: a lack of awareness of what these technologies can offer; insufficient telecommunications infrastructure and Internet connectivity; expensive

ICT access; the absence of adequate legal and regulatory frameworks; a shortage of requisite human capacity; a failure to develop local language content; and a lack of entrepreneurship and business culture open to change, transparency, and social equality.

Many of the problems are symbolized by highly disproportionate rates of e-commerce adoption and diffusion across countries. The obvious digital divide between the information/technology-rich and the information/technology-poor countries is of mounting concern. A major challenge for policy-makers at the national and international levels, therefore, lies in tackling the problem of digital divide and digital exclusion: between rich and poor countries, rural and urban areas, men and women, skilled and unskilled citizens, and large and small enterprizes.

For any country, moving forward on the electronic world map cannot take place without a comprehensive, well-devised strategy at the highest level of government. In developing and emerging economies, one observes a lack of such strategic orientation, in general, and electronic strategic inclination, in particular. Electronic strategies should be better integrated into the overall policy frameworks and strategies of countries. The inflow of foreign investments and international support through development cooperation measures is equally important.

Strategies to improve access to ICT and the Internet, and consequently increase e-commerce adoption and diffusion, include opening up local telecommunication markets to promote competition and creating supportive legal and institutional environments to encourage investment in ICT. The objective should be to decrease the cost of the Internet access for private sector entities and individuals. Guaranteeing the availability of a minimum supply of ICT infrastructure and electricity for remote and rural areas should be considered an important part of those strategies in developing and emerging economies.

In addition, to ensure success of any initiative, human resources development should be at the center of electronic strategies; this necessitates including ICT in the curricula of educational institutions, especially in public ones, and providing training in the workplace to increase IT literacy. To help accomplish some of the objectives of electronic strategies, e-government could be used as a means, including online services offered by governments, and e-business and e-payment operations undertaken through the public procurement process.

UNDERLYING THEORIES

In completing this work, the authors were guided by a number of studies from various disciplines. The IT diffusion literature helped our understanding of the technological, organizational, and institutional factors that affect the diffusion of innovations. Frameworks which focus on country-level Internet diffusion, and are very strong in including dimensions that are especially pertinent to developing and emerging countries were particularly helpful. These included factors describing the organizational context and factors that specifically reflect a view of technological diffusion. Without a specific focus on institutional factors, it is insufficient for studying the diffusion of e-commerce.

We were also guided by research on IT and e-commerce in developing and emerging economies; this line of research considers the many issues that these countries face, factors that are often taken for granted in the developed countries in which most theories of e-commerce and IT diffusion are set. Travica (2002) provides a good framework that captures many of these issues in dimensions that foster more detail and focused analysis.

The main theme of this research was to take a step toward understanding the level of e-commerce diffusion, its determinants and its impact on growth and development in developing and emerging countries. In doing so, a framework that is grounded in strong economic theory was developed. The framework used fundamental concepts central to resource-based and technology diffusion literature and provided a decent understanding of e-commerce adoption and diffusion processes by public and private sector entities in developing and emerging countries.

So far, little research using a resource-based view (RBV) framework has examined strategy differences in the social, cultural and political contexts of developing and emerging economies. As with most resources that create competitive advantage, resources for competitive advantage in developing and emerging countries are intangible. In developing and emerging economies, however, such advantages are difficult to institute without good relationships with national governments.

From a macroeconomic perspective, the RBV sees an economy as a bundle of resources and capabilities. Resources are economy specific assets and competencies controlled and used by countries to develop and implement their strategies. Resources can be either tangible (eg financial assets, technology) or intangible (eg managerial skills, reputation); they can be heterogeneous across economic sectors, and some resources are valuable yet rare, difficult to imitate, or non-substitutable, giving the economy some distinctive core capabilities. Resources that provide sustainable advantage tend to be causally ambiguous, socially complex, rare, and/or imperfectly imitable. Capabilities are defined to be an economy's abilities to integrate, build, and reconfigure internal and external assets and competencies so that it is enabled to perform distinctive activities. The resource-based approach focuses on the characteristics of resources and the strategic factor markets from which they are obtained.

Based on the resource-based theory, economies cannot gain competitive advantage by merely owning and controlling resources. They should be able to acquire, develop, and deploy these resources in a manner that provides distinctive sources of advantage in the marketplace. The traditional conceptualization of the RBV has not addressed or examined the process of resource development. In addition, the traditional RBV is limited to relatively stable environments, which is not usually the case in developing and emerging markets.

In addition to the resource-based approach, the New Institutional Economics (NIE) theory was also used as a foundation for our work. To date, new institutional supporters seem to focus on transaction cost analysis of property rights, contracts, and organizations. The new institutionalism is described as an attempt to extend the range of neo-classical theory by accounting for institutional factors such as governance structures and property rights. The institutional environment is the devized set of constraints that structure political, economic and social interactions. The philosophical foundation of NIE is classical liberalism; it is dominated currently by scholars who cling to the neo-classical core of the discipline, while struggling to broaden its boundaries.

SUMMARY OF THE RESEARCH

This book proposed an empirical/theoretical framework for understanding the level and degree of e-commerce adoption and diffusion in a sample of developing and emerging economies. Basically, a framework that is grounded in resource-based and institutional theories was developed. Based on the framework, a set of hypotheses were developed and tested. The analysis used core constructs that appear central to resource-based, institutional economic and technology diffusion literature and provided a fine-grained understanding of e-commerce adoption processes by public and private sector entities in developing and emerging countries.

Chapter 1 established the context of the book and highlighted the importance of the subject at hand and the importance of the digital economy, including the impact of digitization on economic growth and development, and the various impediments and obstacles facing developing economies in the adoption and diffusion phases of e-commerce.

Chapter 2 reviewed the literature on e-commerce and e-governments. The chapter covered the state of diffusion of e-commerce in developing and emerging economies; as the adoption and diffusion of e-commerce continue to grow in developing economies around the world, it could have significant consequences on the social and economic structures of these countries. The economic, social and political effects cannot be ignored and should be examined closely. In many developing countries, the Internet is quickly displacing older media such as television and newspapers as the prime source of important information for young people. It was stated that compared with developed countries, e-commerce adoption in developing countries has been relatively slow due to obstacles in the online authorization of credit cards, inadequate marketing strategies, and small online population. The lack of interest in e-commerce adoption by several consumer groups is also due to unclear price advantages and a poor supply in this shopping mode. Electronic commerce in the majority of developing economies is currently afflicted by impediments such as low bandwidth, lack of independent gateways for Internet Service Providers (ISPs), an inadequate telecommunications infrastructure, low rate of personal computer (PC) penetration and low tele-density, among others. However, with the expected higher PC or Internet access device penetration levels, the current trend of entry of private ISPs, availability of greater bandwidth and the coming together of e-commerce infrastructure will lead to an explosive growth in the number of Internet and e-commerce users in developing countries.

Assessing the socio-economic influences of an e-commerce adoption is difficult because it requires the use of methods capable of revealing often complex and unpredictable community values. However, the growth of e-commerce has created enormous influence on services, market structure, competition and restructuring of industry and markets. These changes are transforming all areas of society, work, business, and government. The use of ICTs for e-commerce deepens and intensifies the socio-economic divisions among people, businesses and nations. It is often reported that there is a complicated patchwork of varying levels of ICT access, basic ICT usage, and ICT applications among socio-economic groups; many disparities are getting even larger. Disparities in the location and quality of Internet infrastructure, even the quality of phone lines, have created gaps in access. Gaps exist in the adoption of digital technologies among different social groups and firms, depending on income levels, education, gender, and for firms, depending on industry structure, business size (large firms versus small-to medium-sized enterprises (SMEs)) and location.

Chapter 3 covered the RBV literature. As an economic theory, the RBV literature focused on the impact of resources at the micro, firm level; the authors adapted the theory to the macro level of the economy. Simply stated, the RBV of the firm is one of the latest strategic management concepts to be enthusiastically embraced by IT and information management scholars. This book and the empirical analysis carried out maintain that the RBV holds much promise as a framework for understanding strategic information/ knowledge economy issues but cautions that, before it is adopted, it needs to be fully understood.

The chapter outlined the development of the RBV from its origins in early economic models of imperfect competition, through the work of evolutionary economists to the contributions of strategy economics scholars over the past two decades. The chapter also differentiated between and defined the two categories of resources, firms-specific and country-specific. In addition, the relationship between RBV and institutional theories was covered, along with the few attempts to evaluate the experiences of developing economies from a resource-based perspective. It is apparent that research using resource-based theory and examining macro strategy difference in the social context of developing economies is almost absent. Similar to most resources that create competitive advantage at the micro level, resources for competitive advantage at the macro level in developing economies are mainly intangible. The economic literature has paid attention to the revenue-generating promises of developing economies, and as such, has focused, mainly, on big developing and emerging economies such as China, India, and Russia. Consequently, the authors concluded that it is essential to understand the relationship between economic experiences and the changing nature of the institutional environment.

Coverage of four indicators developed by different international entities to measure a country's IT and e-commerce readiness was one of the objectives of Chapter 4. These are the information society index (ISI), the e-government index, the economic freedom index, and the networked readiness index.

The chapter also covered the development of the six hypotheses that were statistically tested later. The set of hypotheses in the current research addressed the determinants of success of e-commerce and e-governments in developing and emerging economies. These identified the human resources, the financial resources, access and technical capabilities of an economy, the strength of the rule of law, the development of cyberlaw, and the existence of a credible payment system.

The first hypothesis stated that a high level of e-commerce diffusion is related to the quantity and quality of human resources available to society; it was stated that training and education are fundamental to the effective use of the Internet and hence to the success of e-commerce. The second hypothesis has to do with the financial resources available to the country. Evidence of a positive relationship between the strength of the financial base of a country and its economic growth is presented in previous studies. In the Information Age, financial investment in Internet-based technologies is positively correlated with economic growth.

The third hypothesis dealt with access to Internet-based resources and technical capabilities. Without access to computers and Internet connections at a reasonable cost, citizens in developing economies will be unable to migrate from traditional markets to electronic markets. The fourth hypothesis deals with the strength and transparency of the rule of law and the role it plays in facilitating the use of Internet-based technologies in a developing country. Law plays a vital role in the transformation and development of societies. A number of reasons have been advanced in the resource-based literature to highlight the role a strong rule of law plays in affecting transactional integrity in an Internet-based society, and thus investment in such markets.

The basis of the fifth hypothesis was the existence of cyberlaw. Due to the unique nature of the Internet, its use creates legal issues and questions, especially in areas related to intellectual property rights and cybercrime. Few countries in the developing world have drafted cyberlaws; and those who have are still struggling to perfect its implementation. In this book, we argue that the existence of cyberlaw leads to the better diffusion of e-commerce, and subsequently to economic growth and development.

The sixth and last hypothesis set forth in this chapter had to do with the existence of credible payment channels. It is argued that payment systems are fundamental to developing Internet-based activities and to the success of e-governments, in particular. Hence, success of any e-commerce project is positively related to the existence of a credible payment system in a country.

Chapter 5 covered data collection and the development and statistical analysis to test the six hypotheses formulated in Chapter 4. This chapter presented the first systematic study on e-commerce adoption and diffusion in a number of developing and emerging economies. The book concludes with a summary, research findings, and recommendation for future research.

CONCLUSION OF THE RESEARCH

Based on our research of the sample emerging and developing countries and their experiences with e-commerce and e-governance, the following main challenges are identified, in addition to the generic challenges cited by economic growth and development authors. Payment mechanisms constitute a major challenge. There are two sides to the payment issue in the countries included in our sample. On the one hand, credit cards, the most popular way of conducting business in consumer exchanges, are not widely used. On the other hand, even if credit cards are used, there are limitations to websites accepting credit card payments. The average credit card penetration rate is 26.3 percent for the 44 countries in our sample. This average drops substantially to 15.9 percent, when the three outliers are excluded from the sample; these are Hong Kong, Korea, and Singapore with credit card penetration rates of 129 percent, 140 percent and 237 percent respectively. This low number can be attributed to a cash-based culture.

In most of the emerging and developing countries, credit card awareness is still in its infancy. In addition, requirements for obtaining credit cards in the majority of these countries are very strict. In some countries, users must maintain bank deposits equivalent to, or around twice of, their credit limit. Since credit cards are the primary method for settling consumer transactions on the Internet, the small number of credit cards necessarily limits the e-commerce market.

A second issue that was recognized during the research phase is the lack of awareness on consumers' part. This constitutes a critical barrier to the implementation of e-commerce in most developing countries. The limited number of Internet users in those countries with an average per capita of 14.3 percent, discourages commercial efforts to create online sites for consumers to buy and sell.

Another problem is the outdated legal system in most of the developing countries. As we have seen from our analysis in Chapter 5, only 26 countries have developed some kind of legislation dealing with cyber issues. Many of these countries, though, are still at the early stages of implementing cyberlaws. It is still debatable whether cyberlaw is so distinctive from other kinds of law that it warrants its own specialty. Nonetheless, cyberlaw is among the hottest new specialties at American law and mass communication schools. Several cyberlaw texts have been published in the United States between 2001 and 2005 to meet the explosive teaching and research demands in the booming field of Internet law. The exact content of cyberlaw is somewhat controversial in that a number of observers agree that it includes many aspects of intellectual property (IP) and technology transfer. It also incorporates the impact of IT on legal processes, electronic aspects of commercial transaction processing, and most aspects of traditional computer law. Beyond this important core, cyberspace is also having significant impact on many traditional areas of law. Given the impact that cyberspace is having on law; the idea of a separate legal field called cyberlaw is becoming a reality.

A number of countries around the world are planning and developing their own information society policies, though operationalized to differing degrees, at different speeds, and in different ways. For e-commerce technology to make the transition from the potential to the actual requires not just that it is technically feasible but there must also be a desire for it, coupled with the ability to pay for it, and the appropriate institutional mechanisms to facilitate its adoption and diffusion. A number of measures to promote e-commerce in developing countries have been identified. These could include establishing a common digital platform to enhance cooperation and knowledge sharing among trading partners across the supply chain, as well as functioning as a route into individual company portals within a sector (Moodley, 2003). They may also require the setting up of support centers or 'incubators' to facilitate suitable country-specific e-commerce strategies. However, the path to e-commerce may be filled with obstacles, particularly when decision makers remain skeptical about its usefulness to overall development and growth. Electronic commerce impediments include limited Internet accessibility, a lack of competition in international telephone traffic that makes access to the international network expensive, a lack of intra-regional infrastructure, and a disproportionate penetration of the telephone in the urban, as opposed to rural, more populated areas. One of the most severe constraints on wider Internet use in low-income developing countries is their limited access to international 'bandwidth', the high-capacity connections needed to transmit the large quantities of digitized information required for full Internet services. Until this bottleneck can be removed, email is likely to remain the dominant use of the Internet in those countries. Developing regions may potentially leapfrog traditional copper and fiber-based land lines and go directly to leading-edge wireless technologies that blend voice and data over the same networks.

In the past 10 years, economists have assessed the impact of a technology developed in an industrialized country which is copied by a developing country. They have shown that the rate of growth of the developing country depends on its initial stock of knowledge and the costs of imitation. A country's readiness for e-commerce depends on network infrastructure and technology diffusion. Electronic commerce growth is fostered by strong growth in infrastructure, including narrow and broadband access, hardware investment and Internet use, but it depends also on the growth of mobile applications, price reductions, service improvement, speed and reliability.

To facilitate the introduction of the Internet and eventually electronic commerce/services, the necessary and sufficient condition is the creation of the communication's infrastructure. For developing countries, investment is one of the main obstacles since most countries rely on foreign funds. In addition to developing infrastructure there is a need to create a sustainable supply of Internet services, including training, marketing, extension into rural areas and support and training for SMEs. To facilitate the diffusion of e-commerce, a necessary condition is the development of e-policies and e-strategies. Telecommunication infrastructure is clearly a necessary but not a sufficient requirement for the development and entry of a developing country into the cyber marketplace. Despite the technology used, the central objective for developing countries is to encourage investment and partnerships with vendors, suppliers, and telecommunications companies outside their borders. This requires a well developed approach using the tools and strategies of an open and fair marketplace.

In addition to the hard resources being considered by many developing countries, a host of soft resources have to be emphasized. The first is the establishment of national policies dealing with the information and telecommunication sector. As noted earlier, communication infrastructure is clearly a necessary, but by no means a sufficient, condition for successful adoption and diffusions of e-commerce. The second soft factor necessary for successful adoption and diffusion of e-commerce in developing economies is appropriate legal norms and standards; laws dealing with consumer protection, privacy protection, and intellectual property rights (IPR) are essential for the successful implementation of e-commerce programs.

Additional issues that countries have to consider embrace recognition of digital signatures and electronic documents, and taxes and tariff collection. The majority of countries in our sample have not studied or created policies or laws to address the issues originating as a result of e-commerce. It is important to state here that the experience of the sample countries in developing a legal system dealing with the digitization of their economies had not been homogeneous a number being much more advanced than others in this respect; namely Brazil, Peru and the UAE, which recently have established national infrastructures for digital certification. In Peru, the national telecom cooperator joined Ecuador as the second Latin American country to develop an infrastructure for digital certificates and allow its consumers to use secure applications for e-services. Customers now can digitally sign and encrypt documents that will build trust in and expand the use of electronic transactions (Tetelman, 2003).

Privacy and information security continue to be one of the most important topics in e-commerce. As the number of transactions over the Internet increase, so does the number of security breaches including data theft, vicious file corruption and even e-commerce site shutdown. Privacy issues would discourage people from using the Internet as a transaction medium, hence reducing telecommunication activities and e-commerce diffusion. For many developing countries, the privacy and information security issues are complicated by the lack of security systems, such as trusted third parties, encryption procedures, and secure telecommunications that would provide the protection needed for e-commerce and e-government to grow. The ability to realize high level of e-commerce diffusion, then, will largely depend on the climate of confidence e-businesses are able to create in their relations with consumers.

The most important aspect of e-commerce is trust. Most likely a product will fail if it doesn't have market trust. Usually the basis of trust is based on risk assessment, while confidence is based on familiarity. Society may become reliant on the product when confidence is achieved. However, not all products achieve this level. Establishing trust in the eminently impersonal environment of the Internet is not straightforward. People are unwilling to give their credit card numbers over the Internet. Also fraud has increased in e-commerce transactions. Consumers also worry that their data privacy will not be valued or respected by the company they are dealing with. Karake Shalhoub (2002) found many solutions to this problem. First of all the combination of data encryption and legal controls will ensure integrity of data that it transmitted. There has to be certain trust policies to establish trust. If governments try to implement certain policies preventing theft of identity, then fraud can be reduced in e-commerce. Most difficulties faced are related to the technical area. A number of trust enhancers were identified by Karake Shalhoub, including the seal of approval from a trusted third party, the appointment of a chief information officer, and the development of a comprehensive clear privacy statement.

The involvement of the private sector in e-commerce should be one of the main objectives of developing and emerging economies because it is the private sector that can create additional jobs and enhanced revenues. Yet many e-commerce initiatives in developing and emerging countries are initiated by the public sector and financially supported by the government. A number of these programs have been very successful, though. The government of Chile has implemented an e-government model that is rapidly diffusing to the private sector. The government's website began as an information portal to the public but rapidly became a facilitator and instigator of e-commerce. In 2001, the Chilean government began its e-procurement portal where smaller businesses compete for public sector contracts, and permitting both private and public sector entities to conduct transactions over the portal. The portal has since become a meeting place where the government provides, free of charge, a cyber market for buyers and sellers to gather and conduct business. This program has enhanced government services through the upgrading of back office systems and the transparency of its processes. The program has motivated businesses to partake in the Internet's development, while increasing their transaction costs efficiency and widening their markets. From our analysis, it is estimated that almost 45 percent of Chile's population are active users of the Internet.

As e-commerce and e-government require technical knowledge and understanding, a lack of education of these technologies is a serious impediment to their adoption. Certain countries lack key elements of education: Internet awareness, understanding of the implications of the

Internet, and skilled workers in IT. Even when people are aware of the Internet, they may not understand how the Internet might improve their lives and therefore oppose it. The erosion of local culture is a prominent issue when discussing e-government. It is therefore the responsibility of regional governments to foster the development of e-commerce (Bonits and De Castro, 2000) and e-government in their areas. Culture influences how people perceive certain things, what they value, and how they interpret the graphical images and lines of text they encounter on a website.

Electronic commerce promises the potential to create and reveal new business opportunities; reduce all types of costs (especially search and transaction costs); increase business efficiency and effectiveness; and improve the quality of life in adopting countries. Given the enormous benefits e-commerce can provide to help the growth and development of any economy, developing and emerging economies should create the necessary conditions to move their economies into the digitized phase. Digitization strategies have to be aligned with existing resources in a particular economy, taking into account the different stages of economic development; the heterogeneous regulatory environments; and the diverse social, economic and cultural frameworks.

It is vital to state here that enhancement capability in e-commerce among regional economies (such as the Gulf Cooperation Council), including through economic and technical cooperation, is needed to enable all developing and emerging economies to reap the benefits of e-commerce. It is recommended that the private sector plays a primary role in developing e-commerce technology, applications, practices and services, and that governments promote and facilitate the development and uptake of e-commerce by providing a favorable environment and the necessary hard and soft resources, such as the legal and regulatory aspects, which is predictable, transparent and consistent, and creating an environment that promotes trust and confidence among e-commerce participants. In addition, governments should promote the efficient functioning of e-commerce internationally by aiming, wherever possible, to develop domestic frameworks which are compatible with evolving international norms and practices, and becoming a leading-edge user in order to catalyze and encourage greater use of electronic means, following the example of the Dubai government.

Electronic commerce cannot flourish without the cooperation of business and governments to ensure the development of affordable, accessible communication and information infrastructure. Furthermore, government and private sector businesses should cooperate to develop and instigate technologies and policies, which build trust and confidence in safe, secure and reliable communication, information and delivery systems, and which address issues including privacy, authentication and consumer protection.

In order to benefit fully from e-commerce, regional developing and emerging economies should strive to work together to build trust and confidence in digital means, and enhance government use; intensify community outreach; promote technical cooperation and experience exchange; where appropriate, work towards the removal of barriers to its adoption; and develop flawless legal, technical, operating and trading environments to facilitate the growth and development of e-commerce.

To accomplish the above, governments in developing and emerging economies should develop programs and action plans aimed at: (1) developing measures and indicators on levels of adoption, use and flows of e-commerce; (2) identifying the economic costs that inhibit increased adoption and diffusion of e-commerce, including those imposed by regulatory and market environment; and (3) considering additional economic and technical cooperation among regional economies to facilitate the adoption and diffusion of e-commerce, and the use and maximization of benefits of e-commerce member economies.

FUTURE RESEARCH

In general, research conducted on developing and emerging economies face a number of obstacles. As a starter, theories deducted and/or applied to developed countries may not be suitable to apply in emerging and developing countries. Sampling and data collection is a big problem in addition to the difficulties researchers face in developing and applying performance measures. Issues have to be addressed concerning the replication of tests and hypotheses used in developed economies in developing and emerging countries. Developing and emerging economies are dynamic and changes occur at a very fast pace in the institutional environment. As a result, cross-sectional studies may produce misleading results concerning the impact of specific policies. To get around this limitation, there appears to be a need for longitudinal studies.

Another limitation of this study is that at present, developing and emerging market economies are not homogeneous, even within the same geographic region. Looking at Middle Eastern countries, one finds clear differences among them in terms of economic, social, and political dimensions. With respect to the independent republics of the former Soviet Union, they have pursued different development paths to transition and have agreed different degrees of progress. Similarly, in East Asia there are clear differences between China and Vietnam on the one hand and other developing countries such as Korea and Thailand, on the other.

In addition, one limitation of the study is that in the current research the analysis was cross-sectional. Static data were used to test for what are, without doubt, dynamic relationships. Longitudinal analysis would have been beneficial, but unfortunately, given the novelty of the subject at hand, the lack of comprehensive longitudinal data precluded such analysis. Studying economies at different points in time may help identify how changes in the independent variables affect the decisions on both behavioral and non-behavioral constructs.

A profound analysis might be made on individual country level, when and if data are available. Studies could be conducted at the sector or industry levels in some economies; such industry-level studies help in the isolation of industry-specific resources, characteristics and peculiarities of diffusion of e-commerce and its impact on growth and development of these industries.

Another recommendation for future research would be to study the relationship between economic structure and level of e-commerce adoption and diffusion in particular countries. Excellent candidates would be countries in Latin America, the Gulf Cooperation Council, and in Asia. This recommendation, however, is more difficult to bring to life in the near future because of the less than perfect data collection methodologies and the less than acceptable coverage of existing economies. For any study to be fruitful and professionally acceptable, information and data have to be collected through questionnaires over a long period of time. This is a lengthy and costly process, but it is professionally challenging.

Another proposition explored in this study concerned the impact of the rule of law in a country on the level of e-commerce diffusion. A country with a strong rule of law is defined as one having a strong court system, well-defined political institutions, and citizens who are willing to accept the established institutions and to make and implement laws and arbitrate disagreements. Many governments and regulatory bodies in developing and emerging countries are starting to recognize the economic potential of e-commerce and e-government and are considering a number of policy initiatives designed to encourage further development and application of this technology. These initiatives include attempts to overhaul or effect amendments to existing laws to deal with the emerging legal issues that e-commerce raises.

For example, in Singapore, various amendments to existing legislation and subsidiary legislation have been put in place rationalizing the existing law to cope with moves in various industries towards the electronic framework. The amendments have collectively dealt with computer and electronic evidence, copyright, income tax concessions for cyber-trading, electronic dealings in securities and futures, electronic prospectuses and deregulation of the telecommunications industry. It was suggested that e-commerce diffusion positively related to the strength and the level of transparency of the 'rule of law' in a particular economy. Weak support emerged for this proposition from the findings. If we accept the NIE theory premise that strong institutional and legal foundations would be conducive to e-commerce adoption and diffusion, then we should have found strong support from our statistical analysis. One reason for the lack of support might be the result of less than perfect data. Almost all researchers and practitioners agree that assessing the level of diffusion of e-commerce will be greatly hindered by the lack of reliable and accessible data. Two problems exist in this respect, which prevent the possibility of multiple studies building on each other. The first is that most of the data are unavailable for analyses by other researchers. The second problem concerns inconsistency across data sources with respect to the data collected. As a matter of fact, deciding what data to collect is much more difficult than collecting the data. In general, the majority of developing and emerging countries have not devized systems to track investments and expenditures on e-commerce technology separately from other areas. The information, if it exists, is usually combined with general investment in IT or general operating and capital investment information.

More work is also needed on the interface between relationship development strategy and e-commerce technology strategies. It is the firm conviction of the authors that devising well articulated e-strategies will lead to higher rates of e-commerce adoption and diffusion in our sample countries. How are strategies developed in electronic contexts and what is the impact of such context on new and existing strategies? Should a country's management strategy be altered under electronic conditions? These are critical questions that have yet to be addressed in e-commerce strategy.

REFERENCES

Bonits, N. and A. De Castro (2000), 'The first world congress on management of electronic commerce: review and commentary', *Internet Research: Electronic Networking Applications and Policy*, **10**(5), 365–74.

Karake Shalhoub, Z. (2002), *Trust and Loyalty in Electronic Commerce: an Agency Theory Perspective*, New York, NY: Quorum Publishing.

Moodley, S. (2003), 'Whither business-to-business electronic commerce in developing countries? The case of the South African manufacturing sector', *Information Technology for Development*, **10**, 25–40.

Tetelman, M. (2003), *Foundations of Electronic Commerce for Development: A Model for Development Professionals*, Washington, DC: Academy for Educational Development.

Travica, B. (2002), 'Diffusion of electronic commerce in developing countries: the case of Costa Rica', *Journal of Global Information Technology Management* **5**(1), 4–24

Index